Smart Leadership for Higher Education in Difficult Times

Smart Leadership for Higher Education in Difficult Times

Edited by

David W. Breneman

University of Virginia, USA

and

Paul J. Yakoboski

TIAA-CREF Institute, USA

In association with TIAA-CREF

Edward Elgar

Cheltenham, UK • Northampton, MA, USA

Published by
Edward Elgar Publishing Limited
The Lypiatts
15 Lansdown Road
Cheltenham
Glos GL50 2JA
UK

Edward Elgar Publishing, Inc.
William Pratt House
9 Dewey Court
Northampton
Massachusetts 01060
USA

A catalogue record for this book
is available from the British Library

Library of Congress Control Number: 2010930117

ISBN 978 1 84980 303 8

Typeset by Servis Filmsetting Ltd, Stockport, Cheshire
Printed and bound by MPG Books Group, UK

Contents

Figure and tables

FIGURE

TABLES

Contributors

AUTHORS

J. Michael Adams became Fairleigh Dickinson University's sixth president on July 1, 1999. Previously he was academic dean at Drexel University in Philadelphia for 15 years. He also led the United Nations Pathways Program and the creation of Global Virtual Faculty™, comprising scholars and professionals from around the world who contribute to the classroom via the Internet. Dr. Adams began his academic career at the State University of New York (SUNY) at Oswego, where he received the SUNY Chancellor's Award for Teaching Excellence. He also served as a United States Congressional Fellow, working on higher education legislation and advising United States congressional leaders. In 2008, he was named President-Elect of the International Association of University Presidents (IAUP) and is an IAUP representative to the United Nations. He also serves on the UN/IAUP Commission on Disarmament Education, Conflict Resolution and Peace and is a National Council member of the United Nations Association of the United States of America. The author of nine books, Dr. Adams' most recent work is *Coming of Age in a Globalized World: The Next Generation*, published in 2006 with co-author Angelo Carfagna. Dr. Adams holds a B.S. from Illinois State University, Normal; an M.S. from University of Illinois, Urbana; and a Ph.D. from Southern Illinois University, Carbondale.

Geoffrey Bannister, Ph.D. served as president of Butler University from 1989 to 2000 and as president of Schiller International University from 2008 to 2009. Prior to becoming president at Butler, Bannister served for 18 months in the newly created office of executive vice president. Bannister was also the dean of the College of Liberal Arts and the Graduate School of Arts and Sciences at Boston University from 1978 to 1988.

David W. Breneman is University Professor and Newton and Rita Meyers Professor in Economics of Education at the University of Virginia. Prior to that he served from 2006 to 2009 as Director of the Public Policy program at the Frank Batten School of Leadership and Public Policy. From 1995 to 2007 he served as Dean of the Curry School of Education at the

University. He is an economist and authority on the finance and economics of higher education. His four decades of experience include service as a professor, college president, think tank scholar, and dean. He currently teaches courses in the Center for the Study of Higher Education. He has taught a seminar in the Frank Batten School on Advanced Policy Analysis and he regularly teaches Higher Education Finance in the Curry School. Kalamazoo College awarded an Honorary Doctor of Humane Letters to Dr. Breneman in 2008. The Council of Independent Colleges (CIC) recently presented Breneman with the Award for Outstanding Service. This award honors his efforts toward "insuring a robust future for private higher education" and recognizes the numerous contributions he has made to higher education, specifically in the area of financial aspects of private liberal arts colleges. His recent writings focus on the vexing issues of state financing of public higher education and on recessions and higher education.

Kent John Chabotar became president and professor of political science at Guilford College in Greensboro, North Carolina in 2002. Previously, he served as vice president for finance and administration, treasurer and senior lecturer on government at Bowdoin College. Chabotar is on the governing boards of the Community Foundation of Greater Greensboro and the Southeastern Center for Contemporary Art. He has been on the faculty of the Harvard Institutes for Higher Education since 1983. Chabotar's most recent publications include a book on strategic finance for the Association of Governing Boards of Universities and Colleges (2006) and commentaries on financial decision making in tough economic times in *Inside Higher Ed* (2009), *The Chronicle of Higher Education* (2009), and *Change* (2010). Dr. Chabotar holds a B.A. from Saint Francis University in Pennsylvania and M.P.A. and Ph.D. degrees in Public Administration from the Maxwell School at Syracuse University.

Michael M. Crow became the 16th president of Arizona State University (ASU) on July 1, 2002. An academic leader and educator, designer of knowledge enterprises, and science and technology policy scholar, he is guiding the transformation of ASU into one of the nation's leading public metropolitan research universities, an institution that combines the highest levels of academic excellence, inclusiveness to a broad demographic, and maximum societal impact – a model he terms the "New American University." Under his direction the university pursues teaching, research, and creative excellence focused on the major challenges and questions of our time, as well as those central to the building of a sustainable environment and economy for Arizona. He has committed the university to social embeddedness and global engagement, and championed initiatives that have led to record levels of diversity in the student body.

During his tenure ASU has marked a number of important milestones, including the establishment of major interdisciplinary research initiatives such as the Biodesign Institute, the Global Institute of Sustainability, the Flexible Display Center, and the Center for the Study of Religion and Conflict; the establishment of more than a dozen new interdisciplinary schools; an unprecedented research infrastructure expansion; and the announcement of the eight largest gifts in the history of the university. According to the National Science Foundation, ASU is now ranked among the top 20 leading research universities in the nation without a medical school, and according to one authoritative international assessment ranks among the leading 100 universities globally.

Prior to joining ASU, he was executive vice provost of Columbia University, where he also was professor of science and technology policy in the School of International and Public Affairs. As chief strategist of Columbia's research enterprise, he led technology and innovation transfer operations, establishing Columbia Innovation Enterprises (now Science and Technology Ventures), the Strategic Initiative Program, and the Columbia Digital Media Initiative, as well as advancing interdisciplinary program development. He played the lead role in the creation of the Earth Institute at Columbia University, and helped found the Center for Science, Policy, and Outcomes (CSPO) in Washington, DC, a think tank dedicated to linking science and technology to optimal social, economic, and environmental outcomes. In 2003 CSPO was re-established at ASU as the Consortium for Science, Policy, and Outcomes. Dr. Crow has been a senior advisor to the United States Department of State and Department of Commerce on matters of science and technology policy in areas related to intelligence and national security. A fellow of the National Academy of Public Administration and member of the Council on Foreign Relations, he is the author of books and articles relating to the analysis of research organizations, technology transfer, science and technology policy, and the theory and practice of public policy.

Mary Cullinan was named president of Southern Oregon University in August 2006. She previously served as provost/vice president for academic affairs and professor of English at Stephen F. Austin State University in Texas. From 1981 to 2003 Dr. Cullinan served in several capacities in the California State University System, both at CSU Hayward (now CSU East Bay) and CSU Stanislaus. She is the author of three books: *Susan Ferrier*; *Business Communication: Principles and Processes*; and *Business English for Industry and the Professions*. She has also co-edited an anthology, "American Women Writers: Diverse Voices in Prose Since 1845." Her most recent article is titled "Lemonade from Lemons: Gaining Strength from Financial Crisis," published in the American Council on Education magazine, *The Presidency* (Spring 2009). Dr. Cullinan received her B.A. from the University of Pennsylvania and her M.A. and Ph.D. in English Literature from the University of Wisconsin.

Roger W. Ferguson, Jr. is President and Chief Executive Officer of TIAA-CREF, the leading provider of retirement services in the academic, research, medical and cultural fields and a Fortune 100 financial services organization with $426 billion in combined assets under management. Mr. Ferguson served as Vice Chairman of the Board of Governors of the United States Federal Reserve System. He was a voting member of the Federal Open Market Committee, served as Chairman of the Financial Stability Forum, and chaired Federal Reserve Board committees on banking supervision and regulation, payment system policy and reserve bank oversight. Prior to joining TIAA-CREF in April 2008, Mr. Ferguson was head of financial services for Swiss Re, Chairman of Swiss Re America Holding Corporation and a member of the company's executive committee. From 1984 to 1997 he was an Associate and Partner at McKinsey & Company. He began his career as an attorney at the New York City office of Davis Polk & Wardwell. Mr. Ferguson is a member of President Obama's Economic Recovery Advisory Board and served on the Transition Economic Advisory Board. He is also a member of the Boards of Trustees for the Institute for Advanced Study, Carnegie Endowment for International Peace, the New America Foundation, and Memorial Sloan-Kettering Cancer Center. He is on the Board of Directors of Brevan Howard Asset Management LLP and the Partnership for New York City, and a member of the Council on Foreign Relations, the Economic Club of New York, the Harvard Law School Visiting Committee, and the Group of Thirty. Mr. Ferguson holds a B.A., J.D. and a Ph.D. in economics, all from Harvard University.

Bobby Fong became the 20th president of Butler University in June 2001, where he also holds a tenured appointment as Professor of English. He was previously Dean of the Faculty and Professor of English at Hamilton College (1995–2001), and Dean of Arts and Humanities and Professor of English at Hope College (1989–95). From 1978 to 1989 he was a member of the English department faculty at Berea College. He received his A.B. in English from Harvard University (1973) and his Ph.D. in English from UCLA (1978), where his dissertation research formed the basis for his lifelong scholarship in the works of Oscar Wilde. He is the editor of *Poems* *and Poems in Prose*, volume one in the Oxford English Texts edition of the *Complete Works of Oscar Wilde*, designated by *Choice* as one of the outstanding academic books of 2000. He is also the author of essays and monographs on literature, higher education, religion, and baseball. He has served on the Board of Directors for the American Council on Education and is currently a member of the Board of Directors for the Association of American Colleges & Universities, the Council of Presidents for the Association of Governing Boards, and the Board of Directors for the Council for Higher Education Accreditation. He was encouraged to go into higher education administration by a mentor who observed, "A professor controls the climate of teaching and learning in his own classroom; an administrator can affect the climate of teaching and learning across a campus."

Robert Charles Holub assumed his role as tenth chancellor of the flagship campus of the University of Massachusetts (UMass) Amherst on August 1, 2008. Previously he was provost and vice chancellor for academic affairs at the University of Tennessee's flagship campus in Knoxville. Most of Holub's professional life was spent at the University of California Berkeley, where he worked for 27 years. He was a full professor and held several administrative offices. During his tenure as chair of the German Department, the National Research Council ranked the department the best in the field. He also served as dean of the Undergraduate Division of the College of Letters and Science. Holub's academic interest is in nineteenth and twentieth century German intellectual, cultural, and literary history. He has written 12 books and more than 100 articles and essays on issues ranging from early nineteenth century German realism to postwar examination of the Holocaust. Dr. Holub earned a bachelor's degree in natural science from the University of Pennsylvania in 1971. At the University of Wisconsin–Madison, he earned a master's degree in comparative literature in 1973, a master's in German in 1976, and a doctorate in German in 1979.

William English Kirwan became the third chancellor of the University System of Maryland on August 1, 2002. He served as President of The Ohio State Univesity for four years (1998–2002) and President of the University of Maryland, College Park for 10 years (1988–1998). Prior to his presidency, he was a member of the University of Maryland faculty for 24 years. In May 2006, Dr. Kirwan was appointed to serve on the Knight Commission on Intercollegiate Athletics and became co-chair of the commission in May 2007. He also serves on the Board of Directors of the Council for Higher Education Accreditation; chairs the College Board's

Commission on Access, Admissions, and Success in Higher Education; and is a member of the Business-Higher Education Forum. Dr. Kirwan is also a member of the Board of Directors of the Greater Baltimore Committee, the Economic Alliance of Greater Baltimore, and the Maryland Business Roundtable for Education. Dr. Kirwan received his bachelor's degree in mathematics from the University of Kentucky and his master's and doctoral degrees in mathematics from Rutgers, The State University of New Jersey, in 1962 and 1964 respectively. In 2002, Dr. Kirwan was elected to the American Academy of Arts and Sciences. He is co-editor of the book *Advances in Complex Analysis* and has published many articles on mathematical research. On February 15, 2007, Dr. Kirwan became the 16th recipient of the Maryland House of Delegates Speaker's Medallion, which recognizes Maryland citizens who have demonstrated exemplary service to the House and to the State of Maryland. The TIAA-CREF Institute wishes to congratulate Dr. Kirwan on being recently honored with a 2009 Carnegie Corporation Academic Leadership Award.

Devorah Lieberman is Provost and Vice President for Academic Affairs at Wagner College. She assumed this position in January 2004, having been the Vice Provost and Special Assistant to the President at Portland State University in Portland, Oregon. Dr. Lieberman sees herself as both an academician and an administrator. As an academic and a scholar she continues to publish in the higher education literature and to present in higher education venues. Her publications have included edited books, chapters, journals and articles addressing institutional change, international studies, intercultural communications as well as faculty development. Her most recent publications have focused on academic institutions as learning organizations, issues of diversity in higher education, and creating community-based learning opportunities. Her academic grounding in intercultural communication keeps her deeply connected to diversity issues and internationalization on her campus and throughout higher education. Her work with civic education is closely tied to her commitment to educating the whole student while connecting theory to practice. Dr. Lieberman received her Ph.D. in Intercultural Communication (1984) from the University of Florida and concurrently received her certification in Gerontology.

Gregory M. St. L. O'Brien is Principal of The Higher Education Group, a consulting practice. O'Brien served as president of the 18 locations that constitute Argosy University from 2004 to 2008. Before joining Argosy, he served as chancellor of the University of New Orleans, where he also taught psychology and public affairs. Previous positions include provost and vice president of academic affairs at the University of South Florida, provost of the University of Michigan–Flint and dean of the School of Social Welfare at the University of Wisconsin–Milwaukee. Dr. O'Brien was also the director of the Human Services Design Laboratory at Case Western Reserve University in Cleveland, as well as an associate in psychiatry at the Laboratory of Community Psychiatry at Harvard Medical School. Dr. O'Brien is vice chair and member of the Board of Directors for the Council for Higher Education Accreditation, and formerly served as Chair of the Board of the National Association of State Universities and Land Grant Colleges, chair of the NCAA Presidents' Commission and president of The American College of Mental Health. Dr. O'Brien was inducted into the Junior Achievement Business Hall of Fame in 1999 and has received the United States Navy's Meritorious Service Award. He received a Ph.D. and master's degree in social psychology from Boston University.

Eduardo Padrón has served since 1995 as President of Miami Dade College (MDC), the largest institution of higher education in the U.S. with more than 170,000 students. Padrón has engineered a culture of success that has produced impressive results in student access, retention, graduation, and achievement at MDC which enrolls and graduates more minorities than any other institution in America. In 2009, *TIME* magazine included him on its list of "The 10 Best College Presidents." He is nationally respected for his advocacy on behalf of underserved populations in higher education. Padrón has also championed innovative teaching and learning strategies. His report, *A Deficit of Understanding*, highlights the funding crisis that threatens access for low-income and minority students.

Padrón is the immediate past chair of the board of the Association of American Colleges and Universities (AAC&U) and is vice chair and chair-elect of the board of the American Council on Education (ACE). He served on AAC&U's *Greater Expectations* panel that re-examined baccalaureate education in the U.S. President George W. Bush nominated him to the National Institute for Literacy Advisory Board. More recently, he represented the U.S. at UNESCO's World Conference on Higher Education at the invitation of the Obama administration, and President Obama appointed him Chairman of the White House Initiative on Educational Excellence for Hispanic Americans. In addition, Padrón currently serves on the boards of the Business/Higher Education Forum, League for Innovation in the Community College, RC 2020, the Collins Center for Public Policy, College Board Advocacy and Policy Center, 2010 White House Fellows Selection Panel, the International Association of University Presidents, the Federal Reserve Board of Atlanta (Miami

Branch), and the Council on Foreign Relations. Most recently, he was appointed to the White House/Congressional Commission of the National Museum of the American Latino.

Dr. Padrón earned his Ph.D. from the University of Florida, and he is the recipient of numerous honorary doctorates and awards. The recent list includes the 2008 *Charles Kennedy Equity Award* (Association of Community College Trustees), the 2008 *Reginald Wilson Diversity Leadership Award* (American Council on Education) and the 2008 *Innovator of the Year* (League for Innovation in the Community College). He is a prolific writer with numerous publications to his credit and serves on the editorial boards of *The Presidency, University Business,* and *Campus Technology.* In addition, he is a guest columnist for *Hispanic Magazine* and *The Miami Herald.* Padrón has been featured in *People* magazine as one of the world's most influential Hispanics, in *Hispanic* magazine's list of most powerful Latinos, and in *PODER* magazine's report on "Movers and Shakers."

Charles B. Reed is chancellor of the 23-campus California State University system, the country's largest system of higher education. As chancellor for the past 11 years, he has improved access to the CSU, especially among ethnic minority students; created the system's first stand-alone doctoral degree; created strong accountability measures; established a system-wide commitment to community service and civic engagement; and developed stronger collaborations with K-12 schools. The CSU's mission is to provide high-quality, affordable education to meet the ever-changing needs of the people of California. Before joining the CSU, Dr. Reed served as chancellor of the State University System of Florida and, earlier, as chief of staff to the governor of Florida.

Craig Swenson joined Argosy University as President-designate in September 2007 and officially became President on January 1, 2008. Swenson was previously Provost and Academic Vice President at Western Governors University in Salt Lake City, UT. Prior to that he was Provost and Senior Vice President for Academic Affairs for the University of Phoenix system, where he had also served as a Senior Regional Vice President, and as a Campus Vice President/Director. He joined that institution's faculty in 1998 and was recipient of its Distinguished Teaching Award in 1989.

Swenson is a member of the Board of Directors of the Council on Higher Education (CHEA) and serves on the United States Army Educational Advisory Committee, advising the Secretary of the Army on education and training matters. He was a member of the National

Advisory Committee on Institutional Quality and Integrity (NACIQI), advising the United States Secretary of Education on matters related to accreditation and to the eligibility and certification process for institutions of higher education. Additionally, he was a non-federal negotiator for the United States Department of Education 2007 Negotiated Rulemaking Process. He serves as a peer reviewer for the Higher Learning Commission of the North Central Association, one of the nation's six regional accrediting associations.

Dr. Swenson holds a bachelor's degree in Journalism and Mass Communication from the University of Utah and a master's degree in Organizational Communication from Brigham Young University. His Ph.D. in Education was awarded by Walden University. He has published frequently in the areas of higher education, organizational management, distance learning, and faculty development. He has also served as a consultant for large corporations and non-profit organizations.

Stephen Joel Trachtenberg is president emeritus and university professor of public service at The George Washington University (GW). He served as George Washington's 15th president from 1988 to 2007. Mr. Trachtenberg moved to George Washington from the University of Hartford, where he had been president for 11 years. Previously he held positions as vice president for academic services and academic dean of the College of Liberal Arts at Boston University. He also served as the special assistant to the United States Education Commissioner, Department of Health, Education and Welfare. Mr. Trachtenberg is a member of the Council on Foreign Relations, Phi Beta Kappa and the Board of Directors of the Chiang Chen Industrial Charity Foundation in Hong Kong, the Bankinter Foundation in Madrid and the Ditchley Foundation in England. He is a Fellow of the American Academy of Arts and Sciences and a Fellow of the National Academy of Public Administration. Mr. Trachtenberg chairs the Rhodes Scholarships Selection Committee for Maryland and the District of Columbia and has published five books. He earned a bachelor's degree from Columbia University, a J.D. from Yale University, and a Master of Public Administration degree from Harvard University.

Jane Wellman is the Executive Director of the Delta Project on Postsecondary Costs, Productivity and Accountability, a research and policy organization located in Washington, DC. The Delta Project's mission is to improve productivity in higher education through more effective management of resources without compromising student access or quality. Established in 2007, the Delta Project has produced two national reports on trends in college costs and prices, and has developed and made publicly available a database with over 20 years of revenue and spending data for over 2,000 public and private nonprofit institutions. Ms. Wellman is widely recognized for her expertise in state fiscal policy; cost analysis; strategic planning; state and federal regulation of higher education; accountability metrics and performance reporting; and quality control including accreditation. She is a member of the Board of Directors for the Association of American Colleges and Universities, and a member of the Board of Trustees for Argosy University.

Paul J. Yakoboski is a Principal Research Fellow with the TIAA-CREF Institute. He conducts, manages and communicates research on issues such as income and asset management in retirement, defined contribution plan design, the preparation of higher education faculty for retirement, managing faculty retirement patterns, options for funding retiree health care, and research on issues related to strategic management in higher education. He is also responsible for the development and execution of Institute symposiums on such issues. In addition, Yakoboski serves as director of the Institute's Fellows Program and editor of the Institute's *Trends and Issues* and *Advancing Higher Education* publication series. Prior to joining the TIAA-CREF Institute, he held positions as Director of Research for the American Council of Life Insurers (2000–04), Senior Research Associate with the Employee Benefit Research Institute (1991–2000) and Senior Economist with the U.S. Government Accountability Office (1989–91). He is a member of the American Economic Association and serves on the editorial advisory board of *Benefits Quarterly*. He previously served as Director of Research for the American Savings Education Council (1995–2000). Between 1986 and 1988, he served as an adjunct faculty member at Nazareth College (Rochester, NY). Yakoboski earned his Ph.D. (1990) and M.A. (1987) in economics from the University of Rochester (Rochester, NY) and his B.S. (1984) in economics from Virginia Tech (Blacksburg, VA).

CONFERENCE PANELISTS AND MODERATORS

J. Michael Adams (see list of authors)
Kent John Chabotar (see list of authors)
Jared Cohon, President, Carnegie Mellon University
Molly Corbett Broad, President, American Council on Education
Michael M. Crow (see list of authors)
Mary Cullinan (see list of authors)

Madeleine d'Ambrosio, Vice President, TIAA-CREF Institute
Roger W. Ferguson, Jr. (see list of authors)
Elson S. Floyd, President, Washington State University
Bobby Fong (see list of authors)
E. Gordon Gee, President, The Ohio State University
David Gergen, Professor, Harvard University; Editor-at-Large, U.S. News & World Report; Senior Political Analyst, CNN
Robert C. Holub (see list of authors)
Muriel A. Howard, President, AASCU
Elizabeth Huidekoper, Executive Vice President for Finance and Administration, Brown University
William E. Kirwan (see list of authors)
C. Alan Korthals, Director of Client Support, Kaspick & Company, LLC
Devorah Lieberman (see list of authors)
John Lippincott, President, Council for Advancement and Support of Education
Gregory O'Brien (see list of authors)
Eduardo J. Padrón (see list of authors)
Charles B. Reed (see list of authors)
Stephen Joel Trachtenberg (see list of authors)
Jane Wellman (see list of authors)
Blenda Wilson, Former President, Nellie Mae Foundation; Former President, California State University–Northridge

Foreword

Roger W. Ferguson, Jr.

From 2007 it has been especially challenging for leaders in higher education. More students of all ages are applying to college, in an effort to improve skills and acquire new credentials for an uncertain job market. Yet public and private resources to meet this demand have declined, while rising tuition and fee levels over many years have left limited headroom for further increases.

Colleges and universities have acted decisively to address budgetary challenges and restructure the way they deliver an outstanding education to a diverse and growing student population.

Hiring freezes, furloughs, early retirement packages, and federal research funding are helping to bridge short-term budget gaps. Long-term strategies include three-year degree programs; online courses and degree offerings; research and academic partnerships with other institutions at the K-12, community college, and university level; and a greater international focus.

As the higher education community continues to grapple with an uncertain economy and long-term structural challenges, the TIAA-CREF Institute will be an intellectual partner, leading research into how colleges and universities can build on their strengths and reposition themselves for future success. In November 2009, the Institute hosted "*Smart Leadership in Difficult Times*," a conference of university presidents, chancellors, academic deans, researchers and other leaders, to discuss innovative answers to questions being asked on many campuses.

We are grateful for the contributions of 150 scholars and leaders, thirteen of whom have adapted their presentations for inclusion in this book. Their chapters analyze the economic outlook for higher education and highlight several ways colleges and universities can establish an affordable model of rigorous, relevant education.

Higher education has long been a source of innovation and fresh thinking about many areas of society. The task ahead is to apply the same mindset internally, focusing on the future of a sector that is vital to

American achievement. TIAA-CREF and the TIAA-CREF Institute look forward to continuing our partnership with all who are thinking boldly about the future of higher education.

Introduction

Paul J. Yakoboski

As the U.S. economy emerges from the severest recession in a generation, the harshest effects of the economic downturn are likely ahead for higher education as campus leadership focuses on enrollment, affordability and fundraising. Most colleges and universities have implemented significant expense reductions, such as cuts or consolidations in academic departments and programs, reorganizations in administration, and increases in class sizes and teaching loads. While not accustomed to lay-offs or furloughs, a number of colleges and universities have taken such steps. Institutions have also slowed or canceled capital projects to limit additions to debt or preserve liquidity.

With large questions regarding the long-term ramifications of the recession unanswered for higher education, the TIAA-CREF Institute hosted the Higher Education Leadership Conference, "Smart Leadership in Difficult Times" in November 2009. The conference brought together presidents, chancellors, other senior campus officials, higher education researchers and thought leaders, and the senior management of TIAA-CREF to examine pursuit of higher education's mission moving forward in a resource-constrained environment. The economic success of individuals and the U.S. economy as a whole, as well as the vitality of America's democracy, are directly dependent in a global society on colleges and universities fulfilling their core missions of education, research and service.

During his keynote address at the conference, David Gergen, Professor at Harvard University, Editor-at-Large with U.S. News & World Report, and Senior Political Analyst with CNN, argued that there will be no return to the old normal for the economy as it emerges from this recession. Praising colleges and universities as the crown jewel of America, he maintained the paramount role of higher education if America is to successfully adapt to the new normal in a global economy and society. Furthermore, he observed that the same macro-level forces are leading to a new normal in higher education as well.

Gergen maintained that colleges and universities must confront the reality that the increasing cost of a higher education, combined with decreasing public funding, led to the current crunch in their collective budgets. He noted that while the cost of health care has risen 250 percent over the last 25 years, the cost of higher education has increased over 400 percent. Budget duress is forcing college and university boards to rethink their business model. He argued the need for a model that can address challenges such as providing a rich experience in the best tradition of a liberal arts education where students study under professors with doctorate degrees, using the internet to save money while preserving the quality of student's experience, and recognizing that innovation is key to thriving in a globally competitive environment.

This volume was inspired by the conference presentations and dialogue, and all chapters are authored by conference participants. Several themes that emerged during the conference are further explored throughout this volume:

- There will be no return to the pre-recession status quo in higher education. In fact, the new normal confronting higher education is not driven by the economic recession, but rather by demographics and globalization. The United States must increase the share of its population receiving a higher education if it is to lead and succeed in the emerging global order and economy.
- The new normal entails innovating to meet the needs for higher education among a growing population of potential students from disadvantaged socioeconomic backgrounds, many of whom are ill-prepared for a college education and unaware of how to access it, and a population of mid-career students seeking to retool or reinvent themselves for the labor market.
- The environment of the new normal is constrained resources as public funding for higher education remains tight, fundraising remains difficult, endowments recover slowly, and pressures mount against current rates of tuition increases.
- Innovation in higher education must involve partnerships with the K-12 sector and better coordination between two-year and four-year institutions. It also means rethinking the development and delivery of curriculums to a student generation that communicates and learns differently than any prior generation.
- Engaging faculty will be crucial for the success of any change strategy.

Many parties will wish to return to the old normal, but fulfilling the mission of higher education will require implementing change in the face of opposition, gaining support from key stakeholders, and maintaining morale in the process.

Chapter 1 of this volume, authored by David Breneman, University Professor at the University of Virginia and co-editor of the volume, examines the question of whether the business model of higher education is broken. In the realm of higher education, Breneman interprets "broken" to mean an inability to provide a college-level education for all citizens able to benefit and an inability to develop the new knowledge necessary for the United States to lead and compete in the global economy. The question and the issues it raises are central to the topics addressed throughout the remainder of the volume. Furthermore, if higher education's business model is broken, then how should colleges and universities change and adapt?

In the chapter Breneman explores arguments on both sides of the question. Evidence supporting the proposition of a broken business model includes rates of tuition increases that are unsustainable without pricing hundreds of thousands of students out of a higher education, severe budgetary challenges despite such tuition increases, and a lack of organizational flexibility and adaptability in the face of these challenges.

On the other side, evidence cited against a broken business model includes steady enrollment rates among high school graduates and enrollment levels at historic highs. Affordability does not seem to be an issue as long as individuals can borrow to fund their investment in higher education, but many families do not, or cannot, view higher education as an investment. The argument is also outlined that very low, subsidized tuition levels were economically inefficient since they benefited not only those in need, but also those who could afford a college education at a market price. High tuitions with need-based financial aid are viewed as more efficient. Finally, for-profit institutions are not seen as direct competition for traditional college and university students; they are best viewed as expanding the market for a higher education to new population segments.

In Chapters 2 and 3, chancellors of two large state university systems, Brit Kirwan of the University System of Maryland and Charles Reed of the California State University System discuss the challenges faced by public higher education in the new normal and how public higher education must respond. Both consider it imperative, despite difficult economic times, for colleges and universities to serve a broader population of students, in particular, under-represented minorities and low income students.

In Chapter 2, Kirwan spells out three key challenges facing higher education – completion, cost and competitiveness. He foresees too many high school graduates failing to earn a college degree in the future, with serious repercussions not only for the individual, but for the United States in today's global economy. He sees the completion challenge as at least partially driven by costs with many college-ready and capable students priced out of a higher education.

Subsequently, Kirwan elaborates on specific problems that must be addressed by public higher education. In particular, he notes the existing gap between high school graduation requirements and college-entrance expectations, a gap that can be especially large for those from disadvantaged backgrounds. Kirwan calls for a recognition by higher education of its responsibility to students before they even enroll on campus. This means a significant change in the relationships between four-year colleges and universities, the K-12 system and community colleges, with a focus on enhancing teacher training and development, improving student learning, and making higher education a desirable, realistic and achievable goal irrespective of a student's socioeconomic background. As part of this response, Kirwan also calls upon colleges and universities to refocus financial aid so it is based on need, not merit.

In Chapter 3, Reed elaborates on higher education's greatest challenge in his view – "helping underserved students, ethic minority students, and low-income students to graduate from high school, start college, graduate, and move into the workforce." He discusses efforts in California, a majority-minority state, to address this challenge with fewer resources than ever. Reed maintains that K-12 teacher preparation and development must be a priority for public colleges and universities; beyond recruiting individuals and training them well, this means developing effective classroom pedagogies. Reed also outlines efforts in California to improve student readiness for college-level work before their arrival on campus. He also explains California State University's (CSU) efforts to proactively reach into the communities where underserved students live to assist with college preparation and to motivate a desire to pursue a college degree. Reed argues that colleges and universities have a responsibility to do more than "simply holding the door open" for such students. He also outlines the need for a reengineered student experience on campus to enable and promote degree completion by these students.

Michael Crow, President of Arizona State University (ASU), begins Chapter 4 by describing his view of a deep-rooted lack of innovation in higher education that has led to what he sees as design flaws in colleges and universities and shortcomings in the overall model of higher education. Combined with public disinvestment in higher education, this has led to a lack of access, particularly for the disadvantaged. But beyond mere access, Crow maintains that more individuals must be educated successfully at higher levels of attainment than is typical today.

He then proceeds to argue the need for "perpetual innovation" in the evolution of higher education, particularly research universities which he contends should be understood as "comprehensive knowledge enterprises committed to discovery, creativity, and innovation." He presents the case study of the reconceptualization of ASU as pioneering the model for the "New American University" which is "an egalitarian institution committed to academic excellence, inclusiveness to a broad demographic, and maximum societal impact." Design aspirations guiding the reconceptualization include creating a culture of academic enterprise and knowledge entrepreneurship, pursuing use-inspired research, transcending disciplinary limitations, becoming a force for societal transformation, and advancing global engagement.

Crow explains that the reconceptualization of ASU has resulted in four differentiated campuses, each with a clustering of related but distinct colleges and schools, including two dozen transdisciplinary colleges and schools that are complemented by transdisciplinary research initiatives. ASU has also expanded access to all qualified students, including those "who do not conform to a standard academic profile" and those lacking the financial means to pursue a four-year degree. In addition, ASU has established differentiated learning platforms within disciplines to offer students multiple pathways to a given degree.

In Chapter 5, Eduardo Padrón, President of Miami Dade College (MDC), emphasizes the theme of organizational effectiveness in mission driven institutions dedicated to "student learning, research for the good of society, a ready workforce and strong communities." Padrón maintains that evaluation of institutional effectiveness must consider access to a higher education experience and completion of the requirements for a college degree, as well as the finances of the college and university. He argues that the reemergence of a strong middle class in America depends on wide access to higher education, especially for those individuals from disadvantaged socioeconomic backgrounds.

Padrón outlines how technology and demographics, especially the growth of the Hispanic population, are impacting higher education. He explains that the Hispanic population is younger and significantly less educated relative to the United States population as a whole. Padrón maintains that higher education must respond by partnering with public K-12, especially in urban areas, and argues that such partnerships send youth a message that going to college is essential and doable. Once students from disadvantaged backgrounds are enrolled, colleges and universities must be "intentionally intrusive regarding academic progress" to maximize the chances of completion.

While technology is a crucial element in planning higher education's future, Padrón maintains that it is the most challenging to address and manage given the pace of change involved. For this reason technology planning must be incorporated into the overall institutional planning process and it must address faculty support and professional development as well as effective student learning.

Padrón then moves on to a broader discussion of the planning process on campus, which he believes should serve as "a source of clarity regarding the direction of the institution, and just as importantly, an opportunity to engage members of the college or university community in setting that direction." Done well, Padrón maintains the planning process creates ownership throughout the institution. Planning at MDC starts from an articulation of the ideal regarding the institution's mission and that ideal is then translated into a practical and accessible plan.

In the following two chapters, Mary Cullinan, President of Southern Oregon University (SOU), and Robert Holub, Chancellor of the University of Massachusetts – Amherst, share their experiences as new presidents who needed to bring immediate, dramatic change to their institutions.

Cullinan begins Chapter 6 by outlining major challenges confronting higher education – state disinvestment, tuition increases and student debt, negative perceptions, and a less-educated populace. She then presents Southern Oregon University as a case study of a public institution in the process of adapting to its "new normal." Upon her arrival in 2006, SOU was in precarious financial shape with enrollment below target and low financial reserves. Financial retrenchment entailing organizational restructuring and lay-offs was necessary. Two years later, SOU's finances had been stabilized. Ironically, this retrenchment better positioned SOU to face the economic challenges of 2008–09.

Cullinan outlines key components of the process followed by SOU – listening and communicating with all the university's constituencies, making the budget process more transparent, recreating and filling a team structure necessary to make difficult decisions for repositioning the university, planning and branding a unified vision and mission for the university, restructuring and redefining positions while decreasing the number of administrators and instructors, addressing enrollment and other revenue streams, pursuing partnerships that match SOU's mission and strategic plan, and maintaining campus morale.

In Chapter 7, Holub discusses the beginning of his tenure shortly before the financial crisis. Part of the UMass–Amherst financial gap was addressed through common strategies, such as increased fees, hiring freezes and travel restrictions. Holub explains that in striving to move beyond such typical actions, the most challenging endeavor has been reorganizing the university's administrative structure. The merger of certain functions in the Provost and the Chancellor's offices was straightforward, but attempts to reorganize the university's nine colleges and schools have been problematic, as described by Holub.

The reorganization strategy, based on both academic rationale and financial necessity, was met with faculty objections driven by, in Holub's description, considerations of impacts on individual units, as opposed to consideration of the best interest for the campus as a whole. Holub's merger strategy was supported in the sciences where faculty were doing similar work, but not elsewhere. A committee of department chairs made recommendations to Holub which he viewed as insufficient to save the necessary dollars or achieve the desired academic synergies. At this juncture, a new College of Natural Science has been created from merged departments, but other planned mergers have been delayed pending more study.

Holub shares several lessons for campus leaders regarding reorganization – personal contact is as important as rational arguments in making the case for change, saving money is not necessarily enough to gain faculty support, faculty buy-in for reorganization is dependent on research and curricular possibilities, institutional history matters greatly, identify and work with faculty leaders who share your vision for the institution, and make the budget and budget process transparent.

Chapters 8 to 11 present views from several leaders of private, non-profit colleges and universities. Michael Adams, President of Fairleigh Dickinson University (FDU), begins Chapter 8 by arguing that higher education is highly resistant to change and discussing reasons for the prevalence of this resistance. He notes that basic fear and uncertainty are powerful deterrents to change, especially on campus. He then relates this resistance to recognition of the need for internationalizing American campuses.

How then to initiate and accelerate change? Adams explains that change is often triggered by external pressures. But he maintains that it need not and should not be this way in higher education. He argues that colleges and universities must be more agile and that empowering faculty is key – ". . . faculty entrepreneurial thinkers who can best adapt to the particular needs of their constituents and their times while remaining true to the institutional goals."

Adams then explains that forces of globalization are currently exerting the greatest pressures for change in higher education, but colleges and universities have generally been slow to respond. He states that "education must be global, or we risk being irrelevant." This means preparing students to be global citizens and Adams outlines the FDU model for providing a global education. He explains that a new institutional mission "to prepare world citizens through global education" was developed in 2000, and all mission-driven changes and initiatives since have been spearheaded by FDU faculty.

Kent Chabotar, President of Guilford College, begins Chapter 9 by noting the danger and risk inherent in predicting the future for higher education, and then proceeds to make several observations regarding future campus revenue streams. First, tuition and fees will continue as the primary revenue source for private colleges and universities. Furthermore, they will likely continue growing as a share of revenue, but not because of continued tuition increases in the ten percent range, rather because other revenue sources and budgets will grow more slowly. Second, Chabotar expects increased tuition discounting and more pressure to secure endowment support for this aid. He also sees an increase in the practices of unbundling and price discrimination as they relate to tuition. Third, colleges and universities will receive more funding from bequests, planned giving and life income trusts, with more of those gifts directed to areas of greatest need. Fourth, Chabotar does not expect sources that have helped offset losses for higher education in previous financial downturns – full-pay students, endowments and government funds – to do so to the same degree this time.

In addition, Chabotar anticipates more use of program prioritization based on standards such as student demand, centrality to mission and cost. He also believes that there are lessons to be learned from the for-profit sector, such as the value of course standardization in selected cases. Finally, Chabotar believes that private colleges and universities must be strategic with respect to growth so that new capital costs do not negate the financial gain from increased enrollments.

In Chapter 10, Bobby Fong, President of Butler University, explains that any consideration of the implications of the "new normal" for colleges and universities must distinguish across institutional sectors, types and missions. For privates, Fong offers a basic taxonomy of institutions along two dimensions – well-endowed versus tuition-dependent and selective admissions versus more open enrollment. The fundamental assumption regarding well-endowed, selective institutions that a large endowment is an unmitigated good has been undercut. When a disproportionately large share of an institution's operating budget is funded by its endowment, a large drop in the endowment value stresses the ability to sustain programs and personnel levels. Moving forward, Fong expects such institutions to use endowments less for ongoing operations and more for one-time initiatives. In turn, this could mean tuition and enrollment increases.

Well-endowed, less-selective institutions typically use endowments to underwrite financial aid which helps fill classes. In this case, a significant endowment drop eliminates the competitive advantage of relatively generous aid packages, making it harder to achieve enrollment targets. This can place such institutions in a precarious position as they may experience deterioration in the size and profile of future entering classes.

Fong next explains that tuition-driven, selective institutions that have been able to maintain their enrollments are experiencing relatively few problems. Since endowments account for only a minor share of operating budgets (for example, six percent in the case of Butler), the impact of endowment drops has been minor. Such institutions should continue to flourish if they maintain their enrollment levels. Fong notes, however, that resistance to continued tuition increases was an issue prior to the economic downturn and will remain a challenge moving forward.

Tuition-driven, non-selective institutions may be the hardest hit according to Fong, and he foresees the possibility of closures in this sector if economic stresses continue. A spiral can ensue as enrollment decreases necessitate cuts in programs and personnel, but such cuts make it harder to attract and retain students.

Fong then argues that higher education in the United States can best serve the needs of individual students if colleges and universities focus on maintaining their institutional distinctiveness. Each institution needs to deliberately define its mission and focus on its comparative advantages according to Fong.

In Chapter 11, Devorah Lieberman, Provost and Vice President for Academic Affairs at Wagner College, argues that culture drives the success of a college or university. Furthermore, a college or university must evolve and adapt to its changing environment. But this necessitates culture change and culture change is dependent upon faculty. Lieberman concludes that it makes sense then to invest in strategies to nurture and sustain faculty commitment to the institution.

After considering research regarding faculty career motivations and current job satisfaction, Lieberman argues that faculty development must be an ongoing process throughout an individual's career. She first discusses strategic faculty recruitment based on program and departmental needs, but also with a vision of the evolution in courses, pedagogy, student demographics, market demand for graduates, and competition with peer institutions. Next she focuses on professional development broadly defined as "an ongoing process that evolves the capacity of individuals to achieve their personal goals and intellectual passions while meeting institutional expectations set for performance of their duties."

Lieberman then outlines Wagner College's faculty development strategy which is based on four principles – (1) active learning requires continuing evolution of the pedagogy, (2) professional growth is a developmental process, (3) development includes social interactions where institutional information is exchanged, and (4) finding renewal and meaning in work is critical to continued growth and development. These principles lead to a multi-pronged approach including personal support, financial support and structural support, along with intentional venues for promoting collegiality. Lieberman discusses Wagner's programs along each of these dimensions and expresses her institution's view that these commitments are particularly important to maintain during periods of economic and political uncertainty.

In Chapter 12, Jane Wellman, Executive Director of the Delta Project, exhorts colleges and universities to drop assumptions that get in the way of change; assumptions such as "it is impossible to control costs without harming quality" and "money equates with excellence." She notes that research reveals little correlation between spending and performance.

Wellman begins the chapter by explaining that higher education is stratified economically, with a relatively small cluster of institutions having access to significant resources. She notes that privatization was the dominant revenue trend in the 1990s with tuition increasing in relative importance as a source of general revenue. While the majority of private higher education is heavily tuition dependent, the growth in access to private resources (endowments and gifts) spiked considerably among a handful of institutions during the 1990s. By 2006 these revenue sources accounted for approximately 40 percent of operating revenues among these institutions which collectively enrolled approximately ten percent of students across higher education. Wellman explains that endowment revenues had not historically funded general operating expenses and gifts were typically assigned to special functions, so this development represented a paradigm shift for these institutions.

Wellman warns that higher education can not look for revenue solutions to structural spending problems. She argues that higher education must manage its resources to support increased educational attainment and that it cannot retreat from collective responsibility for serving public needs simply because there is not as much money. She does not view recent levels of tuition increases as sustainable. Furthermore, she maintains that unless higher education reigns in tuition hikes and increases transparency regarding its fiscal stewardship, it will not turn the tide of negative public perceptions that are the excuse as much as the reason for disinvestment of public resources.

She also argues that higher education must increase the focus on learning productivity so that courses and credits accumulate towards degrees in a more efficient manner; she cites Delta Project research estimating that 40 percent of the cost of degree production at the undergraduate level is attributable to excess credits earned by graduates and attrition. Along these same lines she later lauds the for-profit sector's emphasis on a structured curriculum and student counseling.

Chapter 13 focuses on the for-profit, or in the terminology of the chapter authors, the investor-owned sector of higher education. Gregory O'Brien (Principal of The Higher Education Group and former President of Argosy University), Craig Swenson (President of Argosy University), and Geoffrey Bannister (former President of Schiller International University and Butler University) maintain that investor-owned institutions address the pressures facing higher education differently than public and non-profit private institutions, and therein lies lessons for the latter.

The authors begin by noting that similarities across sectors far exceed the differences, and they discuss some widely held assumptions across institutional types regarding short-term versus long-term focus, faculty roles in curriculum development and governance, and the pressures for consistency and uniformity in course offerings. From there, O'Brien, Swenson, and Bannister detail differences that have evolved in the investor-owned sector, along with the lessons to be learned from these differences –

- Operating with agility and just-in-time decision-making
- Emphasizing scalability
- Making student needs the priority
- Using adjunct faculty purposefully
- Developing metrics for every aspect of operations
- Evaluating new initiatives as capital investments with a cost-benefit perspective
- Decision-making based on mission focus and clarity
- Understanding and targeting the market of potential students
- Collaborating while competing

The authors explain that there are sound reasons for the growth of investor-owned colleges and universities, and lessons for the rest of higher education in understanding that success.

In Chapter 14, Stephen Trachtenberg, President Emeritus of The George Washington University (GWU), concludes the volume with a set of observations and arguments pointing to the peril of a well-ingrained resistance to substantive change in the higher educational model in the absence of financial necessity. He maintains that administrators and academics see few if any new solutions to the structural problems confronting higher education operations and governance.

Trachtenberg argues that common practices in colleges and universities are not unchangeable. For example, he argues that an undergraduate degree should not take four years to earn and he then makes several suggestions on how to address the time to degree challenge. But he sees such proposals as non-starters within the higher education community and relates the resistance to even considering the idea at GWU.

Trachtenberg also makes the case that the structure of the research university does not realistically make sense for, nor does it benefit, the majority of state universities and the students they serve. On the administrative side of higher education, Trachtenberg argues that a vast oversupply of Ph.D.'s continues to be produced relative to demand in the liberal arts and social science academic labor markets. He also questions the teaching loads of many senior tenured professors. He views much of this as resulting from a reticence among senior administrators to take on the faculty who typically wield great power over changes in governance. Nonetheless Trachtenberg remains hopeful that American higher education will overcome this grim moment as it has ones before.

CONCLUDING THOUGHTS

As noted by Roger Ferguson, President and CEO, TIAA-CREF, in his keynote presentation during the conference, there are a limited number of levers – lay-offs, salary and hiring freezes, benefit reductions, certain structural reorganizations and postponement of major initiatives – that colleges and universities can pull to work through the current economic crisis in the short-run. In the face of what he projects to be a likely lengthy and challenging economic recovery, Ferguson maintained that while such actions make sense today, they can perversely make progress more difficult tomorrow.

The good news, as demonstrated by the dialogue throughout the course of the conference, is that the higher education business model is evolving and creative strategies are emerging to address the long-term strategic challenges recognized by the leadership of higher education; challenges that are primarily related to, but not restricted to, access, cost and effectiveness, particularly for individuals from poor socioeconomic backgrounds. As further noted by Ferguson, while higher education is dealing with stressful and difficult times, it is showing the kind of resilience and creativity that one would expect of a leading sector in the United States economy.

1. Is the business model of higher education broken?

David W. Breneman

In recent years, several industries in the United States have struggled with failing business models. The examples are numerous: automobile manufacturers, newspapers, electronics manufacturing, textiles, clothing, shoes, and airlines, to name but a few. Recently, the business model concept has been applied to non-profit organizations as well, including colleges and universities. In that framework it's legitimate to ask whether, and to what extent, the business model of higher education is broken, or unsustainable, in its current form. This chapter, originally prepared for The Miller Center of Public Affairs at the University of Virginia as background for their National Debate and Discussion Series, provides a context for the chapters that follow.

When the business model concept is applied to for-profit industries, the focus is primarily on the survival of firms in the industry. In most cases, there is limited public interest in preventing firms from failing, as new suppliers, often with lower production costs or new technologies, enter the marketplace, displacing older industries and providing consumers with newer, often better, products.[1] Non-profit higher education differs from the case of for-profit firms, however, in that a public interest exists in the education of our citizens, not only for careers but for civic and community leadership. Both public and non-profit private institutions of higher education, and their students, receive billions of dollars in public subsidies to ensure adequate investment in the nation's human capital.[2] For institutions charged with broad public purposes, many would argue that the concept of a broken business model must be enlarged to consider how well these broader purposes are being achieved. Even if the majority of institutions manage to survive, it is possible that in so doing they may fail to accomplish the public purposes for which they were founded and have been supported historically.

In addition to providing educational opportunity for all citizens able to benefit, the nation also relies on higher education for developing new knowledge and sharing that knowledge through education, public service, and supporting economic development. Evaluating the higher education business model must, therefore, consider not just the solvency of the providers but also their ability to meet these vital social responsibilities. This chapter discusses the financial and organizational challenges confronting the higher education industry, and threats to its ability to perform effectively. Those who assert that the business model is broken argue that shifts in the way higher education is financed render it increasingly unaffordable to many students, and that institutional incentives toward increased status and prestige distort internal resource allocation in wasteful and inefficient ways. Others argue that the benefits of higher education accrue primarily to the recipient, and thus it is desirable (and efficient) for students to pay a higher share of the cost, borrowing if necessary to make that investment. The next section provides information relevant to these positions, followed by key "pro" and "con" arguments on the topic.

BACKGROUND

Many of us aged 60 or more remember when tuition in public higher education was extremely low, or even non-existent, as state governments provided the bulk of operating support for state colleges and universities. That pattern of high state support, and low (or no) tuition, began to change in the 1980s, as the state share of institutional budgets began a secular decline that continues to this day, although with some ebb and flow corresponding to the business cycle.[3] Measured in constant (2008) dollars per full-time equivalent (FTE) student, state support in public institutions in 1985 was $7,269; in 2005, that number had fallen to $6,445, a drop of 11.3 percent.[4] Institutions responded to the declining share of state support by seeking funds from other sources, including philanthropy and research support, but the primary source they could directly increase was tuition. Over the same time period noted above, net tuition revenue (gross tuition and fees minus state and institutional aid and tuition waivers) climbed from approximately 22 to 36 percent of public institution educational revenues (the sum of state appropriations plus tuition).[5] The College Board reports in its 2009 publication on college costs that public four-year in-state tuition and fees average $7,020 and that total expenses for a residential student for one academic year averages $19,388.[6] (The comparable figure for private four-year schools is $39,028.) At these rates, students and families are looking at a sticker price of roughly $80,000 for a public four-year degree, and nearly $160,000 for a private four-year degree, a sharp and dramatic increase in prices from the world of 30 years ago.[7]

The National Center on Public Policy and Higher Education has examined college affordability in a somewhat different fashion. Figure 1.1 compares the growth in current dollar prices of tuition and fees to the growth of median family income and to a variety of other spending categories.[8] While median family income in the period 1982–2006 rose by 147 percent, college tuition and fees soared by 439 percent, outstripping all of the other expenditure categories listed. The Center then compared net college costs (tuition, room and board minus financial aid) at public four-year and two-year colleges to median family incomes by quintile, lowest to highest (see Table 1.1). In the relatively short time period from 1999 to 2007, public four-year costs jumped from 39 to 55 percent of the median income of the lowest income quintile families, an indication of how rapidly college costs are outstripping ability to pay.

What we have witnessed over several decades has been a steady shifting of the costs of public higher education from the general taxpayer to the student and family. Public institutional leaders initially decried this trend, but as state government budgets have slipped further and further into structural deficit,[9] many college leaders have given up hope that the country will ever return to a time of significantly higher state support and lower tuition. Talk of privatization of higher education is now often heard, and although somewhat exaggerated, that term certainly appears to describe the direction that finance is taking.[10] The concern, obviously, is that rising prices, even when offset to some degree by financial aid, will discourage many low and middle income young people from considering college a realistic option, thereby lowering our national educational level, reducing future economic growth, and undermining the promise of equal educational opportunity.

Coupled with this concern is the claim that higher education cannot (or will not) control its cost increases, and thus the production cost of higher education (not the same as tuition) also rises at rates above the Consumer Price Index (CPI). As a consequence, some argue that in the face of declining state support, colleges have chosen to pass on costs to students rather than seek operating efficiencies to reduce costs. It has also been argued that the growth of federal student aid, in the form of Pell Grants and Guaranteed Student Loans, has contributed to rising tuitions, either by analogy to the third-party payer argument applied to medical costs, or by arguing simply that the existence of financing has enabled the colleges to raise prices sharply.

Economists have made two principal arguments to explain why educational costs increase at 2–3 percent above the rate of inflation annually. The first argument, put forward by William Baumol and William Bowen, is that the very nature of educational production, essentially a handicraft activity, precludes productivity gains, but wages of faculty nonetheless

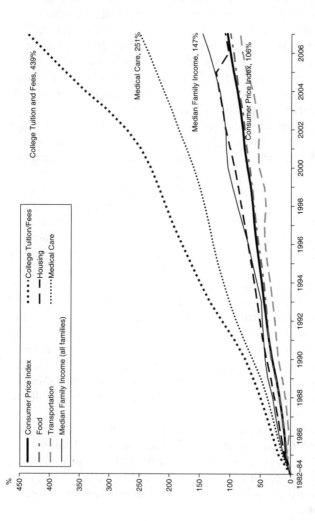

Notes: Growth rate is calculated from a baseline average of 1982, 1983, and 1984. Data are from 1982 to 2007. All industries, except median family income, are components of the CPI.

Source: Measuring Up 2008: The National Report Card on Higher Education, The National Center for Public Policy and Higher Education (2008). Data from the Bureau of Labor Statistics, Consumer Price Index, All Urban Consumers. Median Family Income is from U.S. Census Bureau, Current Population Survey, Annual Social and Economic Supplements, and American Community Survey.

Figure 1.1   Growth rate of tuition and fees relative to family income and other spending

Table 1.1   Net college cost as ratio of median family income

	1999–2000	2007–2008	% increased
At public 4-year colleges and universities			
Lowest income quintile	39%	55%	16%
Lower-middle income quintile	23	33	10
Middle income quintile	18	25	7
Upper-middle income quintile	12	16	4
Highest income quintile	7	9	3
At public 2-year colleges			
Lowest income quintile	40	49	9
Lower-middle income quintile	22	29	7
Middle income quintile	15	20	5
Upper-middle income quintile	10	13	3
Highest income quintile	6	7	2

Note: Net college cost is tuition, room and board, minus financial aid.

Source: Measuring Up 2008: The National Report Card on Higher Education, The National Center for Public Policy and Higher Education (2008). Data from the Bureau of Labor Statistics, Consumer Price Index, All Urban Consumers. Median Family Income is from U.S. Census Bureau, Current Population Survey, Annual Social and Economic Supplements, and American Community Survey.

rise, resulting in a steady increase in the unit cost of production.[11] The second argument, advanced by Howard Bowen, is that higher education has an endless array of worthy activities seeking support, and thus institutional leaders raise all the money they can, and spend it all on these valued activities.[12] Under this argument, the only way to reduce cost is to reduce revenue, for the institutions are constrained only by the non-profit requirement that costs do not exceed revenues. A related argument is that higher education is a "positional" good in that its value to the recipient is a function of its scarcity at the highest levels of quality and prestige, and thus ambitious students will pay virtually any price to attend a highly selective college or university.[13] Another way of stating this point is that a handful of highly selective institutions face a virtually price-inelastic demand curve, coupled with heavy demand for places, so that one might wonder, for example, why Princeton's tuition is not higher than it already is. These price-leaders, by this argument, provide an umbrella over the entire price structure, and allow other institutions to settle in at somewhat lower levels, sheltered by the higher prices of the leading institutions.

For those students who do enroll, a shockingly large percentage, close to one out of every two, will fail to complete the bachelor's degree.[14] Thus, even if a student gains access to higher education, a problem remains with poor completion rates. Compared with other developed countries belonging to the Organisation for Economic Co-operation and Development (OECD), the United States has slipped to 15th in college completion, just as we have slipped to 7th place among OECD nations in the percentage of young adults (18–24) enrolled in college.[15] These international comparisons indicate that the performance of our "system" of higher education has declined relative to peer countries, and that we have lost the first-mover advantage that we had for a generation in developing mass higher education before other countries. Many of them have caught up and are surpassing us now on these key measures of educational attainment.

A final point to mention as background is the growing concern many knowledgeable observers have about the financial future of the public research university. It is unclear whether states will be able to provide the resources that they did in earlier days to keep their public research universities competitive with the best private universities and, increasingly, with rapidly advancing research universities abroad. While the principal focus of this debate will be on student access and completion, our ability as a nation to remain competitive in scientific and engineering research is key to our economic future, and we no longer have as dominant a position as we did in the latter half of the previous century.

THE MODEL IS BROKEN: SUPPORTING ARGUMENTS

A key argument supporting the proposition that higher education's business model is broken is found in the divergent growth trends of tuition versus median family income; it seems implausible that this can be sustained. Economist Herb Stein famously proposed Stein's Law in the 1980s – "If something cannot go on forever, it will stop." A reasonable argument, therefore, is that colleges and universities will be unable to continue raising tuition at the rates of the last two decades without pricing hundreds of thousands of students out of the market. Various estimates have been made of the price and income elasticity of demand for higher education, and the research clearly indicates that the laws of economics are not overcome in this instance. Higher price, all else equal, means lower demand. While many efforts at the state, federal, philanthropic, and institutional levels have been made to cushion price increases for many students, the fact remains that higher education absorbs a growing portion of most family incomes. The effects of this changing pattern of finance include increased student borrowing and higher debt burdens, longer hours spent working for pay while enrolled, increased part-time attendance, and lower completion rates. While it is impossible to state with precision how many potential students will not enroll because of current and prospective pricing policies, we know that many students and families are reluctant to borrow heavily for something as uncertain and risky as higher education, a factor particularly true of families without prior college or university experience. Such families make up a growing portion of the relevant population, which puts the current financial model increasingly at odds with much of the population meant to be served.

A related aspect of this argument about diminished opportunity is the behavior of institutions which, even with increased tuition, still face budgetary problems. Increasingly, public colleges and universities have been cutting enrollments in response to sharp drops in state support.[16] Many campuses are also cutting course sections and course offerings, making it difficult for students to enroll in courses needed to graduate on time. Growing use of adjunct, part-time faculty is widespread, as a budgetary move to save money, but often at the expense of quality and consistency of instruction. Student support services, such as counseling and advising, have been scaled back at many institutions, thus reducing the resources that can help student retention. All of these institutional adaptations to declining budgets mean that even at current growth rates, tuition has not been able to fully offset the decline in state support; another sign of a failing business model.

The privatization discussion earlier needs to be qualified by noting that only a handful of highly selective public flagship universities can hope to succeed at becoming "privately financed public universities," and even for that handful, the potential is limited. A small number of state universities have significant endowments and a history of successfully raising large amounts of private money; similarly, a very small number of state universities have the capacity to raise tuition to private market levels, typically in professional schools such as Law and Business. For the vast majority of public two-year and four-year institutions, however, these sources of revenue are pipe dreams at best. Privatization is simply not a serious option for maintaining a strong and effective public higher education system, and thus the attempt to move in that direction for most institutions is not a viable business model.

A word should be said about the several hundred private, non-profit colleges and universities that collectively enroll over 20 percent of all students in the United States. A relatively small number of these institutions have sizable endowments and excess demand for enrollment, but most have modest endowments, are heavily dependent upon tuition, and struggle annually to fill their entering classes. Analysts have been forecasting the demise of hundreds of these small undergraduate colleges for years, but they have proved to be remarkably resilient and innovative in finding ways to survive. They have, for example, altered curricular offerings rapidly in response to shifting student interests, and have become expert at price discrimination by using financial aid as a tool for enrollment management.[17] Each year a few of these small colleges close their doors, or merge with a stronger, nearby institution, but they are not "too big or too important to fail," and policymakers are not likely to intervene to save those that falter financially. A handful of closures does not imply that the private sector business model is broken; however, their need to attract students from higher income families means that many of them will be unable to enroll substantial numbers of low-income, first-generation college students in future years. As such, from a national, policy perspective, their business model limits their ability to serve the broader public purposes of access and opportunity.

While much of the discussion has centered on the search for new and increased revenues, one might also note that a business model can be broken if the institutions are unable to innovate and alter their production processes as a way to lower costs while sustaining quality. Higher education is not known for organizational flexibility and adaptability, and the tendency among most colleges and universities when confronted with recessions and reduced support has been to cut costs temporarily through pay and hiring freezes, reduced travel, buying fewer books for the library, and so forth, while waiting for things to get better.[18] Few institutional leaders have undertaken the hard tasks of rethinking the university strategically and systematically reallocating resources to permanently lower costs. This "hunker down and pray for better times" approach has worked during past recessions, but it may not work as well going forward. In their recent report on United States higher education, Moody's Investors Service comments that: "Given their reduced resources, colleges and universities will need to consider a fundamental restructuring of their business models to regain financial stability. Responses like freezing hiring, furloughing faculty members and suspending capital projects are all short-term solutions."[19] Given that few leaders have demonstrated the ability to make such fundamental changes, one might argue that the business model is broken, or at best, highly vulnerable to extended periods of economic decline.

From the narrow perspective of institutional survival, the business model of higher education is not broken. Few institutions, public or private, are likely to close in coming years, and the social need for higher education will increase, not diminish. From the perspective of meeting the public purposes of access, opportunity, affordability, completion, and international competitiveness, however, one can make a strong case that current methods of financing and organizing higher education are not well aligned with our national needs. In that sense, the business model is definitely broken.

THE MODEL IS BROKEN: ARGUMENTS AGAINST

A key argument against the proposition of a broken business model in higher education is simply to point to current enrollment levels, which have never been higher, at 18.2 million students in 2007.[20] Furthermore, enrollment rates of recent high school graduates have not dropped, as one might expect if the proposition were accurate: "The rate of college enrollment immediately after high school completion increased from 49 percent in 1972 to 67 percent by 1997, but has since fluctuated between 62 and 69 percent."[21] If the business model were broken, numbers such as these would not be possible. Effective demand for higher education has not declined, and these figures demonstrate that students are finding a way to pay for college.

A central part of the argument that the business model is broken is based on the assumption that affordability has been severely compromised by rising tuition. The National Center for Public Policy and Higher Education, in its biennial report on state performance, *Measuring Up*,[22] had 49 of the 50 states with an 'F' on affordability, and yet millions of students are still enrolling. An economist might argue that there can be no true affordability problem provided students do not face credit constraints that limit access to loan capital. The argument (analogous to that made for the social benefits of perfectly competitive markets) is that students can calculate the increased income they will earn with a college degree, and thus will be motivated to invest in themselves via borrowing so long as the rate of return is positive. Like so many other theoretical models, the kernel of truth in this position is swamped by numerous limitations on such rational calculations in the real world. Future earnings are uncertain and subject to wide variation, students may be unable to predict their success in an academic environment, many students and parents are risk-averse and reluctant to borrow, time horizons are often shorter than required by the investment model, and credit constraints do exist in the student loan market. Nonetheless, the argument has the merit of highlighting two distinct ways to view affordability – as investment, in which case current income is irrelevant, or as a purchase analogous to consumption, in which case current income is highly relevant. Most economists would argue strongly for the investment approach, but interestingly, the needs-analysis system built into federal, state, and private student financial aid programs encourages the consumption view of affordability. (*Measuring Up* also uses that view, relating college costs to family income.) All of this is to argue that defining affordability is far from simple, but ignoring the investment dimension overstates the problem.

One might also argue with the belief that the United States needs to increase the number of college graduates substantially over the next decade or so.[23] If the market needs more graduates, then wage differentials between high school and college graduates will increase, thereby sending a signal to potential students that enrolling in college is a wise investment. So long as the financial rate of return on a college degree exceeds the interest charged for student loans, then the market can be expected to function effectively in determining the "right" number of college graduates.

A further argument is that low (or no) tuition is a highly inefficient way to subsidize higher education enrollments. The shift since the 1980s has been from a low tuition, high appropriation model to a high tuition, high student aid model. By concentrating financial aid on individual students based on financial need, subsidy dollars are allocated more efficiently than by providing across-the-board subsidies to all students regardless of income, as the older model did. The low-tuition model, it is argued, effectively awards a scholarship to all students enrolled, regardless of income, an allocation policy that few would adopt in designing an efficient scholarship program. Thus, the new model is designed to use subsidy dollars to get the most for the money. Students from wealthy families are able to pay the higher tuition, and thus the low tuition of the old model was simply a dead-weight loss in that it did not influence their enrollment behavior.[24] The epic battle in the early 1970s over federal student aid, and whether it should be directed to students or to institutions, hinged on a similar consideration, and was decided in favor of direct grants to students, based on financial need.

Two further issues have been proposed as threats to traditional higher education and its business model. First, might not technology and the digital revolution have a negative impact on universities similar to that experienced by the newspaper industry? Might not online learning systematically replace face-to-face teaching and learning in the classroom? Might not entire introductory courses be developed online and used as substitutes for faculty-taught courses at many institutions? While it is true that technology is having an impact on the education process of both traditional universities and for-profit providers, the results thus far are decidedly mixed, both educationally and financially. Hybrid courses that involve a mix of online and face-to-face instruction are growing in use, and may represent the most promising direction for future development, but the wholesale replacement of faculty, or the erosion of markets for traditional instruction, have not yet occurred, and seem unlikely to happen. Pure online programs seem most effective for older, part-time adult students, who can work at home one course at a time; for younger students, the benefits of living on campus as a full-time student retain considerable appeal. Steadily increasing costs of residential higher education, however, might induce some shift to online programs, but most observers think this effect, if it occurs, will be modest.

Another perceived threat to traditional higher education has arisen in the last decade or so in the form of regionally accredited, degree granting, for-profit institutions, with the University of Phoenix as the poster child for that movement. Indeed, during the current recession, the for-profit sector has generally continued to grow and perform well on the stock exchanges, while traditional institutions have suffered significant revenue loss. Some of the early claims about the impact of the for-profit sector appear, in retrospect, to have been linked to the false belief that they were all, and only, online providers, and that digital technology would erode face-to-face instruction, as discussed above. Subsequent research has indicated that they are significant niche players, and particularly successful with older, adult students, a group largely ignored by many traditional universities. As such, they compete with some universities that rely on the adult market, but there is little evidence that they will become a viable substitute for most students.[25] In general, they appear to extend the market for higher education to populations who otherwise might not enroll at all.

CONCLUDING OBSERVATION

The arguments supporting the proposition of a broken business model in higher education stress the social functions of higher education and the belief that, even if most colleges and universities survive, their accomplishments under the evolving model will be much less than a just and progressive society needs from its institutions. The arguments opposing the proposition stress the value of increased market orientation for higher education and the sense that the evolving model is designed to produce an efficient allocation of resources. To a degree, the different perspectives can be viewed as representing the age-old trade-off between equity and efficiency, but that would oversimplify matters. The first position includes an efficiency concern that the nation runs a risk of under-investing in higher education relative to economic needs, while the second position suggests that if subsidies are accurately targeted on the needy, social justice is thereby served.

NOTES

1. Recent exceptions to this rule would be large banks and related financial institutions, deemed "too large to fail," as their demise would have crippled the nation's financial system.
2. A growing for-profit sector of higher education also exists, currently enrolling about seven percent of students in postsecondary education. These institutions receive indirect subsidies through federal financial aid to their students. Their special case will be discussed subsequently.
3. Thomas J. Kane, Peter R. Orzag, and David L. Gunter, "State Fiscal Constraints and Higher Education Spending: The Role of Medicaid and the Business Cycle," Discussion Paper No. 11, Urban-Brookings Tax Policy Center, May 2003.
4. State Higher Education Executive Officers, *State Higher Education Finance, FY 2008*, Boulder, CO, July 2009, p. 18.
5. Ibid., p. 22.
6. http://www.trends-collegeboard.com/college_pricing/1_2_total_student_budgets.html?expandable=0
7. These figures are before any financial aid that students might receive, although such aid is increasingly loans, not grants.
8. http://measuringup2008.highereducation.org/print/NCPPHEMUNationalRpt.pdf, p. 8.
9. National Association of State Business Officers, *Fiscal Survey of the States, Fall 2009*, and http://www.rockinst.org/pdf/government_finance/state_revenue_report/2010-01-07-SRR_78.pdf
10. Christopher C. Morphew and Peter D. Eckel (eds), *Privatizing the Public University*, Baltimore: The Johns Hopkins University Press, 2009. The University of Virginia, for example, is often referred to as a "privately financed public university."
11. The argument was first developed in William Baumol and William Bowen, *Performing Arts: The Economic Dilemma*, New York: Twentieth Century Fund, 1966, and extended to higher education. See William J. Baumol and Sue Anne Batey Blackman, "How to Think About Rising College Costs," *Planning for Higher Education*, vol. 23, Summer 1995, pp. 1–7.
12. Howard R. Bowen, *The Costs of Higher Education*, San Francisco: Jossey-Bass Publishers, 1980.
13. Henry Hansmann, "Higher Education as an Associative Good," in Maureen Devlin and Joel Meyerson, (eds) *Forum Futures: 1999 Papers 11-24*, Foundation for the Future of Higher Education, 1999.
14. William G. Bowen, Matthew M. Chingos, and Michael S. McPherson, *Crossing the Finish Line*, Princeton: Princeton University Press, 2009. Also, see http://www.edtrust.org/
15. http://measuringup2008.highereducation.org/print/NCPPHEMUNationalRpt.pdf, p. 6
16. http://www.google.com/search?client=safari&rls=en&q=cuts+in+university+enrollment&ie=UTF-8&oe=UTF-8
17. See David W. Breneman, *Liberal Arts Colleges: Thriving, Surviving, or Endangered?*, Washington, DC: The Brookings Institution, 1994, and Michael S. McPherson and Morton Owen Schapiro, *The Student Aid Game*, Princeton: Princeton University Press, 1997 for discussion of these issues.
18. College and university behavior may have inspired the observation that "Hope is not a strategy."
19. Moody's Investor Service, "Annual Sector Outlook for U.S. Higher Education for 2010", January 2010.
20. National Center for Education Statistics, *Digest of Education Statistics 2008*, Washington, DC: US Department of Education, 2009, p. 278.
21. http://nces.ed.gov/fastfacts/display.asp?id=51

22. http://measuringup2008.highereducation.org/print/NCPPHEMUNationalRpt.pdf, p. 11.
23. See the paper by William Zumeta, "Does the U.S. Need More College Graduates to Remain a World Class Economic Power?" prepared for the first debate in this Miller Center series, for discussion of labor-market needs for college graduates.
24. Some analysts argue, however, that as costs are shifted to students and families and as these costs increase more rapidly than family income, middle class families demand a larger share of financial aid, resulting in tuition tax credits, state and institutional merit aid, and more borrowing, thus offsetting some of the benefits of the need-based approach.
25. David W. Breneman, Brian Pusser, and Sarah E. Turner, (eds) *Earnings from Learning: The Rise of For-Profit Universities*, Albany: State University of New York Press, 2006.

2. Macro-challenges of the national imperative facing higher education

William E. Kirwan

From my perspective, there are three key challenges facing higher education – especially public higher education – in America today. First is the challenge of "Completion." Under current conditions and trends, far too few of American high school students will ultimately become college graduates. This threatens not only America's standing in the world, but the cultural and social fabric of our nation, personified in the "American Dream" that each generation will do better than the previous generation. Second is the challenge of "Cost." With college costs growing at twice the rate of inflation by some estimates, too many college-ready, college-capable students are being priced out of our institutions. It is imperative that action be taken – at the campus level, state level, and federal level – to overcome the obstacle of cost. Finally, we must address the challenge of "Competitiveness." In the latter half of the twentieth century – often dubbed "The American Century" – the university community was at the heart of research and development in the United States, resulting in an era of learning and discovery that brought progress and prosperity to the academic sector, the American economy, and society as a whole. We must recapture that spirit and reestablish our institutions as engines of progress.

THE COMPLETION CHALLENGE

President Barack Obama has set an ambitions educational goal: By 2020, the United States will once again have the highest proportion of adults with a college degree in the world. Although there has been significant analysis – and skepticism – as to the feasibility of reaching the president's goal within his stated timeframe, what must not be lost are the audacious aspirations he has put forth and their importance for our nation.

In 2008, I chaired the College Board's Commission on Access, Admission and Success, which produced the report "Coming to Our Senses." While the commission's goal was slightly more modest than the president's – by

2025, 55 percent of our nation's young adults should receive a postsecondary degree – the thrust of our report and its recommendations very closely mirror the president's proposal and the rationale behind it. The State Higher Education Executive Officers, the Lumina Foundation, and the Gates Foundation, among others, have embraced similar goals of dramatically improving United States graduation rates. The challenge of achieving any of these goals is enormous, but there can simply be no doubt as to their importance for the future wellbeing of our nation.

For most of the twentieth century, the United States was the world's leader in education, with the top high-school and college completion rates. These gave us a huge global advantage in the quality of our workforce. Sadly, this is no longer the case. Currently, only 39 percent of the 25 to 34 year-old cohort has a postsecondary degree, placing the United States 10th among the industrialized nations in such completion rates. If we stay on our present course, given the rising proportions of under-represented minorities among college-age youth and given their lower participation and success rates in higher education, our population's proportion of degree-holders would drop from 39 percent to below 30 percent by 2025. This would mean that the United States would have gone from first to last in postsecondary completion rates among industrialized nations over the past several decades. This growing educational deficit is perhaps an even graver threat to our nation's future wellbeing than is the current fiscal crisis.

Regardless of the specific benchmark – the president's goal of having the world's highest proportion of students graduating from college by 2020, the College Board's goal of a 55 percent college-completion rate by 2025, or something in between – achieving success rests on several factors. They include our ability to rethink education as a continuum rather than as a series of segments; the corresponding willingness to make strategic investments across the education spectrum; and – ultimately – our capacity to bring about fundamental change in the role played by higher education.

Simply funneling more unprepared high-school graduates into our colleges is not the solution. Having more children begin their educational journeys prepared to learn and putting more seventh and eighth graders on the path to college is part of the answer. To accomplish this, we must focus on the youngest students, then move forward – plugging the numerous "leaks" in the educational pipeline along the way – as we map their paths to higher education.

The National Association of System Heads (NASH) and the think tank Education Trust have conducted research that illuminates those leaks in the pipeline: The United States' on-time, high-school graduation rate stands at 73 percent; the college-going rate at 67 percent; and the six-year college graduation rate at 55 percent – leaving us with only about 40 percent of American adults 25 years or older holding a college degree. For African-American and Latino students, the numbers are lower across the board, resulting in a 26 percent and an 18 percent college completion rate, respectively.

To achieve a result in line with the President's goal, roughly 50 percent of the adult population would need to have a two- or four-year degree by 2020. According to an analysis by the Delta Cost Project and the National Center for Higher Education Management Systems (NCHEMS), at current annual degree-production rates, we would produce about 27 million recipients of college degrees by the end of the coming decade, some 10 million degrees short of the President's goal. That's the bad news. But this gap can be closed if our nation has the will and dedicates the resources to do so. Indeed, the Delta Project/NCHEMS analysis shows that if the high-school graduation rates, college-going rates, and degree-attainment rates nationwide each rose to the levels currently produced by the "best performing" states, the president's goal would be reached.

While moving these three indicators in tandem will unquestionably be a significant challenge, with adequate investments and enlightened policy changes, this certainly can be achieved.

As we have come to understand, the foundation for college graduation is laid well before a child enters primary school. Growing evidence suggests that children who attend high-quality, pre-K programs begin kindergarten equipped with larger vocabularies, the basic building block of language and learning. Likewise, a fundamental understanding of mathematics – the language of science – must be developed in the earliest grades.

To that end, as the College Board's report recommends, states need to provide universal, voluntary access to high-quality, pre-school programs for three- and four-year-olds. Children who attend pre-school tend to graduate from high school and college and move into the middle class at much higher rates than those who do not. It is encouraging that President Obama has identified pre-school as a major element of his educational agenda, providing $5 billion in the American Recovery and Reinvestment Act for early-learning programs, including Head Start and Early Head Start.

While moving students into middle school and through high school, we must work to build and support their college-going aspirations. More attention must be paid to providing middle-school students with the counseling and guidance they need to begin preparing for college. If students do not begin the proper course sequences during middle school that lead to high-school courses that prepare them for college-level work, their paths to higher education will be blocked before they even realize it. In many school districts, however, there is one college-prep counselor for every

2,000 students. In fact, we need one counselor for every 250 middle-school students if we are serious about enhancing not only the college-going rate, but also the college-completion rate.

These initial steps – additional funding and additional staff – are best classified as evolutionary. Recognition of what works and the political will to direct the necessary resources toward those efforts are what government is designed to accomplish. While they are important first steps, they will only get us part of the way to our goal. Laying the groundwork that will dramatically reverse our present course and re-establish the United States as the undisputed world leader in higher education will require revolutionary change.

If our nation is to move toward President Obama's goal, it is incumbent on the higher-education community – public and private, two-year and four-year institutions alike – to re-evaluate its structures; re-engineer its operations; place a much higher priority on affordability, access and completion; and establish genuine partnerships with the K-12 community.

A major problem impeding progress on student access and graduation is the gap that exists between high-school exit requirements and college-entrance expectations. This gap leads to unacceptably high levels of remedial education at our nation's colleges and universities. A recent study by the National Center for Education Statistics estimates that 30 percent of students moving from high school to postsecondary education must begin with remedial courses. The figure for students beginning in community colleges is over 40 percent.

College-completion rates for students who start their postsecondary careers with remedial-education courses are abysmal. A study by the Texas Higher Education Commission showed that only 16 percent of Texas students who began college with a remedial course attained a four-year degree within six years.

Fortunately, a major initiative has been undertaken – sponsored by the National Governors Association, the Association of Chief State School Officers, and Achieve, Inc., with support from the College Board and American College Testing – to produce a higher percentage of college-ready, high-school graduates. Forty-six states have joined to develop and implement "college-ready" standards. The creation of those standards is an important first step, a necessary but not sufficient condition for improvement. What also must happen is that states need to insist that faculties from higher education and the K-12 sector come together to ensure that the content in courses for high-school seniors aligns with first-year college courses. We will have achieved success in this area when the transition from the 12th grade to the first year of college is as seamless as the transition from the 11th grade to the 12th grade.

But aligning the curriculum is only one step if we are to move toward President Obama's laudable goal. Active and seamless articulation partnerships with community colleges are also essential. Other innovative approaches that have the demonstrated ability to enhance higher-education access must be integrated into our program offerings. These include greater use of online instruction and the development of regional education centers that offer courses from multiple campuses in a centralized location.

Colleges and universities also need to give much greater attention and priority to teacher-preparation programs. "Rising Above the Gathering Storm," the 2007 report from the National Academy of Sciences, is the latest in a series of clarion calls for a substantial increase in highly qualified teachers for our nation's K-12 classrooms, especially in STEM disciplines (science, technology, engineering, and mathematics). The remarkably successful UTEACH program at the University of Texas shows what can be accomplished when a university makes producing trained teachers a priority.

Along these same lines, we need a fundamental change in the way colleges and universities view themselves. The idea of higher education as "the Academy," separate and apart from the K-12 community, must be rejected. We cannot tell the K-12 community it is their job to get students ready for college and then our job to get them through college. We must recognize that we have a vital role to play before students enroll in our institutions; we have an obligation to help prepare them at the front end. Individual campuses and entire systems must establish partnerships with primary and secondary schools to enhance teacher training and development, improve student learning, and keep the promise of higher education a realistic, desirable, and attainable goal.

Finally, as the College Board's report recommends, colleges and universities need to better understand why students leave their institutions without earning degrees. Most universities invest heavily in marketing for new students, but too few have devoted the same kind of attention and resources to figuring out why their graduation rates are not higher. An impressive study by the Education Trust demonstrates that this kind of analysis, coupled with intervention strategies, can produce dramatic results.

THE COST CHALLENGE

Of course, it is impossible to "de-couple" the issue of college completion from the issue of college cost. According to the United States Department of Education, 400,000 qualified high school graduates put off attending college each year due to cost. In addition, about one in five students who do go to a four-year college or university end up dropping out, with financial stress being the prime cause. And the average college graduate faces nearly $21,000 of debt upon graduation, with the debt load among low-income students even more burdensome.

We need to attack the affordability issue on multiple levels, including funding, financial aid policies, grant practices, student loan regulations, and other innovative approaches.

First and foremost, however, it is incumbent upon university systems, institutional presidents, and governing boards to work internally to bring the rising costs of colleges under control. By streamlining administrative expenses, cutting energy costs, using instructional faculty resources more effectively, and eliminating duplication, we can show a top-to-bottom commitment to keeping higher education affordable.

This is being done in some places, including the University System of Maryland (USM). Five years ago, as an earlier economic downturn resulted in a sharp decline in state support for the USM, our Board of Regents launched the Effectiveness and Efficiency (E&E) initiative. E&E involved a systematic reexamination and reengineering of both our administrative functions and academic processes to reduce costs, enhance access, and raise the student completion rate, while also protecting quality.

The fiscal and academic impacts of this effort speak for themselves. Administratively, we have removed more than $130 million in direct costs from our budget, while experiencing significant additional savings through cost avoidance. Academically, USM's four-year and six-year graduation rates are well above national averages for public universities and time-to-degree across the USM is at its best level ever, averaging less than four-and-a-half years. Also, since the first full year under E&E, enrollment at USM institutions has increased by 15,000 students.

Along with cost-cutting, E&E employs innovative approaches to deliver educational opportunities in a cost-effective manner. One especially promising approach is course redesign following the model espoused by Carol Twigg and the National Center for Academic Transformation. This model makes better use of technology and teaching assistants and has proven effective at teaching larger groups of students at lower cost in several fields. Such efforts are under way within USM and have resulted in both improved student performance and substantial savings in instructional costs.

Although there is no universal approach that would be effective for systems and campuses nationwide, our actions certainly have broader applications and have been recognized in many national publications as a model, singled out as a "success story" by the United States Department of Education, and specifically endorsed by President Barack Obama.

Beyond pure "stewardship," we must also reverse the recent trend of favoring merit-based aid at the expense of financial aid based on need. I am all for recognizing merit, but the primary recipients of financial aid must be students who would otherwise not be able to afford college. In Maryland we have institutionalized this emphasis on need-based aid by adopting a system-wide policy goal of having the lowest income students graduate with 25 percent less debt than the institutional average, in effect reversing the ratio that existed a few years ago. With this goal in place, the University System of Maryland has seen need-based financial aid increase by more than two-thirds over the past few years.

This approach must manifest itself at the federal level as well. Along these lines, in 2008 the House of Representatives passed the Student Aid and Fiscal Responsibility Act, which aims to reduce the excessive subsidies provided to student loan companies. The Act aims to use that money – literally tens of billions of dollars – to make college more affordable and accessible for low- and middle-income families with an additional increase in Pell Grant funding. In addition, creative incentives are called for, such as providing campuses with additional funding as low-income and first-generation students progress toward a degree. Such incentives implemented at the federal level would have a significant impact.

USM's internal actions have not gone unnoticed by state leaders; and the support has truly been bipartisan. When E&E was first initiated, our efforts won strong support from Republican Robert Ehrlich, who was governor of Maryland at the time. In the years since, Democratic Governor Martin O'Malley has continued to commend our efforts. After being singled out for significant budget cuts in the early 2000s, which triggered increases in the system's average tuition of almost 40 percent over four years, the system is now established in both Maryland's executive and legislative branch as a funding priority. While we have certainly not been held harmless during this most recent recession, we have not been targeted for a disproportionate share of cuts. In fact, the combined impact of savings generated through E&E and state support has enabled USM to hold tuition flat for the past five academic years, during which time we moved from the sixth highest tuition in the nation down to a projected 21st.

THE COMPETITIVENESS CHALLENGE

When President Obama announced his educational goal of having the United States lead the world in college completion, he emphasized the reason why that goal was so vital: "In a global economy where the most valuable skill you can sell is your knowledge, a good education is no longer just a pathway to opportunity, it is a prerequisite."

We all recognize that education for its own sake is central to our mission. An understanding of history, an appreciation of art and literature, insight into philosophy, and an awareness of world cultures are indispensable aspects of a civilized society. We have an obligation to make sure our graduates have the cultural and intellectual underpinning necessary to enable them to take their place as enlightened leaders. At the same time, we have an obligation to ensure that our graduates are prepared to meet the rigorous challenges of the new economy armed with the knowledge and skills they need to compete in an ever-changing and increasingly-competitive workplace. As is the case with the completion challenge, the competitiveness challenge must be addressed across the educational spectrum, with the STEM disciplines – science, technology, engineering, and mathematics – the most important.

In the most recent Programme for International Student Assessment (PISA) tests – administered by the Organisation for Economic Co-operation and Development (OECD) and considered the world's most comprehensive and rigorous international comparison of student achievement – the challenges facing the United States were made clear. In "scientific literacy," students from the United States ranked 21st out of 30 OECD countries, in "mathematics literacy," 25th, and – perhaps most troubling – in "problem solving," 24th, with one half falling below the threshold of problem-solving skills considered necessary to meet emerging workforce demands.

With America's educational prowess declining, so too is America's economic leadership in the global marketplace. This was highlighted in an essay titled "Is America Falling Off the Flat Earth?" written by Norman Augustine, chair of the National Academy of Sciences committee that produced the "Rising Above The Gathering Storm" report. He observed in that 2007 document that nearly 60 percent of the patents filed with the United States Patent and Trademark Office in the field of information technology now originate in Asia. Further, in 2000, the number of foreign students studying physical sciences and engineering in U.S. graduate schools surpassed – for the first time ever – the number of U.S. students in those fields. And the United States has become a net importer of high-technology products.

There can simply be no argument that we must improve educational attainment if the United States wants to be the world's leader in creativity, innovation, and the knowledge economy. In addition, critical challenges extending beyond economic prosperity, such as addressing global climate change and advancing life-saving medical research, also hinge on producing a well-educated populace.

With the most innovative and most creative faculty, America's university community sets the standard in education. If we don't step up and lead this effort there is little chance we will be able to overcome this challenge. As the "Rising Above the Gathering Storm" report noted, America is in danger of losing its economic leadership position in the global marketplace. And I often note that the very first goal listed among this report's recommendations was to "Increase America's talent pool by vastly improving K-12 science and mathematics education," calling for 10,000 new STEM teachers per year for 10 years . . . reaching "1 million minds." And the second goal was to strengthen the skills of 250,000 current teachers. This recommendation leads the way despite the fact that this wasn't a report focused on education per se. The official title was "Rising Above the Gathering Storm: Energizing and Employing America for a Brighter Economic Future." It was in many ways an economic development document produced by a business-heavy group. But more and better teachers were at the top of their recommendations.

There is the potential for genuine momentum, but it is incumbent upon America's universities, as the primary engines of education, discovery, and progress, to fully adopt a more active – more "hands-on" – relationship that reaches across the entire educational spectrum. If we adopt this outreach-based model, we can enhance the teaching and learning of mathematics – the language of science – in the earliest grades, we can put more middle school students on the path to higher education, and we can better align high school math and science graduation requirements with incoming college requirements.

If we take such steps, the flow of students onto our campuses will be far more "STEM-literate," which will open up vast new horizons for them as they embark upon their college careers. In addition, the stream of graduates we produce will be better positioned to take their place as STEM educators and STEM professionals, which would have the dual effect of enhancing primary education going forward and boosting our economic competitiveness. Finally, the size and scope of the research conducted will be significantly enhanced, with a broader impact on the economy and on society.

These are not "pie-in-the-sky" recommendations; these are things happening – at various levels – at college and university campuses across the nation. For example, the University System of Maryland is working in cooperation with the United States Department of Education, the National Science Foundation (NSF), and private partners to improve STEM education at all levels. Our efforts are enhancing teacher development and student experiences in the sciences, addressing the under-representation of minorities in STEM fields of study and professions, implementing strategies to increase both STEM graduates as well as STEM educators, and creating pathways to college for middle and high school students.

In a global economy where knowledge is the coin of the realm, and discovery the most prized commodity, America's research universities can – and must – become fully engaged in creating a seamless educational continuum that makes STEM a priority on every level. Given the fact that tomorrow's economy is taking shape at research universities today, such a commitment will not only strengthen our nation educationally and economically in the short term, but will also position America to reclaim its status as a global leader in these two most vital areas.

CONCLUSION

The economic turmoil of recent years has given rise to speculation regarding the end of America's ability to compete in the global economy. Historians note the decline of world powers, both ancient and modern. They cite the ancient empires of Egypt, Greece, and Rome, as well as twentieth century superpowers such as France, Britain, and the Soviet Union. America's "managed decline" and China's "peaceful rise" are spoken of as certainties. While it would be foolish in the extreme to overlook this possibility, it would also be a mistake to take such potential developments as given.

While there can be no doubt that we face significant challenges, the United States also possesses tremendous strengths. Chief among these strengths is our outstanding system of colleges and universities. In fact, as I have noted, this area represents America's best avenue to enhance our ability to compete and maintain our position of leadership in the world.

According to the Academic Ranking of World Universities compiled by Shanghai Jiao Tong University, 17 of the world's top 20 universities are in the United States. Across the globe, the best and brightest students aspire to attend American colleges and universities. This, in turn, makes the United States the center of gravity for all types of scientific research. For example, in 2007, almost one-third of all research expenditures were in the United States. As a result, America is not only dominant in the lab, but also in the ability to deliver innovations to the global marketplace. These factors are reflected in our economic standing. According to The World Bank, in 2008 the world's GDP stood at $60.6 trillion. The United States accounted for almost one-quarter of that figure.

If we as a nation step forward to address the challenges of completion and cost with a sustained focus on our colleges and universities, we can not only maintain our considerable strength in higher education, academic research, and market innovation, but also enhance America's global competitiveness for the foreseeable future.

3. Expanded access to public higher education: challenges for the twenty-first century

Charles B. Reed

When the 2009 Higher Education Leadership Conference was first convened, higher education leaders from across the United States were asked to talk about the challenges ahead for colleges and universities. The question before us: What is the "new normal," and how will colleges and universities need to operate differently than we have in the past?

At this point, we are almost all in agreement that colleges and universities cannot afford to maintain business as usual right now. In fact, the only thing we know for sure about the "new normal" is that things are going to continue to change, and we are never going back to the way things were 25, 50, or 75 years ago.

To understand where we are headed, consider the following about the United States economy, workforce needs, and demographics. First, the importance of a college degree is higher than ever. We're facing a crisis in the United States because of our failure to get enough of our young people into higher education. The Association of Public and Land-Grant Universities has reported that in Japan, Korea and Canada, more than 50 percent of young adults hold college degrees. In the United States, only 41 percent of young adults hold those degrees.

Recognizing this shortfall, President Obama in his 2009 State of the Union address set a goal of having the highest proportion of college graduates in the world by 2020. The reasoning was that we must have more of our young adults earning degrees if we want to enjoy the same kinds of economic success and stability that we have experienced during previous decades. This marked the first real admission by an American president that we are no longer the global leader in higher education access and educational attainment. Furthermore, this statement indicated that we can no longer continue doing business as usual in the world of higher education policy. As many of us have believed for a long time, we must do more than simply argue at the federal level every two to four years about how much to increase Pell Grant maximum awards or the aggregate subsidized loan cap for undergraduate students. This limited discourse has resulted in stagnant progress for our nation while much of the rest of the world has developed new and more innovative policies for helping students earn degrees.

However, while we set our sights on this important goal, our country is undergoing a major demographic shift. In California, a majority-minority state, the student population is growing fastest among traditionally underserved groups, such as people from ethnic minorities, those for whom English is a second language, or those who are the first in their families to attend college. This trend is expected to continue across the United States in the next few decades. To meet President Obama's higher education goal, we are going to have to reach this rapidly growing segment of our population. We need to figure out how to enroll more of these hard-to-reach students in college, and help them succeed once they get there. That is why the future of access in higher education essentially boils down to how well we can serve the underserved.

But it gets more difficult: With the current economic slowdown, both public and private universities are facing a situation where resources are tighter than ever. This means that we are called upon to serve more hard-to-reach students with fewer resources. And at a time of recessionary cutbacks, many institutional budgets are facing more than just "a little cut here and a little snip there." Some universities – especially public institutions, which are inextricably tied to the state's budget – are losing entire portions of the budget, while at the same time being asked to do more with less.

On top of all of this, college affordability is down. The College Board has reported that tuition and fees are going up for both public and private universities, and it is rising faster than ever. In these difficult times, we need to remember who will suffer first and most from the effects of our belt-tightening: the young people who are traditionally under-represented in our student population.

Put together, all of these factors add up to a very difficult situation for helping more young people earn college degrees. At the 23-campus California State University (CSU), the largest four-year university system in the country, we are confronting these issues head-on, day after day. With nearly 450,000 students, 48,000 faculty and staff members, we are one of the most diverse and most affordable university systems in the country. And as the primary source for baccalaureate degrees for California students, we will need to serve California's rapidly expanding populations of underserved and minority students. Yet as a part of a state that is facing a budgetary crisis, we are currently managing one of the toughest budget situations we have ever encountered. That is why we have had to manage this challenge with a multi-faceted approach that focuses on understanding our incoming students and managing our limited resources with the most efficiency. The following describes how we are attempting to tie together all of these challenges and come up with a coherent plan for the future.

K-12 CURRICULUM

To begin to address these challenges, we believe we need to extend our reach beyond higher education, to look at reforms in the K-12 system. One almost universally acknowledged fact is that many students in the K-12 system are not being properly prepared for higher education. All educators – and that includes those in higher education – need to do a better job of getting kids ready for college sooner. Our role is to be clear about what our expectations are for incoming students, and to get out into high schools and middle schools to make sure that students have the right information and the right coursework.

This task begins with teacher education. It is the responsibility of the entire university to prepare teachers. Teacher preparation needs to be on the front burner for our presidents, provosts, deans, and department chairs. Everyone has to realize the importance of producing great teachers – not just good teachers – so that children learn what they need to know to succeed from grade to grade and into college. The quality of education that those students receive is a measure of how well prepared they will be when they arrive at our colleges and universities.

At the California State University, which prepares 60 percent of California's teachers and nearly 10 percent of the teachers in the country, this issue is of paramount importance. We became the first university system in the country to conduct a comprehensive first-year teacher evaluation study for all of our teaching graduates. Our surveys show that we do a good job, but we know that we still need to make progress in reaching a different population. We need to be innovative in how we reach these students and families, many of whom have never been to college and who do not speak English as a first language.

For example, we are working closely with "Just for Kids," which has statistical data on schools across the state. They have compared schools with identical characteristics, and are able to show which schools are having better success at teaching students. We have given that information to our provosts so that they know which schools need more professional development. Then we are able to model what those good teachers are doing for the other schools.

We are also working to find ways to encourage more college students to go into teaching, especially in math or science. We are looking at ways to make teaching more attractive financially, and we are working to develop more opportunities for those students to have hands-on math and science experience that they can pass along when they become teachers.

Additionally, we are making it simpler for more future teachers who come from non-traditional backgrounds to complete a teaching credential. Our CalState TEACH program offers a unique opportunity for qualified candidates to earn their teaching credential without attending traditional college classes. The curriculum is delivered online using web, print and CD-ROM materials. The prospective teachers share ideas through web-based "class discussions," and get professional feedback through on-site coaching from mentor teachers and CSU faculty. More than 700 prospective teachers were enrolled in the program this year, and nearly 3,300 have completed the program since it was created in 1999.

Continuing with our efforts to work with K-12 schools, we are committed to ensuring that students are offered a rigorous college preparatory curriculum, beginning as early as sixth or seventh grade. By high school, students need to have Algebra I, Algebra II, and trigonometry. We should not be wasting their time (or ours) by offering dumbed-down "almost math" or "someday it will be math" offerings. We supported the governor and the State Board of Education's adoption of Algebra I as the math standard for all of California's eighth graders even though it was not a popular position to take. We must set high expectations and standards for our students – and when we do, they will almost always surprise us by meeting those expectations.

Students also need more disciplined work on oral and written communications. The employers that hire our graduates consistently tell us that they want students who can communicate well in a variety of settings, both orally and in writing. That is why we must preserve reading and writing assignments across the middle and high school curriculum.

Despite these and other efforts, when students begin college-level work, many are still under-prepared. The California State University shoulders a tremendous amount of responsibility when it comes to remedial education. The numbers of incoming freshmen needing some kind of remedial help in math or English hover at around the 50 percent mark. We honor our responsibility to help those students. However, to whatever degree we can, we want to help them get the assistance they need before they get to the university. They should not have to spend their college time and money doing the work they needed to do in high school, and the state should not have to spend that money either.

In response to this challenge, we have worked with the California Department of Education and the State Board of Education to create a voluntary test known as the Early Assessment Program, or EAP. The test incorporates our placement standards into the California Standards Tests for English and math. It is designed to help 11th grade students get a "snapshot" of their math and English proficiency. If the EAP shows that that a student needs more work, they can use their time in 12th grade to brush up on the skills they need for college.

We have created many opportunities for high school students and teachers to get extra assistance in these areas if they need it. For instance, we have two websites, www.csumathsuccess.org and www.csuenglishsuccess.org, to help students prepare for college readiness in those subject areas.

In 2009, for the fourth consecutive year, the results from the EAP showed an increase in the overall number of students tested. Of the 466,303 11th graders who took the California Standards Test in spring 2009, a record 369,441 (79 percent) also took one or both of the CSU's Early Assessment tests. This is good news for us because it means that students are voluntarily choosing to be tested so that they can assess their college readiness. The end result is that these students will get the help they need in a timely fashion, and they will not have to waste their time on remedial courses once they come to us. This should enable them to arrive at our campuses ready to succeed.

Finally, while my colleagues and I have been working closely with K-12 educators about how to bridge the transition between high school and college, we have repeatedly encountered an idea that sounds radical but may not be as extreme as it sounds: get rid of the 12th grade, and send students straight to college. The reality is that for most students, the 12th grade year is simply a waste of time. We could save our schools and our students a year's worth of school by making sure that their time is meaningful in 11th grade and then moving them straight ahead. Although we are nowhere near moving forward with this idea, we believe it should be on the table as a possible solution for the "wasted year" problem that drags students down at a critical point in their education.

CSU OUTREACH EFFORTS

As we move on to talking about the transition between high school and college, we need to look more closely at the outreach efforts that universities have undertaken. One unfortunate reality about colleges and universities in this rankings-driven age is that universities tend to be focused on prestige, not on serving students. Often this translates to "outreach" that does nothing more than lip service to the groups of students who truly need advice and support to get to college. Instead we need to focus on our greatest challenge: helping underserved students, ethnic minority students, and low-income students to graduate from high school, start college, graduate, and move into the workforce.

The United States Census Bureau has found that of every 100 white kindergartners, 93 graduate from high school, 65 go to college, and 33 get a bachelor's degree. Of 100 black kindergartners, 87 graduate from high school, 50 go to college and 18 get a bachelor's degree. Of 100 Latino kindergartners, 63 graduate from high school, 32 go to college, and 11 get a bachelor's degree. This breakdown offers a stark illustration of the discrepancies in degree attainment, and the need to significantly raise the number of black and Latino students who get their degrees.

But the simple fact is that reaching out to underserved students requires more than simply holding the door open. Universities need to reach out to their neighborhoods and find out who the real incoming students are. They need to start as early as fifth or sixth grade to give students a sense of purpose and direction from a young age. They must also go into the communities populated with underserved students and actively assist them with college preparation.

For these kinds of outreach efforts, the greatest burden will fall on our regional serving institutions. These institutions will have the most important role to play because of costs. Most of these students can't just pack up and move to a dorm in Michigan, for example, or Connecticut. Although many nationally ranked institutions have the capability to offer large financial aid packages that could make a move more feasible, many students still choose to stay local because of family or other work responsibilities.

At the California State University, we have been working on the challenge of reaching underserved students for several years. A main focus of our work has been reaching out to students in places where they live and gather.

CSU Super Sundays

One of our most successful efforts has been the "Super Sunday" college information sessions we hold at African-American churches. This unique initiative was formed in 2005 through a partnership with local leaders of church, civic and business organizations and the CSU working together to promote a college-going culture among African American students. Every year, on two Sundays in February, leaders from the CSU and local communities gather at churches to send the message from the pulpit about the lifetime value of higher education and the need to begin preparing for college while in middle school and high school. Following Super Sunday services, CSU outreach staff and church education counselors provide information about college applications and financial aid. Students are also introduced to CSU Mentor, the online application website for prospective students.

The sessions have expanded each year to include companion events that fill the weekend. In 2009, we reached 72 churches, with congregations totaling 92,500 people. The total applications received also indicate that we may be having an impact: Applications from African American students have gone from 8,700 to 12,300 over the four-year period since we began.

Parent Institute for Quality Education (PIQE)

Another traditionally underserved group is students of Latino heritage, particularly those who are English learners and who are the first in their families to attend college. In 2006, the CSU created a statewide partnership agreement with PIQE (the Parent Institute for Quality Education), an organization that helps parents of Latinos and other underserved students prepare their children for higher education. Through the PIQE program, parents complete a nine-week class about how to help their children succeed in school and prepare for college. Many participants have never graduated from any school. When they finish, the children of the participants get a college ID card showing that they are conditionally admitted to the campus, as long as they complete the college requirements. The CSU has committed $1.7 million through 2009 to support PIQE's parent involvement program in the CSU's 23 campuses.

Additionally, we are working to reach students from the underserved Asian groups – Vietnamese, Hmong, Pacific Islanders, and others – at Asian-American community centers, which are some of the best places to reach parents and families.

College Planning Tools

To help students prepare for college admissions – especially those with limited access to college planning assistance – we have developed several additional tools. CSU Mentor (www.csumentor.edu) is a free online resource designed to help students and their families learn about the CSU system. The program helps students select a CSU campus to attend and create a plan to finance higher education. It also allows them to apply for admission online.

We have featured CSU Mentor widely, especially on our "Road to College" tour, a statewide campaign that empowered students, parents, teachers and counselors with information about how to prepare for college. Our customized 40-foot biodiesel tour bus loaded with laptop computers traveled to high schools, college fairs and the CSU's counselor conferences throughout the state. At each stop, students, teachers, and counselors explored the CSU's 23 campuses, learned about the admissions process, received information about financial aid, and talked to CSU experts.

We have also developed a widely popular and award-winning "How to Get to College" poster. This poster outlines the coursework and preparation that students need to prepare for college beginning in sixth grade, along with resources for applying for financial aid. We have distributed over three million posters. They are currently available (for distribution, and for viewing online) in English, Spanish, Chinese, Vietnamese, Korean, Hmong, Russian, and Tagalog.

Additionally, the CSU is part of the statewide Troops to College initiative, which is an academic outreach and enrollment plan to help California's 60,000 veterans attend colleges and universities.

Through these and other outreach efforts, we appear to be making a difference. This year, in the priority application period for enrollment, the CSU saw a total increase of 20 percent in first-time freshmen applications over the prior year. Driving this increase is a nearly 40 percent rise in applications by Asian American students, and a nearly 30 percent rise in application by Latino/Latina students. First-time freshmen applications among African American students also rose by 17 percent.

However, while the CSU has done much to increase student access and degree attainment, particularly among low-income students, we cannot be content with maintaining current levels of progress. Closing achievement gaps at every level of the educational pipeline will require each university to accept greater responsibility for setting high expectations for student success. This will require better use of data to diagnose and confront the causes for student failure; more proactive advising; more aggressive outreach to students in academic trouble; and more attention to student financial aid that will help students cut back on work to be able to focus on education as their primary priority.

UNIVERSITY-LEVEL CHANGES

Once we successfully reach these students and help them make their way to college, we need to consider internal changes that will help us better meet the needs of our students. At the CSU, for example, we are not dealing with the traditional 18 to 22-year-old students:

- The average undergraduate age is 24.
- Only 8 percent live on campus.
- Approximately 61 percent are dependent on parents.
- About 12 percent are married.
- Nearly one-quarter have dependents.
- Three out of four have jobs, and almost 18 percent work more than 30 hours per week.
- Nearly 35 percent are in the first generation in their family to attend college.

These types of incoming students will be likely to need non-traditional assistance and support. For example, they may not need the regular advising services in terms of which courses to take, but they may need special support in finding classes that meet their schedule, identifying times to use university computer labs, and exploring various sources of financial aid to allow them to continue their education.

To meet these students' needs, one of the most obvious changes involves offering more classes on evenings and weekends. This can serve the dual purpose of helping us reach more students who have full- or part-time work responsibilities, and helping us make better use of our facilities. Additionally, we need to offer more courses with an online component that would allow students to "attend" class remotely, from their home or place of work.

But we also need to start thinking outside the box about how to make important changes that will allow us to serve more students and run our operation with greater efficiencies. Some ideas include:

- Rethinking the 120-credit hour standard and reducing the credit requirement where appropriate;
- Moving the baccalaureate degree to three years when feasible;
- Improving the community college transfer process to avoid duplication of coursework and save students time and money;
- Offering more university-level courses at community colleges that may be closer to where our students live and work;
- Charging different tuition for different disciplines to reflect expected income and ability to pay back student loans (that is, business should cost more than teacher education).

One frequently overlooked element is the need to be aware of how our institutions are viewed externally by policymakers and the public. For example, along with many of our university colleagues, we have criticized short-sighted state policies such as mandatory sentencing laws that have sapped critical state funding away from universities and into the state prisons. However, when we continue to portray ourselves to state policymakers as victims, the resulting reaction is often less than sympathetic. In California right now, there is no extra money to be found, whether we deserve it or not, and so by painting ourselves as victims we do little to earn respect in Sacramento. Instead we need to become more positive in outlook and more entrepreneurial in focus, continuing to build and earn support from our business and community backers.

One way to help the public understand the importance of what we do is by demonstrating our institutions' productivity and importance to the economy. For example, a survey that the CSU did in 2005 showed that our university system had a direct economic impact on the state of $7.46 billion. For every $1 the state invests in the California State University, the CSU returns $4.41. That's a four-fold return on investment. We continue to emphasize these points when promoting the university among policymakers and supporters. While our results are large given the size and scope of our university system, every college and university will by definition have some economic impact on its community – an impact that the institution should attempt to quantify and share.

Unfortunately, for colleges and universities facing budgetary challenges, the short-term solution is almost always to raise tuition. In 2009 the College Board reported that college tuition and fees rose across the board, and the price tag is rising faster than ever. Those price increases appear even bigger after adjusting for inflation. Plus – and this is even harder to justify – public universities are using about two-thirds of their grant money for merit rather than financial need.

To the outside observer, these price increases reflect careless spending rather than need. When people learn of these fast-paced tuition increases, public sentiment turns against our universities, and this will hurt us in the long term. To combat this we must reprioritize our aid money to ensure that it goes to the neediest students. Additionally, we must be more transparent about our needs in terms of additional support for helping these students, as well as the steps we are taking to improve efficiencies and become more productive. If tuition increases are reasonable, incremental, and justified in terms of the additional help they provide for needy students, they will be better understood and accepted by the public.

FEDERAL ISSUES: TITLE I EXPANSION

We also need to take a deeper look at the role of federal funding for the neediest students. The conundrum that we are facing is that we are mostly operating with reduced budgets, but we need to enroll more students who need additional help.

The answer may lie in a form of federal assistance that was first proposed more than 30 years ago. In the early legislative history of what is now the Pell Grant program, Congress envisioned what would have been a two-pronged federal aid process for economically disadvantaged students who were headed to college: grants to the students (which became Pell Grants), and grants to the institutions to help educate those students.

This institutional aid program, authorized in 1972 but never funded, was known as the "cost of education allowances." It was based on a similar concept found in Title I funding for K-12 schools: the widely accepted premise that economically disadvantaged students cost more money to educate than students from wealthier backgrounds. Title I was created to provide supplemental federal funding to elementary and secondary schools with above average numbers of lower-income students. In a parallel effort, these "cost of education allowances" were designed to provide supplemental resource support to colleges and universities where large numbers of Pell Grant recipient students were enrolled.

The irony now is that not only is there no federal support for institutions in this area, there are actually widespread disincentives for universities to assist students from disadvantaged backgrounds – especially the lower-cost state institutions that serve the most students. Current national ratings systems such as the popular *U.S. News & World Report* rankings indirectly encourage universities to reduce their lower-income student enrollments by rewarding higher graduation rates, admissions selectivity, and other variables that promote institutional prestige above common purpose. Many state authorities have also begun prioritizing very simplistic institutional measurements such as graduation rates without any regard for the aggregate numbers of graduates or the socioeconomic status of the students educated at the various institutions.

A federal Title I-type program for higher education:

- Would provide a flat institutional grant per lower-income student to every college and university that meets a minimum enrollment of 20 percent;
- Would provide a federal grant to higher education institutions the same way that schools receive federal grants to help the Title I students;
- Would help admit, retain, and graduate our Pell grant recipients (who would continue to receive Pell Grants).

If this institutional grant program were put back on the table, the effect would be profound all across the country, and perhaps most notably in

California. More than 600,000 California students receive Pell Grants, and approximately 123,000 of those students are at the California State University alone. With more federal dollars to help our universities support those students, we would be better equipped to offer them appropriate counseling, remedial education, and computer support services at every step along the way. The ultimate goal, of course, would be to help more students earn degrees, make their mark in the workforce, and bolster the economy.

Making a big commitment like this is not such a far-fetched idea. In fact, given President Obama's goal for returning to higher education preeminence by 2020, there is no better time to put this idea back on the table. If we are going to solve the problem of reaching more economically disadvantaged students, this administration needs to provide federal funding for these "cost of education allowances."

While this idea has been advanced by the California State University, it has earned support from national higher education leaders, as well as from the American Association of State Colleges and Universities, and from the College Board in its recent report, "Rethinking Student Aid." Our hope is to continue to promote the idea and make a national push for a renewed federal commitment to institutional aid.

CONCLUSION

Earlier this year, the higher education community celebrated the 150th anniversary of the Morrill Act, which provided a major boost to American higher education by creating land-grant colleges. When the Morrill Act was signed 150 years ago, the United States was going through similarly tough economic times. However, President Lincoln and some far-sighted lawmakers knew that investing in higher education would reap rewards.

Today's dilemmas require a similarly far-sighted commitment on behalf of American students. These proposals, especially for a college-level Title I program, are not simply pie-in-the-sky ideals. If we don't address the needs of our underserved students by establishing a new direction for higher education, we will neglect the needs of a massive segment of our country's population. This will harm the students, the economy, and eventually our own institutions.

If we are going to meet President Obama's goals for higher education, we are going to have to make a serious investment in our students and in the universities who serve them. That is why we must understand the needs of our incoming students, adapt our services to help meet their needs, and give them greater opportunities to complete their degrees and find success in the workforce. By understanding the current educational environment and adapting to it, we will ensure success for our students, strengthen our universities, and give more fuel to the economy with young people who are prepared for success in the workforce.

4. Beyond the "new normal" in American higher education: toward perpetual innovation

Michael M. Crow

As the United States negotiates its recovery from the near meltdown of global economic markets, most institutions of higher education are engaged in some form of damage control and reassessment. Confronted by continuing fallout from the repercussions of the fiscal crisis, many colleges and universities are retrenching as if under siege while others are focused on restoring equilibrium. Still others are determined to seize the moment as an opportunity to restructure their academic organization or administrative mechanisms, generally with the intent of becoming more "efficient." Much of the discussion surrounding the implications of the downturn for the academy has been couched in terms of a desire to attain to some condition of "new normalcy" in higher education.

I would maintain that any intent to seek a new normalcy in higher education is inherently misguided because such an objective suggests that conditions were tenable prior to their disruption by the economic dislocation. Indeed, I would argue that we must strike the notion of "normal" from the lexicon of American higher education because for decades the status quo has been characterized by progressive ossification and disinvestment. In my usage of the term, "ossification" refers to the lack of innovation in the organization and practices of our colleges and universities, and "disinvestment" refers to the progressive decline in investment, particularly from the public sector, in the infrastructure of higher education. It is the lack of innovation, however, even more than lack of investment that perpetuates existing "design flaws" and encourages the formation of new ones. Unless we come to some more lucid understanding of the design flaws in our academic institutions and the shortcomings in our overall model of higher education, our best efforts to turn crisis into opportunity will prove insufficient.

Perhaps the chief consequence of the confluence of ossification and disinvestment is lack of access to higher education. The momentum of increased access to higher education by a wider demographic that marked the course of the past century has faltered in the past several decades, with the result that more and more students who would most benefit from access to this most obvious avenue of upward mobility – those whom we might categorize as "disadvantaged" or "underrepresented" – choose not to pursue, or are not aware that the option exists to pursue, a high-quality four-year university education (Bowen, Chingos, and McPherson, 2009). Inasmuch as our quality of life, standard of living, and economic competitiveness are intrinsically interrelated to the contributions of our universities, for the first time in our national history we risk broad decline as a consequence of the insufficient evolution of our institutions and the disinvestment that characterizes our policies toward higher education (Adams, 2009; Cole, 2009; Crow, 2008a).

Despite America's success during the past century in establishing what is justifiably regarded as the world's leading system of higher education – a decentralized system that led to the formation of a plurality of institutional types engaged in what has been described as a highly competitive but extremely productive "academic marketplace" (Graham and Diamond, 1997) – the nation's educational infrastructure remains dangerously underbuilt and undifferentiated. And despite our success at establishing the gold standard for academic institutions, our colleges and universities, both public and private, have not evolved sufficiently in response to the progressively accelerating complexity across all sectors of global society that we must now regard as a permanent condition.

The status quo in American higher education was inadequate long before the economy proved that our sense of mastery over the course of events was not fully justified. While the present recession is symptomatic of what I perceive to be a growing complacency in American society, academic institutions have generally been similarly content to base their self-esteem on the accomplishments of the past. The many indicators of inadequacies in higher education have been well documented in any number of specialized reports replete with recommendations for incremental improvement or even drastic reforms. In a keynote address to the American Council on Education, for example, Gordon Gee, president of Ohio State University, expressed with particular eloquence the imperative for "radical reformation" for our colleges and universities: "The choice, it seems to me, is this: reinvention or extinction" (Gee, 2009). No one would argue that some measure of change is not essential, but we are nowhere near the sort of broad consensus or collective sense of urgency that would transform analysis into action.

In the following, I largely confine my focus to American research universities, which, I contend, should be understood as *comprehensive knowledge enterprises committed to discovery, creativity, and innovation* (Crow, 2010). While there are approximately five thousand institutions of higher education in the United States, no more than one hundred or so, both public and private, are categorized as major research universities in the classification established by the Carnegie Foundation for Higher Education. I argue that the only antidote to the gradual erosion of our standard of living and quality of life is what in the more restricted context of technological innovation and economic competitiveness has been termed "perpetual innovation," referring to innovation in ideas, products, and processes (Kash, 1989; Crow, 2007). More broadly, I maintain that the concept of perpetual innovation should guide the evolution of organizations and institutions, especially colleges and universities. As a case study in institutional innovation in higher education, the following also offers a summary account of selected aspects of the reconceptualization of Arizona State University (ASU), initiated in 2002. As president of ASU, I have guided the task of pioneering the foundational model for what we term the "New American University" – an egalitarian institution committed to academic excellence, inclusiveness to a broad demographic, and maximum societal impact (Crow, 2002, 2010; "A New American University," 2008).

A LACK OF INSTITUTIONAL INNOVATION: DESIGN FLAWS IN THE AMERICAN RESEARCH UNIVERSITY

The American research university assumed its present form in the final decades of the nineteenth century. With the consolidation during this period of the discipline-based departmental organization we take for granted as the norm, significant further development in the organizational structure of the institutional form largely stagnated (Crow, 2008a; Atkinson and Blanpied, 2008). Undergirding the strict disciplinary organization of knowledge is a social organization hidebound by behavioral norms of astonishing orthodoxy. Along with entrenchment in disciplinary silos has come a fixation on abstract knowledge for its own sake as well as the proliferation of increasingly specialized knowledge, which comes to produce diminishing returns on investment as its impact on the world is measured in smaller and smaller ratios. Rather than exploring new paradigms for inquiry, academic culture too often restricts its focus to existing models of academic organization (Committee on Facilitating Interdisciplinary Research (U.S.), 2005).

Following the Second World War, American research universities assumed a leadership position in the discovery and dissemination of the new knowledge that drives the global economy and provides those of us in advanced nations with the standard of living and quality of life we have come to take for granted (Graham and Diamond, 1997). While research universities are comprehensive in scope and the magnitude of their impact transforms nearly every aspect of our lives, their contribution to economic development is most closely associated with scientific discovery and technological innovation (Atkinson and Blanpied, 2008; Cole, 2009).

The quality of life and standard of living Americans take for granted has in fact been shaped by a trajectory of economic competitiveness that to a remarkable extent has been the product of scientific discovery and technological innovation (Blakemore and Herrendorf, 2009). Such discovery and innovation is primarily the product of the teaching and research that takes place in our colleges and universities. Public sector investment in the infrastructure of higher education – and thus investment in human capital – during the twentieth century produced a level of educational attainment that served as a catalyst to innovation and thus American competitiveness in the global knowledge economy (Goldin and Katz, 2008). Yet with our success, public investment in higher education has progressively declined (Heller, 2006; Hossler et al., 1997; McPherson and Shulenberger, 2008). American higher education cannot assume that its competitive position in the world is unassailable (Douglass, 2006). This erosion corresponds to a slackening in the pace of innovation and diminishment of our national competitiveness (Committee on Prospering in the Global Economy of the Twenty-First Century (U.S.), 2007).

The lack of innovation in the organizational structures of our colleges and universities is matched by insufficient differentiation between distinct categories of institutions as well as a stultifying homogeneity among institutions of the same type. The elite universities and colleges in our nation, both public and private, have established and maintained a gold standard for higher education that all others feel compelled to emulate, but institutions today must overcome their identification with this historical model of elitism and isolation from society. While conventional wisdom suggests that all great universities must function equally as centers for humanistic and social scientific scholarship as well as world-class science, engineering, and medical research, not every institution can support a comprehensive spectrum of programs and should instead seek differentiation and adapt to be of greater value to its constituents. Research-grade universities are but one of a number of institutional types in American higher education, but even such institutions must develop distinctly different competencies if our national innovation system is to remain robust. Our nation requires variation and not replication in all types of institutions – public universities, private universities, liberal arts colleges, regional colleges, community colleges, professional schools, technical institutes, as well as for-profit enterprises focused primarily on workforce training. Institutions must advance unique and differentiated research and learning environ- ments that address the needs of students with different levels of academic preparation and differing types of potential. Moreover, with the advent of ubiquitous information technology as an enabler of universal custom- ized education, the monopoly on higher learning once held by universi- ties is vanishing (Crow, 2006). Distance learning provides an important complement or for some an alternative to the traditional undergraduate experience.

While the intrinsic impetus to advance innovation distinguishes the research university from other institutional forms in higher education, institutions committed thus primarily to innovation restrict the potential of their contribution unless they explicitly embrace a broader societal role (Crow, 2010). We are daily confronted by urgent challenges of unimagina- ble complexity, yet our academic culture remains equivocal regarding the outcomes of its teaching and research. If research universities are to create knowledge that responds to the grand challenges of our epoch – social justice, poverty alleviation, access to clean water, sustainable development – these institutions must integrate their quest to advance discovery, crea- tivity, and innovation with an explicit mandate to assume responsibility for the societies they serve. If our universities are to understand and respond to their multiple constituencies and advance broader social and economic outcomes, the continued evolution of our knowledge-producing enterprises becomes imperative (Bok, 1982; Duderstadt, 2000; Kerr, 2001; Kitcher, 2001; Rhodes, 2001; Sarewitz, 1996).

A LACK OF ACCESS AND THE PROBLEM OF SCALE

No national leader before President Barack Obama has so fully under- stood the transformational role of higher education in realizing both individual success and our collective societal ideals. But in order for the United States to achieve the ambitious objectives for educational attain- ment he specifies – the president envisions an America where all children graduate from high school and most go on to college – we must first build a higher education infrastructure adequate to the task. Unfortunately, our colleges and universities, both public and private, lack the capacity to offer access to the number of qualified applicants seeking admission. The issue of access is far more urgent than most realize, even those on the national stage charged with advancing higher education policy. More to the point, however, mere access is in itself inadequate and will not produce desired results unless we educate greater numbers of individuals successfully and also educate at higher levels of attainment. Concomitant with building access, thus, we must also unleash evolutionary change in our institutions. What is required is a new model for our colleges and universities, a new set of assumptions that encourage institutions to innovate and differentiate and become useful to their local communities and regions while at the same time seeking solutions to global challenges.

America's educational infrastructure remains little changed from the mid-twentieth century and is unable to accommodate projected enrollment demands in real time and at scale. More and more Americans of all ages, socioeconomic backgrounds, levels of academic preparation, and differing types of intelligence and creativity are seeking enrollment in our colleges and universities, overwhelming a set of institutions built to accommodate the needs of the United States prior to the Second World War. More and more students who would most benefit from access to higher education – those whom we might categorize as "disadvantaged" or "underrepresented" – are denied access for lack of means or choose not to pursue a baccalaureate degree for lack of understanding the implications associated with the decision (Bowen, Kurzweil, and Tobin, 2006; Douglass, 2007; Goldin and Katz, 2008; Haskins, 2008; Haskins, Holzer, and Lerman, 2009).

While the direct correlation between educational attainment and standard-of-living and quality-of-life indicators has been widely documented (Mortenson, 1999), leading American institutions of higher education have almost without exception during the course of the past half-century become increasingly *exclusive* – that is to say, they have chosen to define their excellence through admissions practices of exclusion. While our leading universities, both public and private, consistently dominate global rankings, our success in establishing excellence in a relative handful of elite institutions does little to ensure continued national competitiveness, especially when one considers the disproportionately few students fortunate enough to attend our top schools. In this sense, academic elitism has become a defensive posture and abdication of implicit responsibility.

It is generally taken for granted that there are two types of universities: the small cadre of elite institutions that focus on academic excellence and discovery, and the majority of less selective schools that offer access yet often provide little more than the most standardized instruction. Institutions that focus on academic excellence generally admit only a fraction of applicants, many of whom come from privileged socioeconomic backgrounds and have enjoyed undeniable advantages. The majority of students are thus expected to attend less competitive schools (Bowen,

Kurzweil, and Tobin, 2006; Golden, 2006). In terms of the growing social and economic stratification between those with access to a quality higher education and those denied opportunity, this implicit calculation is not only shortsighted but is certain in the long run to exacerbate inequality and injustice in our society (Bowen, Chingos, and McPherson, 2009).

If we continue to exclude a high proportion of qualified applicants from access to quality education by the excessive and sometimes arbitrary "culling" of the admissions processes of elite universities, we deprive individuals with immense promise of opportunities to attain their potential. Individuals thus deprived, whether through lack of funds or available seats represent not only personal opportunity lost but also the diminishment of societal economic prosperity. Such individuals will most likely earn lower wages and generate fewer jobs than they would have as graduates (Hill, Hoffman, and Rex, 2005). And because untold numbers of high school students lack the necessary qualifications even to submit applications to top universities and colleges, institutions have no recourse but to assume the additional responsibility to improve K-12 schools in their communities. A recent report on high school graduation rates in the fifty largest cities in the United States underscores the urgency of the problem: according to the study, seventeen of the nation's fifty largest cities had graduation rates lower than 50 percent (Swanson, 2009). Not only must we make more of an effort to understand how to educate greater numbers of individuals successfully, but we must also endeavor to instill in students the potential to become productive citizens. A willingness to assume responsibility for the development of this socioeconomic dimension in undergraduates should become intrinsic to the societal mission of colleges and universities.

The problem of scale is an important dimension to analysis and endeavor in higher education that has not been sufficiently examined. I believe we do not understand either the implications of scale or how to shape questions at an appropriate scale in order to advance society and our institutions. With the population of the United States exceeding 308 million and projected to soar to 440 million within the present planning horizon, it is remarkable that no new universities of any significant scale are being conceptualized and built to meet enrollment demand, nor have existing institutions undertaken plans for significant expansion. Relative to the scale of our nation, the entire cadre of elite institutions, both public and private, operate on a limited bandwidth of engagement. Their lack of impact derives in part from their lack of capacity to adapt in response to the needs of society at scale. All of the engineers, scientists, doctors, and teachers that our nation will require in the decades ahead will inevitably come from the rank and file of American citizenry across all classes. Yet where will so many students attend college in the numbers this nation urgently requires? Unless benefactors unexpectedly come forth to endow new private universities of international stature and scope, with current trends there is little hope that state legislatures will allocate sufficient investments to build new institutions or expand existing schools at sufficient scale.

Public policy throughout the nation perpetuates a tiered system that determines the lives of students according to arbitrary admissions criteria like class rankings and standardized test scores. The University of California is perhaps the nation's leading system of higher education and in some cases limits its freshman applicant pool to the top four percent of graduating high school classes. As a consequence of the enactment of Proposition 209, which prohibited consideration of race, ethnicity, and gender in admissions, UCLA admitted only 249 African American applicants to its 2006 freshman class of more than 4,800, of whom only about one hundred enrolled. While UCLA had historically maintained among the highest levels of minority enrollment in the UC system, and has since redoubled efforts to boost enrollment of ethnic minority students, given the ethnic and racial diversity of California and especially Los Angeles, such admissions practices represent a demographic distortion. Current constraints in admissions to UC system campuses attributable to the economic downtown have made recent headlines, but the progressive exclusion of more and more applicants has been ongoing for decades. According to enrollment reports from the California Postsecondary Education Commission cited by John Aubrey Douglass (2007, p. 127), the ratio of admits to freshman applicants to UC Berkeley from 1975 to 1995 declined from 77 percent to 39 percent. Since higher education is the means by which a skilled workforce is produced and the source of economic growth and advances in society both for the benefit of the individual and the collective, such trends augur a reduction in our quality of life in the next generation.

TOWARD ACADEMIC ENTERPRISE AND ECOLOGIES OF INNOVATION

Most of us correlate innovation primarily with the scientific discovery and technological advancement springing from the research enterprises of our colleges and universities, but innovation must also be understood to take place at the organizational or institutional level. If research universities seek only to recover normalcy and regard change and evolution as recourses of last resort, then we ignore the potential inherent in institutional innovation. In their quest for recovery and advancement in the wake of the downturn, research universities face increased competition in their effort to secure limited resources. While the most important competition takes place for the best ideas, competition is ongoing for research dollars and private investment and also the best students, faculty, and administrators. In this fiercely competitive milieu, colleges and universities must embrace "real-world" entrepreneurial speed, resilience, and ingenuity. A change in institutional mindset such as I describe represents an evolutionary process or a process of institutional innovation. With my formulation of the research university as a "comprehensive knowledge enterprise," I seek to underscore the potential inherent in the concepts of "enterprise" and "entrepreneurship," which through some elitist logic have been marginalized in the discourse of the academy. Generally associated with the private sector, entrepreneurship is critical to the advancement of innovation (Schramm, 2006).

While the capital that business and industry produce is measured in economic terms, our task in academia is to produce both knowledge capital and human capital. All of these concepts are closely interrelated because knowledge capital actually produces human capital through a process of "academic enterprise." If universities are to sustain their contributions to the development of new ideas, new products, and new services that yield substantial economic value, they must maintain their levels of investment in research infrastructure and R&D despite the downturn, guided by the resiliency required to negotiate ongoing technological change. In our accustomed effort to focus on discovery and the production of increasingly specialized knowledge, many research universities underestimate their capacity to advance desired outcomes or to create useful products and processes and ideas with entrepreneurial potential (Geiger, 2004). While the commercialization of university research is the most obvious avenue to move academic research at the "edge of newness" from the laboratory to the marketplace, our expansive usage of the concept of academic enterprise embraces all creative expression of intellectual capital and knowledge-centric change. Entrepreneurship is the process of innovation and spirit of creative risk-taking through which the knowledge and ideas generated within universities are brought to scale to spur social development and economic competitiveness. Academic enterprise thus inspires discovery, creativity, and innovation – the intellectual capital that is the principal asset of every college and university.

In order to maximize the potential for innovation, institutions must organize to exploit complementarities and establish new degrees of connectivity, both internally and externally, with stakeholders in the public and private sectors. Consistent with Gordon Gee's call for universities to become "transinstitutional" (2009), entrepreneurial universities must become highly networked, with contacts and working alliances with business, industry, and government, as well as individuals and organizations concerned with innovation and economic development. Participation in such an ecosystem of networked connectivity and cooperation creates many pathways for innovators to move ideas from conception to reality. When the organizational arrangements of an institution are conducive to innovation and a network of relevant collaborative relationships has been established, one perceives a well-rounded innovation infrastructure and the university becomes part of a larger ecology of innovation (Crow, 1998; Kash, 1989). Through such collaboration national systems of innovation integrate with global knowledge exchanges (Niosi, Saviotti, and Crow, 1993).

A PROTOTYPE FOR INSTITUTIONAL EVOLUTION: A NEW AMERICAN UNIVERSITY

As president of Arizona State University since July 2002, I have guided an effort to pioneer a foundational model for a New American University. Such self-determination has meant embracing fundamental change: we have confronted the complexities associated with advancing robust institutional innovation in real time and at scale. The operationalization of the vision represents an effort to compress a process of institutional evolution that might otherwise have taken more than a quarter of a century into a single decade (2002–12). The challenge was considerable since in its present form ASU is the youngest of the roughly one hundred major research institutions in the United States, both public and private, and, with an enrollment approaching seventy thousand undergraduate, graduate, and professional students, the largest American university governed by a single administration. An organization as large and complex as a major research university operating in one of the most rapidly growing metropolitan regions in the nation would face daunting challenges during the implementation of any large-scale planning adjustment but a comprehensive top-to-bottom reconceptualization of an institution such as we have accomplished is without precedent.

Our efforts to operationalize the vision of a New American University in Arizona were shaped by the imperative to accommodate the demands and requirements of the unique setting and demographic profile of the institution. As one of the fastest-growing states in the nation, Arizona will continue to experience large increases in its college-age population but boasts an insufficient four-year college infrastructure to accommodate that growth. Arizona's economy is insufficiently diverse to accommodate

its population expansion, and the state is confronted with major challenges associated with its environment, health care, social services, immigration, and the performance of K-12 education. As is already the case
in California, where minorities already constitute a majority, within the
near term no single demographic category will comprise a majority of the
population in Arizona. The rapid population growth is accompanied by
rapid cultural diversification, and the unprecedented transformation of
the regional demographic profile requires ASU to offer access, promote
diversity, and meet the special needs of underserved populations.

Situated in the heart of an emerging megapolitan area that stretches
from the Prescott region of central Arizona southward to the border
with Mexico, ASU is the sole comprehensive baccalaureate-granting
university in a metropolitan region of four million projected to increase
to eight million. Demographic projections suggest that the so-called Sun
Corridor will become one of perhaps twenty significant economic, technological, and cultural agglomerations in the United States (Crow, 2008b;
Lang, Muro, and Sarzynski, 2008). Responsibility for higher education
in other large metropolitan regions is shared by a number of institutions.
Metropolitan Los Angeles, for example, boasts major research institutions
such as UCLA, USC, and Caltech, with four additional UC campuses –
Santa Barbara, Irvine, San Diego, and Riverside – within close proximity.
A number of California State University campuses and private institu-
tions such as Occidental College, the Claremont Colleges, and Claremont
Graduate University complement these research universities. And while
Maricopa County has the same population as the state of Colorado,
the latter by contrast boasts the University of Colorado at Boulder; the
University of Colorado at Denver, consolidated now with the medical
school; the University of Colorado at Colorado Springs; Colorado State
University; the University of Northern Colorado; a number of regional
institutions, and some noted private institutions such as the University of
Denver and Colorado College.

In the face of such challenges, the response of most institutions would
have been to retreat and rely on the elite historical models of the past.
ASU instead operationalized the vision of a New American University
while continuing its existing operations. As set forth in the white paper
"One University in Many Places: Transitional Design to Twenty-First
Century Excellence" (2004, rev. 2009), the objective of what we term the
"design process" has been to build a comprehensive metropolitan research
university that is an "unparalleled combination of commitment to academic excellence and major responsibility for the economic, social, and
cultural wellbeing of its community." An interrelated formulation that
we have developed is the expression of our intent to build an institution

"committed to the topmost echelons of academic excellence, inclusiveness to a broad demographic, and maximum societal impact," with the associated tagline "Excellence, Access, Impact." *Newsweek* has termed our experiment at scale "one of the most radical redesigns in higher learning since the modern research university took shape in nineteenth-century Germany" (Theil, 2008). An editorial from the journal *Nature* observes that questions about the future of the contemporary research university are being examined "nowhere more searchingly than at Arizona State University" (April 26, 2007). Accordingly, we invite scrutiny and encourage critique of the process since we consider our effort a definitive prototype or case study in the potential for institutional innovation in higher education.

While in some measure the initiation of our efforts was inspired by the call for a "new university" issued by Frank Rhodes (2001), the implementation of the New American University model we are advancing has in practice been shaped through exhaustive trial and error, a number of course corrections, and our best efforts at the application of common sense. Guided by a series of working drafts of comprehensive strategic plans, our intent has been to expand and intensify the capacity of the university for teaching and discovery in all disciplines while addressing the challenges of burgeoning enrollment with a distributed model. The evolving strategic plan centers on four basic university goals, all of which are interdependent but critical to achieving a set of eight "design aspirations," considered in the following paragraph. The goal of "access and quality for all" recognizes our responsibility to provide opportunities in higher education to all qualified citizens of the State of Arizona without impacting the highest levels of quality. A second goal is the establishment of "national standing for colleges and schools in every field." "Becoming a national comprehensive university by 2012" will build regional competitiveness and national and global distinction to the state and region. The fourth goal recognizes the university's responsibility towards the region it serves, and focuses on "enhancing our local impact and social embeddedness." While the advancement of the university will necessarily always remain a perpetual process, as of early 2010 – more than two years ahead of schedule – we announced that we have not only made demonstrable progress but have in fact accomplished these four basic goals.

The design aspirations guiding the process, applicable to all universities, both public and private, enjoin the academic community to (1) embrace the cultural, socioeconomic, and physical setting of their institutions; (2) become a force for societal transformation; (3) pursue a culture of academic enterprise and knowledge entrepreneurship; (4) conduct use-inspired research; (5) focus on the individual in a milieu of intellectual and cultural diversity; (6) transcend disciplinary limitations in pursuit of intellectual fusion; (7) socially embed the university, thereby advancing social enterprise development through direct engagement; and (8) advance global engagement (Crow, 2002).

ASU has sought to promote access to excellence despite the challenges of burgeoning enrollment with a distributed model, operating from four differentiated campuses of equally high aspiration, with each campus representing a planned clustering of related but academically distinct colleges and schools. "School-centrism" has produced a federation of unique interdisciplinary colleges and schools that are expected to compete for status with peer entities worldwide. Schools are encouraged to grow and prosper to the extent of their individual intellectual and market limits ("One University in Many Places," 2004, 2009).

Traditional academic organization reinforces disciplinary "silo mentality," isolating faculty members from intellectual interaction with those in other departments. The "school-centric" reconceptualization has produced more than two dozen new transdisciplinary schools, including the School of Human Evolution and Social Change; the School of Historical, Philosophical, and Religious Studies; the School of Computing, Informatics, and Decision Systems Engineering; and the School of Earth and Space Exploration. New schools are complemented by major transdisciplinary research initiatives such as the Biodesign Institute, focused on innovation in health care, energy and the environment, and national security; the Global Institute of Sustainability (GIOS), incorporating the world's first School of Sustainability; and the Center for the Study of Religion and Conflict. In the process we have eliminated a number of traditional academic departments, including biology, sociology, anthropology, and geology (Capaldi, 2009). Transdisciplinarity has trumped arbitrary constructs that may once have served certain social or administrative purposes but are no longer useful as we prepare to tackle global challenges (Committee on Facilitating Interdisciplinary Research (U.S.), 2005).

Operationalization of the New American University vision is shaping a unique academic profile at ASU to such an extent that consideration of major dimensions lies outside the scope of the present discussion. In recognition of the immense variability in types of intelligence and creativity that we champion in our student body, for example, ASU has established differentiated learning platforms within given disciplines to provide multiple pathways to a degree. Consistent with our design aspiration to focus on the individual, we have charted one of our campuses, for example, on a course to emerge as one of the nation's leading polytechnics, with programs that provide both theoretical perspective and practical learning experience, preparing graduates for direct entry into the workforce. We are advancing two differentiated schools of engineering, one focused on research and the theoretical aspects of technology and the other on practical application. Tens of thousands of students want to become engineers, yet the average math score on the SAT for students admitted to our traditional research-intensive engineering school is 765, which is to say a score in the 95th percentile. The program on our polytechnic campus responds to the needs of the thousands of students who possess spatial and tactile intelligence and every potential to enter the profession but would ordinarily never be admitted to conventional engineering programs because of their math scores. Similarly, we are advancing differentiated learning platforms through multiple schools of management or business, each with different learning modalities.

To consider a further example, to advance our institutional culture of academic enterprise we have reconceptualized a number of policies and processes associated with the commercialization of university research. Beginning with the establishment of Arizona Technology Enterprises (AzTE) in 2003 as our exclusive intellectual property management and technology transfer organization, we have boosted innovative output with new approaches to technology evaluation, product development, technology marketing, capital formation, operations and management, IP protection, industry relationships, and licensing and commercialization.

But our conception of academic enterprise transcends the commercialization of university research. ASU is building an innovation ecosystem infused with the intent not only to generate new enterprises but also to contribute solutions to the global challenges before us. We have not limited our entrepreneurial education to business and engineering but extended it across our campuses and throughout the disciplines and new interdisciplinary schools and centers. More than one hundred entrepreneurship-related courses are to be found throughout our curriculum, but instead of just teaching relevant courses we embed dynamic mechanisms for entrepreneurial innovation throughout schools and departments. The College of Nursing and Healthcare Innovation, for example, now boasts an innovation and entrepreneurship center, and a major industry-funded center for innovation in news media enhances teaching and research in the Walter Cronkite School of Journalism.

For students who are beginning to formulate a plan of action there are experiential learning opportunities and starter grants available through the Entrepreneur Advantage Project. For student teams ready to launch a venture there is the Edson Student Entrepreneur Initiative, which offers grants in addition to office space, training and mentorship. ASU Technopolis provides fledgling technology and life sciences entrepreneurs with skills and strategies necessary to convert ideas into commercially viable businesses. Guidance is available for product development, business infrastructure development, proof-of-concept capital formation, revenue development, and access to funding. And while it is not uncommon for universities to establish research parks, ASU conceptualized and designed SkySong, the ASU Scottsdale Innovation Center, named for an iconic shade structure that is its signature architectural element. SkySong integrates academia with commerce in a state-of-the-art mixed-use complex for knowledge and technology research and commerce.

At Arizona State University we reject the notion that excellence and access cannot be integrated within a single institution, and alone among American research universities have sought to redefine the notion of egalitarian admissions standards by offering access to as many students as are qualified to attend. Our approach has been to expand the capacity of the institution to meet enrollment demand and provide expanded educational opportunities to the many gifted and creative students who do not conform to a standard academic profile, as well as offering access to students who demonstrate every potential to succeed but lack the financial means to pursue a quality four-year undergraduate education. Socioeconomic disadvantage based on low levels of family income and educational attainment of parents is a barrier to access that should occasion more widespread concern among the general public: According to research conducted by William Bowen and colleagues, the percentage of first generation college students from families with incomes in the bottom quartile of distribution represent no more than 3.1 percent of university enrollment nationwide (Bowen, Kurzweil, and Tobin, 2006, p. 98–99, figure 5.2). In an era when the importance of higher education both to the individual and the collective has never been greater, such lack of representation precisely by those who might most benefit from this obvious avenue of upward mobility is a sad comment on our society.

When President Obama spoke at our 2009 commencement exercises, he was especially excited about our newly established program to ensure that resident undergraduates from families with annual incomes below $60,000 admitted as incoming freshmen would be able to graduate with baccalaureate degrees debt free. During fall semester 2009, the President Barack Obama Scholars program allowed more than 1,700 freshmen an opportunity to pursue their educational objectives. The program epitomizes our pledge to Arizona that no qualified student will face a financial barrier to attend ASU and underscores the success of the longstanding efforts that have led to record levels of diversity in our student body. While the freshman class has increased in size by 42 percent since 2002, for example, enrollment of ethnic minority students has increased by 100 percent, and the number of students enrolled from families below the poverty line has risen by roughly 500 percent. Our success in offering access regardless of financial need is easily one of the most significant achievements in the history of the institution.

CONCLUSION: RECOVERING CORE VALUES OF OUR NATION THROUGH INSTITUTIONAL INNOVATION

Efforts to define a "new normalcy" in higher education in the wake of the recession are misguided because they represent the perpetuation of the ossification that has increasingly marked a sector of society that should be characterized by perpetual innovation. Any further recourse to the business-as-usual approach that has become the norm in higher education is counterproductive to efforts the academic sector must undertake to meet the challenges that confront humanity in the twenty-first century. Any such effort represents not a judicious recalibration but rather a step backwards, both for individuals and the collective. What is required instead is discussion regarding how best to operationalize perpetual innovation. What will be required are new institutional models that offer access to excellence to a broad demographic. But even such access is insufficient unless institutions have the resolve and resources to adequately guide student outcomes. Without sufficient public investment, our schools cannot hope to offer the curricula, programs, student services, and facilities that will produce the graduation rates called for by the president.

President Barack Obama has called on our universities to take on a national agenda: To provide every American with the opportunity to pursue a quality higher education. To help guide our nation through its current crisis. To ensure continued American leadership across all sectors, aided by a renewed focus on science and technology. It is the same agenda we are advancing at Arizona State University with the model of the New American University. This new model for the American research university seeks to recover the egalitarian values of a national university envisioned by the framers of the Constitution.

During the summer of 1787, a nascent republic was just completing its earliest aspirational blueprint, the Constitution of the United States of America. At this watershed moment in the history of the democratic process, delegates from the thirteen colonies considered the possibility of establishing a national university. While the vision for a single preeminent national institution dedicated to the advancement of knowledge and discovery for the collective good was never realized, I would contend that such an institution evolved and flourishes to this day.

Our great public universities collectively comprise a de facto national university. Taken together all public universities produce more than 70 percent of all baccalaureate degree recipients in our nation as well as conducting nearly two-thirds of all federally funded research (McPherson, et al., 2009). It is these institutions that educate the majority of our students in a milieu that advances discovery and innovation and creativity while contributing to the development of a highly skilled workforce and the prosperity of our economy.

There was a time in the life of our nation when average citizens could reasonably hope for access to our great public universities. Following the Second World War, for example, returning veterans could expect to be admitted to institutions like the University of Michigan or the University of California, Berkeley, based on the B-plus average they had earned in high school. With elite universities now limiting enrollment to the very topmost few percent of graduating high school classes, the broad access to the best possible education that could once be taken for granted is now denied. While some may argue on behalf of this putative meritocracy and yet others justifiably challenge its assumptions (McNamee and Miller, 2004), I contend that the real imperative is for higher education to recover the egalitarian tenets inherent in the intentions of the founders of this nation. Since no national university was in fact ever established and higher education in America has instead thrived through the advancement of an astonishing array of diverse and heterogeneous institutions, each more at liberty to establish its own identity than most would even dare to contemplate, those of us in the academy are free to determine for ourselves the meaning of a true public university in all of its varied institutional forms. This, then, is a call for a New American University focused on perpetual innovation and for higher education to serve a higher purpose.

REFERENCES

Adams, James D. (2009), "Is the U.S. losing its preeminence in higher education?" NBER Working Paper no. 15233, Cambridge, MA: National Bureau of Economic Research, August.

Atkinson, Robert D. (2007), "Deep competitiveness," *Issues in Science and Technology* 23, no. 2, 69–75.

Atkinson, Richard C., and William A. Blanpied (2008), "Research universities: Core of the U.S. science and technology system," *Technology in Society*, **30**, 30–38.

Blakemore, Arthur, and Berthold Herrendorf (2009), "Economic growth: The importance of education and technological development," Tempe: W. P. Carey School of Business, Arizona State University.

Bok, Derek (1982), *Beyond the Ivory Tower: Social Responsibilities of the Modern University*, Cambridge, MA: Harvard University Press.

Bowen, William G., Matthew M. Chingos, and Michael S. McPherson (2009), *Crossing the Finish Line: Completing College at America's Public Universities*, Princeton: Princeton University Press.

Bowen, William G., Martin A. Kurzweil, and Eugene M. Tobin (2006), *Equity and Excellence in American Higher Education*, Charlottesville: University of Virginia Press.

Capaldi, Elizabeth (2009), "Intellectual transformation and budgetary savings through academic reorganization," *Change* (July/August): 19–27.

Cole, Jonathan R. (2009), *The Great American University: Its Rise to Preeminence, Its Indispensable National Role, and Why It Must Be Protected*, New York: Public Affairs.

Committee on Facilitating Interdisciplinary Research (U.S.); Committee on Science, Engineering, and Public Policy (U.S.) (2005), *Facilitating Interdisciplinary Research*, Washington, DC: National Academies Press.

Committee on Prospering in the Global Economy of the Twenty-First Century (U.S.) (2007), *Rising Above the Gathering Storm: Energizing and Employing America for a Brighter Economic Future*, Washington, DC: National Academies Press.

Crow, Michael M. (1998), "Organizing to respond to external research opportunities: Dimensions of concern for university collective action," Lawrence: Merrill Advanced Studies Center, University of Kansas.

Crow, Michael M. (2002), "A New American University: The New Gold Standard," Tempe: Arizona State University, available at http://www.asu.edu/president/inauguration/address/

Crow, Michael M. (2006), "The university of the future," *Issues in Science and Technology* 22, no. 2 (Winter): 5–6.

Crow, Michael M. (2007), "Perpetual Innovation: Universities and Regional Economic Development," keynote address, International Economic Development Council (IEDC), Scottsdale, Arizona, September 17, available at http://president.asu.edu/files/2007_0917PerpInnovation.pdf

Crow, Michael M. (2008a), "Building an Entrepreneurial University," in *The Future of the Research University: Meeting the Global Challenges of the 21st Century*, proceedings of the 2008 Kauffman-Max Planck Institute Summit on Entrepreneurship Research and Policy, Bavaria, Germany, June 8–11. Kansas City, MO: Ewing Marion Kauffman Foundation.

Crow, Michael M. (2008b), "Fulfilling the Sun Corridor's Promise: Creating an Economic, Technological, and Cultural Center," foreword to Grady Gammage Jr. et al., "Megapolitan: Arizona's Sun Corridor," Phoenix: Morrison Institute for Public Policy.

Crow, Michael M. (2010), "The research university as comprehensive knowledge enterprise: A prototype for a New American University," in *University Research for Innovation*, 211–225, edited by Luc E. Weber and James J. Duderstadt. Geneva: Economica.

Douglass, John Aubrey (2006), "The waning of America's higher education advantage: International competitors are no longer number two and have big plans in the global economy," Berkeley: Center for Studies in Higher Education, University of California.

Douglass, John Aubrey (2007), *The Conditions for Admission: Access, Equity, and the Social Contract of Public Universities*, Stanford: Stanford University Press.

Duderstadt, James J. (2000), *A University for the Twenty-First Century*, Ann Arbor: University of Michigan Press.

Gee, Gordon (2009), "Colleges face reinvention or extinction," *Chronicle of Higher Education* (February 9).

Geiger, Roger L. (2004), *Knowledge and Money: Research Universities and the Paradox of the Marketplace*, Stanford: Stanford University Press.

Golden, Daniel (2006), *The Price of Admission: How America's Ruling Class Buys Its Way into Elite Colleges – And Who Gets Left Outside the Gates*, New York: Crown.

Goldin, Claudia, and Lawrence F. Katz (2008), *The Race Between Education and Technology*, Cambridge, MA: Belknap Press of Harvard University Press.

Graham, Hugh Davis, and Nancy Diamond (1997), *The Rise of American Research Universities: Elites and Challengers in the Postwar Era*, Baltimore: Johns Hopkins University Press.

Haskins, Ron (2008), "Education and economic mobility," in *Getting Ahead or Losing Ground: Economic Mobility in America*, pp. 91–104, edited by Julia Issacs, Isabel Sawhill and Ron Haskins. Washington, DC: Economic Mobility Project, Pew Charitable Trusts.

Haskins, Ron, Harry Holzer and Robert Lerman (2009), *Promoting Economic Mobility by Increasing Postsecondary Education*, Washington, DC: Economic Mobility Project, Pew Charitable Trusts.

Heller, Donald E. (2006), "State support of higher education: Past, present, and future," in *Privatization and Public Universities,* 11–37, edited by Douglas M. Priest and Edward P. St. John. Bloomington: Indiana University Press.

Hill, Kent, Dennis Hoffman, and Tom R. Rex (2005), "The value of higher education: Individual and societal benefits," Tempe: L. William Seidman Research Institute, W. P. Carey School of Business, Arizona State University.

Hossler, Donald et al. (1997), "State funding for higher education: The Sisyphean Task," *Journal of Higher Education* 68, no. 2 (March/April), 160–190.

Kash, Don E. (1989), *Perpetual Innovation: The New World of Competition*, New York: Basic Books.

Kerr, Clark (2001), *The Uses of the University*, fifth edition, Cambridge: Harvard University Press.

Kitcher, Philip (2001), *Science, Truth, and Democracy*, Oxford: Oxford University Press.

Lang, Robert E., Mark Muro, and Andrea Sarzynski (2008), "Mountain Megas: America's newest metropolitan places and a federal partnership to help them prosper," Washington, DC: Metropolitan Policy Program, Brookings Institution.

McNamee, Stephen J. and Robert K. Miller Jr. (2004), *The Meritocracy Myth*, Lanham, MD: Rowman & Littlefield.

McPherson, Peter and David Shulenberger (2008), *University Tuition, Consumer Choice, and College Affordability: Strategies for Addressing a Higher Education Affordability Challenge*, Washington, DC: National Association of State and Land-Grant Colleges and Universities, pp. 68–69.

McPherson, Peter, David Shulenberger, Howard Gobstein, and Christine Keller (2009), "Competitiveness of public research universities and consequences for the country: Recommendations for change," NASULGC Discussion Paper working draft.

Mortenson, Thomas G. et al., (1999), "Why college? Private correlates of educational attainment," *Postsecondary Education Opportunity: The Mortenson Research Seminar on Public Policy Analysis of Opportunity for Postsecondary Education*, 81 (March).

"A New American University" (2008), Tempe: Office of University Initiatives, Arizona State University, available at http://ui.asu.edu/docs/newamu/New_ American_University.pdf

Niosi, Jorge, Paolo Saviotti, Bertrand Bellon, and Michael Crow (1993), "National systems of innovation: In search of a workable concept," *Technology in Society*, 15: 207–27.

"One university in many places: Transitional design to twenty-first century excellence" (2004, rev. 2009), Tempe: Office of the President, Arizona State University.

Rhodes, Frank H.T. (2001), *The Creation of the Future: The Role of the American University*, Ithaca: Cornell University Press.

Sarewitz, Daniel (1996), *Frontiers of Illusion: Science, Technology, and the Politics of Progress*, Philadelphia: Temple University Press.

Schramm, Carl J. (2006), *The Entrepreneurial Imperative: How America's Economic Miracle Will Reshape the World*, New York: Harper Collins.

Swanson, Christopher B. (2009), "Closing the graduation gap: Educational and economic conditions in America's largest cities," Bethesda, MD: Editorial Projects in Education.

Theil, Stefan (2008), "The campus of the future," *Newsweek* (August 9).

5.   Higher education's mandate: planning for a new generation

Eduardo J. Padrón

THE CONTEXT FOR PLANNING

One decade into the twenty first century, higher education is facing an abundance of challenges. Many concern our own house but more profoundly, the tremors in the greater society continue to shake that house, right to the foundations in many cases. Planning, particularly long-range planning, and our decision-making have become increasingly difficult given the deep changes that continue to occur on so many fronts.

With the economy impinging on every element of society today, the notion of organizational effectiveness looms large for higher education. While the federal government has opened its coffers to assist all levels of education, rigorous performance standards to justify the expense are common practice, as well they should be. And states across the nation, while struggling to adequately support the various tiers of education, have nonetheless demanded an increasing level of accountability.

But before we make across the board cuts, delete entire programs or initiate any other major cost saving plans, the context for decision-making and planning needs to be reconsidered. We sit at the helm of mission-driven institutions, dedicated to student learning, research for the good of society, a ready workforce and strong communities. Revenue and expense may constantly occupy our minds but nevertheless, our eyes must scan the horizon. Never before have we been confronted with the promise, or rather the certainty, of such volatile change that is sure to challenge our understanding and affect the learning environment.

Who enters and who does not enter that learning environment is a critical question that should concern every institution in the country. It should concern us to the point of redefining our notion of effectiveness well beyond our financial ledger. Higher education is a necessary pathway to prosperity and the re-emergence of a strong middle class, and as such, it is incumbent upon higher education's leadership to view planning and priority-setting consistent with the challenges facing the nation.

It concerns President Obama enough that he has proposed to double the education budget, offering unprecedented funding for both K-12 and higher education. He challenged the nation to regain world leadership in the percentage of people gaining a bachelor's degree, which translates to approximately doubling the numbers of 25–34 year olds earning degrees. Today, the United States ranks 10th in the world for the percentage of 18–34 year olds earning an associates degree or higher. Our younger students rank 24th in math literacy and 17th in science as per a 2006 study of 30 of the world's most advanced nations. The President pointed out that Singapore's middle schoolers outperform ours three to one. Two-thirds of our thirteen- and fourteen-year olds cannot read at grade level. And our high school graduation rate has fallen to 10th among advanced nations.[1]

Effectiveness should be considered in this context, and the definition is simple and direct: How successful are we in expanding the existing base of college-going students, and how well do we integrate, support and graduate this new generation that will staff our workforce for years to come?

CHALLENGES IN ABUNDANCE

As noted earlier, the challenges for higher education are utterly tangled with the larger societal quandaries. Today, we live in a two-tiered society with a rapidly dwindling middle class. This is the overriding economic context, certainly, for every urban institution and community college in the nation. It also needs to turn heads in the flagship public and elite private colleges and universities. The gap between rich and poor has not been this wide since the 1920s,[2] with an enclave of the wealthy perched atop a growing population of low-income residents in every metro region of the country.

The future of metropolitan America hangs in the balance today, and that should be a critical factor in defining the effectiveness of our institutions. How will the gap between rich and poor be bridged without a broader avenue of access to the nation's colleges and universities? What remedy exists beyond education, beyond a practical set of tools to navigate the changing workforce?

Because of the staggering advances in technology and the advantages to be gleaned by the users, the prospect we face is a class system like none we have ever witnessed. The fortunate few will become world citizens, connected as never before to economic, social and cultural opportunities, while those for whom the door to education closes will be excluded as never before. These are the realities that are staring us in the face.

Higher education is the fulcrum. The choices we make will determine the severity of the chasm between a new generation of haves and have-nots. We cannot bridge the divide on our own but we can ensure that the other players – government, private industry, the new media, philanthropy and more – know full well the consequences of ignoring the present context.

THE CHANGING DEMOGRAPHIC

The impact of technology is just one of several powerful change agents affecting higher education and the greater society. The United States is not the same country demographically as it was 25 years ago, and even more striking, just ten years ago. The country's current Hispanic population reflects an historic growth surge that promises even greater changes to the overall American social fabric. Our melting pot is very warm once again. The numbers and the accompanying economic and education data have dramatic implications for American education.

In 1970, the United States' Hispanic population was shy of 10 million, or just 4.7 percent of the total population. By 2000, 35.3 million Hispanics called the United States home, amounting to 12.5 percent of the population. The influx has continued and the Census projection for 2010 is 47.8 million Hispanics, up to 15.5 percent of the total United States population. Only Mexico has a larger Hispanic population than the United States. By 2050, the U.S. Census Bureau estimates that the national population will include 102 million Hispanics, or about one-quarter of the United States population.[3]

The numbers are greatest in the expected states of California, Texas, Florida, New York and Illinois. But the highest growth rates are in the South, particularly in Arkansas, Georgia, South and North Carolina, and Tennessee. Each of these states hosts more than 100,000 Hispanics and experienced a growth rate of between 50 and 60 percent between 2000 and 2006. While not as dramatic, very significant increases have occurred in every region of the nation.[4]

Higher education's planning and the nation's education and immigration policies need to seriously heed these numbers. The Hispanic population is much younger than the overall population, but also significantly less educated. The median age of Hispanics is about nine years younger than the overall population, and new traditions of college going are evolving in recent years. However, statistics suggest a steep curve to bring Hispanics in line with the achievement of other ethnic groups in the country, and perhaps most daunting, 25 percent of children younger than five were Hispanic in 2008. All in all, Hispanics comprised 22 percent of children younger than 18.[4]

Approximately 12 percent of Hispanics hold a bachelor's degree or higher, compared with 27 percent of the entire population. Not surprisingly, individual median income lags behind the overall population by a full third, and 21.5 percent of Hispanics live beneath the federal poverty threshold compared to 12.5 percent of the all Americans as of 2007 and 8.2 percent of whites. These numbers, however, were calculated before the recent economic crisis, suggesting that all percentages have risen.[4]

While the African-American population is no longer the largest American minority, many of the same economic and educational challenges are present. In fact, the poverty rate for African-Americans surpasses Hispanics at 24.5 percent. While a significantly higher percentage had earned bachelor's degrees (20 percent), the need to meet a new generation's needs is also evident, with 30 percent of African-Americans aged 18 years or younger.[4]

WORKING WITH THE NATION'S PUBLIC SCHOOLS

The struggles of America's minority and low-income populations are evident in the performance of the nation's public school systems. The graduation rate from the nation's high schools has fallen beneath 70 percent, but much more dire is the state of education in the nation's cities. A report by Editorial Projects in Education in 2009 indicated a high school graduation rate of just 52.8 percent from the school districts serving the nation's 50 largest cities.[5] Couple that statistic with a United Nations' report in 2008 indicating that 81 percent of the American population resided in cities and their suburbs,[6] and you know that the Obama administration's efforts will only begin the remediation.

As president of an open access institution that is the backbone of higher education opportunity in South Florida, I witness – and welcome – a constant flow of underprepared students entering Miami Dade College (MDC). Seventy-four percent require at least one developmental course in basic skills,[7] but MDC's students are not alone in their remedial needs. At colleges and universities across the country, 53 percent of entering students arrive underprepared.[8]

It's foolish to write this circumstance off as K-12's problem, if for no other reason than the obvious – that higher education is enduring the effects of K-12's struggles. But the larger reason is that higher education has something invaluable to share with colleagues and students in the nation's public school systems. First and foremost, the presence of a college or university in partnership with the public schools sends an essential message: Going to college is essential. As important, the attitudes that limit young students' expectations are confronted alongside a realistic introduction to the world of higher education and its expectations.

Such a notion might manifest in a dismissive or "what's the point" attitude, usually masking a fear of not measuring up. Once enrolled, the reality of life in a low-income family kicks in, and leaving college studies to support a family is a decision too often made. At MDC, our effort has been to craft an environment that is intentionally intrusive regarding academic progress, and supportive in engaging students in the life of the campus, with peers, faculty, staff and events. Study after study demonstrates that such an environment pays off in overcoming first year challenges and ultimately, in college success.

But we also need to rethink and re-shape developmental education. That implies more effective entry assessment that better defines a student's deficits in basic skills, beyond "college-ready" or "college-prep." Assessing non-cognitive attitudes that are crucial for college success can help greatly, as well. With developmental needs better defined, the next step is modular learning that targets specific needs. Rather than spending an entire semester in a broad college prep math course, students can focus on a specific deficit such as general math or algebra. All of this, of course, asks us to reconsider the credit hour and reorganize our academic offerings, no small challenge for higher education.

In addition to confronting limiting attitudes, colleges and universities can export the experience and learning gained in addressing the needs of low-income minority students who are often underprepared. These are the graduates of public high schools who were, in many cases, struggling through high school but have succeeded in a new environment.

Early college high schools and the many variations that have demonstrated success are serious avenues to exert an impact on college readiness. In much the same fashion that community colleges partner with universities to develop clear articulation for graduates, an effort to reach back and accomplish the same end result with the nation's public schools is essential. Such an effort is essential to promote the expansion of the college-going base and support successful college careers.

But before that can happen, a nation concerned with college success needs to recognize that we are functioning in a remedial era. The statistics and performance of our young students are not fabrications, and the success of the country in an international marketplace depends on recognizing the work that needs to be accomplished. And that means recognition of the financial costs by both the state and federal governments. The personnel – teachers, advisors, tutors – and technology to support a generation of students whose skills trail their grade level will be expensive.

If effectiveness and efficiency are our focus, consider the implications of short selling developmental needs. In truth, the fallout is nearly impossible to calculate on individuals, families, the workforce and the larger community. The calculation of lost opportunity is unscientific but nonetheless, devastating. But a hint can be gauged from a previous economic impact study of Miami Dade College that measured money saved in public services when education takes the place of so many societal ills. The study calculated aggregate dollar savings of $57.9 million per year for taxpayers in avoided costs for state-supported health care, reduced welfare and unemployment benefits and fewer incarcerations. Educated people simply live healthier and more productive lives. With regard to taxpayer return on investment, the study demonstrated that MDC provided a benefit/cost ratio to the state of 16.5, meaning that for every dollar of tax money invested in MDC at the time of the study returns a cumulative $16.50 over a 30 year period. When viewed in the short term, each dollar invested returned $2.74 over a period of just 7.4 years.[9]

These are the numerical counterpoints to arguments that claim we cannot afford to expand higher education's reach. What we can't afford is the lost human resource and the costs of inaction. These numbers simply verify that spending on education qualifies in every regard as astute investment.

UNDERSTANDING TECHNOLOGY'S IMPACT

The Explosion of Information

Technology qualifies as the most obvious element in crafting higher education's future, and the most difficult to foresee and commit to a plan. The changes in information technology, social networking and a host of technology-based fields are creating entire new careers – and disposing of them – as new innovations shake the marketplace.

Our students are growing up in a social network that has no precedent in our lives. And calling it a social network is tame; it is more like a haze of constantly evolving and very compelling media. Students are adept with the tools of their time but they are extremely vulnerable to the onslaught of information. Clearly, our planning should consider the integration of new technologies and the expansion of the learning environment. Equally important, however, is the foundation in learning that equips students to engage productively with not only a volatile workforce but also a raucous world of information and opinions.

The pure volume of information we are generating is occurring at a rate

that is difficult to comprehend. Researchers have observed that information is expanding at a rate faster than anything else we create or measure
on the planet. Our feeble efforts at "junk e-mail" receptacles are hardly
a match for the onslaught, and our search for faster and faster avenues
of transmission is a constant element of technological growth. As one
blogger pointed out, the rate of growth in information may even be faster
than any biological growth in our current purview.

Researchers at the University of California, Berkeley, in their report
"How Much Information?" measured the total production of all information channels in the world for two different years, 2000 and 2003. That we
don't have a standard fashion of even measuring the growth of information in this digital age is a statement itself, but their efforts demonstrate a
beginning foray into understanding what all of us are confronting.

Their calculations included information found on all analog media such
as paper, film, and tape, as well as in all digital media including hard disks
and chips, and through bandwidth via TV, radio and telecommunications.
The tally focused on unique information, avoiding duplicates of any type.
The tally was 1.5 exabytes in 2000. By explanation, that's equivalent to
about 37,000 times the holdings in the Library of Congress. Three years
later, the annual total had reached 3.5 exabytes, a 66 percent growth rate
in information per year.

How does this occur? The authors offer a period-relevant example.
Consider the 600 percent increase in iPods shipped last year. While that
type of product sales growth is not sustainable, think of all the playlists
developed, new methods of sharing, cataloging, indexing and developing
the information about playlists. This is what Hal Varian, one of the UC
Berkeley researchers calls the "democratization of data."[10] And this is
the tip of the iceberg, perhaps not earth shaking information but a small
lesson in how we are exploding the information pathways. Technorati, a
news site that rates the blogs, estimates the existence of 133 million blogs
since 2002.[11] Back in 2008, Google announced that the number of unique
URLs in their index had reached one trillion. It's also estimated that two
billion Google searches occur each day, up from 10,000 per day in 1998.
And Google recently made public that the company is introducing an
internet connection that acts 100 times faster than the best fiber optic
network we now have.[12]

Economists estimate that physical production grows at about three
percent a year in advanced countries, and as high as seven percent a year in
a dramatically expanding market like China. Information is growing at 66
percent per year, almost ten times as rapidly as physical production. Can
there be any doubt that we have moved into a new era, one that has untold
implications for our institutions and students?[13]

Growing the Institution's Capacity to Engage with Technology

Effective planning for technology must be consolidated into the overall planning process for the institution. To allow technology operations to be planned in any significant degree of isolation is inviting unnecessary costs and waylaying the growth of the core mission. This is not to say, by any means, that the technology sector of an institution does not need its own strategic plan for growth. Everything about technology suggests volatility and rapid change, so the need for strategic long-term planning is crucial, including both internal and external environmental scanning. More than any other aspect of planning, technology poses the challenge of uncertainty and the need for diverse input and a fundamentally sound, if not a conservative approach, to decision-making.

With nearly every higher education institution experiencing the crunch of lean economic times, difficult decisions based on priority-setting conversations are a necessary aspect of planning. Decisions on infrastructure, the backbone of further development, hardware purchases, storage strategies, telecommunications, software purchase and development, and desktop and other upgrades are all part of an increasingly daunting and complex process of seeing as far around the bend in the road ahead as possible. Virtual learning, of course, is an additional aspect, replete with social media and networking innovations, that will require increasing attention in the years ahead. Overall, this reflects an immense menu of growth options and very few institutions can move on all fronts at the same time. In most cases, such growth would be impractical and unwise for reasons beyond economics.

Central to planning, of course, are curriculum and teaching and learning, and critical questions need to be asked to ensure a supportive partnership. The introduction of new technologies in the classroom has influence on textbook selection, assessment practices, state requirements and accountability policies. And beyond these issues is the basic concern with the effectiveness of various tools on learning, faculty facility with the tools and the conduct of the classroom.

Two currently relevant examples of new tools with the potential to greatly influence the learning environment are smart phones and e-books. Both appear to hold immense possibilities for students but major investments should be subjected to a costs/results/durability assessment. The use of these innovations in higher education should be studied internally to ascertain if a particular strategy is effective and warrants consideration of institutional investment. At an institution like Miami Dade College, with a student population that is mostly low-income and poor, such investments, if justified in their durability and effect on the learning environment, can provide students with tools they would not otherwise obtain.

Faculty lead in identifying useful tools but it can be assumed with the proliferation of software approaches that whatever grows to be the dominant platform for a given activity will be challenged by faculty members who uncover a different tool that works better for them. This is inevitable and while innovation and new approaches using technology are absolutely necessary to deliver the best possible classroom experience, the range of tools poses a problem in providing institutional support. This may seem like a small point in overall technology planning but in truth, it is a delicate issue that affects faculty innovation and engagement with students, and just as important, available support for virtual learning. The latter is crucial, particularly with students who may not be adept as independent learners. Overall, ensuring that a community of learners is maintained in education's virtual outpost is imperative.

MDC's Virtual College is now larger than five of our eight campuses, with enrollment exceeding 11,000 students. The ANGEL course management system is the operational backbone of the Virtual College and provides students a full tutorial online that includes a course tour and student user guide. In the ANGEL environment, students can access course content, take quizzes and tests, contribute to discussion forums and chats, send and receive messages, upload assignments and obtain grades and progress reports. Additional support elements include a trouble shooter step-by-step process, information knowledge base of accumulated wisdom from users, and a live chat function.

Support for students, however, is not the only required assist. Technology planning is hardly complete without attention to professional development and support for faculty. Today, MDC offers nearly 400 courses involving 275 faculty. Common sense dictates that training faculty and providing ongoing support to them must be a hand-in-hand development with increased enrollment and extended class offerings. As well, the key element of assessment always looms large with the introduction of new curriculum and teaching methods, and that is certainly the case with all efforts in virtual learning. Support from curriculum strategists and institutional research is essential in moving forward.

Education policy discussions now must include a new area of technology, and to be sure it adds a new dimension to planning. As faculty continue to develop new classes, software applications and teaching methods, intellectual property rights demands clarification. Cyber security policies are an essential conversation and one that needs constant review, similar to the need for technology planning. Right alongside, given the free access that students and staff have to the Internet in the course of college activities, identity theft is an additional issue for consideration. And the larger issue of privacy concerns must be addressed as social media and networks become regular tools within higher education. Last but hardly least, we now have a new arena to track with regard to federal and state policy that will, undoubtedly, exert a major impact on our institutions.

The last concern with regard to policy and planning is the subject of equity. MDC is an open access institution that welcomes high percentages of low-income and underprepared students. It is essential to ensure that technological advances are inclusive and that facilities are available that provide access to the tools and learning environments that are otherwise available via the range of personal computers and mobile devices. To this point in time, computer courtyards on campus have served effectively in providing this access but in some cases, "low-tech/high touch" options need to remain available, consistent with a philosophy that always affords personal contact as a source of support or alternative approach to cyber communication.

TRANSPARENCY, ENGAGEMENT AND OWNERSHIP VIA THE PLANNING PROCESS

In uncertain times, clear information that makes its way to all corners of the institution is invaluable. With the external environment in flux, maintaining transparency and engagement on the inside is necessary for both productivity and morale. It follows that the processes through which we communicate and plan are equally valuable next to the tangible goals and objectives for the institution.

Periods of fiscal scarcity pose challenges to colleges and universities that are not readily apparent, lurking beneath the evidence on a financial ledger. State supported community colleges and universities are no strangers to these periods and it's likely that most have felt the slump in morale hastened by constant belt tightening. Beyond the basic anxiety about job stability, hiring and travel freezes and the reluctance to invest in new programs can sap creativity and generate a malaise that is anathema to a learning environment.

If we cannot control many of the forces that precipitate financial shortages, we can, indeed, manage our response and the impact on our work and learning environments. The planning process should be a source of clarity regarding the direction of the institution, and just as importantly, an opportunity to engage members of the college or university community in setting that direction. This is, of course, true in both tight and well-heeled financial times.

But it's no easy assignment in a large organization. MDC has nearly 6,100 employees, 170,000 students and an eight campus complex to navigate. Engendering engagement in planning must be a systematic and carefully engineered process. And it should include both long-term strategic planning as well as opportunities to evaluate the effectiveness of the action plans on a regular basis.

Planning isn't glamorous but neither is it boring. More importantly, it is an essential practice that lends stability to the organizational community, particularly as noted, during times of economic strife. But above all, participation in the planning process invites ownership at every level of the institution. From a skilled core team representing diverse perspectives to the broad expanse of the entire college community, the experience can be downright exciting.

Planning is, first and foremost, the articulation of an ideal, a clarification of the institution's mission, which should be a grand statement of what is possible. And once again, this is ever more crucial as the balance sheet appears to deny possibility. The simple statement of purpose reminds and rekindles the sense of potential, which implies that the mission and vision of the institution cannot be stated once, and then relegated to an archive until the next strategic plan is formulated five years later.

If the process begins with an ideal, it is then one of translating it into a plan that is both practical and accessible. School and department personnel throughout the institution should gain the benefit of the umbrella of guidance provided by the overall strategic plan. Miami Dade College engages in a systematic, broad based and interrelated planning and evaluation process. Based on a clearly defined mission and vision statement, long-term strategic and annual educational, administrative and student support goals are developed and evaluated as to how effectively the goals are being met, with results suggesting the direction toward improvement.

The Strategic Plan defines the broad, College-wide, long-term goals with measurable objectives. We also evaluate effectiveness on an annual basis through the institutional effectiveness process, which has three levels of reporting and accountability: (1) College-wide effectiveness based on core indicators with annual reporting to the College-wide Academic and Support Staff Council and the College's executive leadership; (2) campus/area effectiveness, via annual goals and priorities developed at annual meetings and planning sessions; and (3) unit effectiveness (academic, student support and administrative areas) measured by area goals and annual reports to deans and vice provosts.

As an example of how we connect the mission and vision to action and evaluation, we ask key effectiveness questions at the college-wide level:

- How accessible are MDC programs and services?
- How affordable are MDC programs and services?
- How well does MDC help students progress through the curriculum to acquire needed knowledge and skills?
- How successful are MDC students in their academic and career pursuits after leaving MDC?
- How satisfied are MDC students with the education and services provided by the College?
- How well does MDC encourage creativity, risk-taking and accountability in employees?
- How well does MDC work in partnership with the community?
- How effectively does MDC use its resources?

Core Effectiveness Indicators have been identified for each of these questions and provide a college-wide focus. Institutional Research (IR) compiles the data for most of these indicators and works with other departments at the College to obtain additional information. These inputs form the basis of the college-wide Institutional Effectiveness Annual Report. Planning and effectiveness efforts also inform and support budget decisions at the College.

MDC is presently formulating its 2010–15 Strategic Plan, and the process relies on collaboration each step on the path to an approved plan. The revised mission and vision statements reflect the College's response to changing times, and have been submitted to college-wide scrutiny and recommendations from the entire College community. Armed with results from internal and external scans, the College has engaged in four planning streams to identify goals that support specific vision statements. Planning streams include facilitated meetings for campus presidents and vice presidents, deans and school heads, and web and in-person town hall meetings for employees and students. Input is analyzed by the college-wide Strategic Plan Coordinating Committee (SPCC) that orchestrates the development of the plan. The completed plan is submitted to the College's executive leadership and Board of Trustees for final approval.

Every organization relies on hierarchical relationships for decision-making and accountability. But effective planning also demonstrates that an organization is a collaboration of perspectives, and each has a vital contribution to make to the overall direction of the organization. Clearly, those with broad and visionary responsibility have no effective means of appreciating the granular needs of the organization on a day-to-day basis, and likewise, those charged with meeting students face-to-face each day will have little chance of forming broad conclusions for the institution's future direction. Valuing and combining these diverse perspectives is a recipe for comprehensive awareness throughout the institution and the essential sense of ownership that powers it forward.

THE REASON WE PLAN

Long ago Plato put forth a radical approach to governance that amounted, in effect, to serious skepticism regarding the practice of citizen democracy. Plato doubted the body politic's grasp – or interest – in the intricacies of economics, military strategy, domestic policy and the like. He felt people were vulnerable to the guile and nebulous talk of politicians, whose commitment to the common good Plato seriously doubted, as well. His remedy was the philosopher kings, those gifted individuals who combined a love of wisdom with a depth of understanding on matters of the day. His utopian ideal never came to pass but he has left us with much to consider.

The Harris research group will never be accused of espousing the teachings of Plato, but their recent study for the Association of American Colleges and Universities (AAC&U) marks them, indeed, as an odd bedfellow. Having asked business leaders what they were looking for in today's college graduates, their report summarized the need with the term "three hundred sixty degree people." It doesn't have the same ring as "philosopher kings" but it's closer than you think. Specific skills in a given field, and yes, technological acumen was in demand, but more than anything, they wanted people who could think critically and solve problems, and work effectively as members of a team. And more – they wanted people who were conscious of cultural diversity and trends in sustainability that might benefit their enterprises. Perhaps anointing our students as philosopher kings is a stretch, but the study, in essence, was offering up a definition of a new world citizen.

Regardless of financial constraints, we can and should plan for this outcome. It would be expensive to do otherwise – for our institutions, our students, the communities in which they will live, and the economies that very much need their contributions.

Redefining Traditional Liberal Learning

We have an opportunity to redefine traditional liberal learning for a new age, making it more relevant to the development of the nation's workforce than ever before. To be successful, such an endeavor should be central to our planning, the core of our efforts around which a constellation of support projects adhere.

MDC has embarked on a comprehensive initiative, now four years in progress, to establish liberal learning outcomes across the curriculum, along with a newly authentic approach to assessment. Like the planning process, it has served to galvanize accountability and ownership among both faculty and staff, this time around the very teaching and learning elements that define the institution.

We have agreed on ten learning outcomes that every student should master and that clearly articulate what it means to gain an MDC education. The outcomes reflect the "360 people" that business leaders are seeking, and include effective communication; quantitative analytical skill; problem solving, critical and creative thinking and scientific reasoning; dexterity with new volumes of information; cultural awareness; civic and social responsibility; the application of ethical thinking; technological acumen; environmental awareness; and an appreciation for aesthetics.

Faculty have developed real-world, performance-based assessment tasks with accompanying rubrics at four levels of achievement. These have served as global indicators of how well our students are performing collegewide on the outcomes, and guide the faculty in attending to weaknesses in achievement. Discipline-specific assessments are also in progress utilizing many of the approaches developed for the learning outcomes.

In addition, faculty have engaged in an in-depth curriculum mapping project, identifying how effectively each of MDC's 2,000 courses addresses the ten learning outcomes. Campus dialogues also identify gaps in courses and degree offerings, and institutional research plays an ongoing and crucial role in analyzing and validating the assessments, while conducting student focus groups and studying the effects of student motivation and effort as factors that influence assessment results.

CONCLUSION

Whether the coffers of higher education are full and programs are flourishing – or not – the value of what our institutions achieve across the country looms large. Given what has clearly defined itself as an inverse cycle that swells enrollment as the economy struggles, it might be concluded that higher education holds an acute potential during recession. The Secretary of Education, Arne Duncan, said as much in stating repeatedly that the nation needed to "educate its way out of the economic crisis." Certainly, the President intoned as much when he projected the United States to once again lead the world in the percentage of people earning baccalaureate degrees by 2020.

These are the grand aspirations of those with an unbridled perspective, but it is those of us in the everyday trenches who move the needle.

As the economy and even the greater society are transformed, it's clear that higher education has become more essential than ever to navigate an altered workforce terrain.

We are, then, faced with the contradiction of leading a resurgence in the face of limited resources that would have us stand pat and retrench. But this is why we plan, because far from being a tedious and narrow exercise, it is, in fact, the arena of vision and creation, the intersection of big ideas and heroic undertakings. Planning is about facing reality without being mesmerized by its apparent limits. Ultimately, it is an exercise of renewal and reaffirmation of purpose. It is an opportunity to recognize resources that may very well be more important than those that appear or not on a financial ledger.

NOTES

1. Alliance for School Choice (2009), "Education in America: A nation still at risk," available at http://www.allianceforschoolchoice.org/UploadedFiles/ResearchResources/EdInAmerica_NationAtRisk_04202009.pdf, pp. 2–3.
2. CNN (2007), "Gap between rich, poor seen growing," citing Internal Revenue Service data, October 12, available at http://money.cnn.com/2007/10/12/news/economy/income/index.htm
3. U.S. Census Bureau, 1970, 1980, 1990, and 2000 Decennial Censuses; Population Projections, July 1, 2010 to July 1, 2050, available at http://www.census.gov/population/www/socdemo/hispanic/hispanic_pop_presentation.htm
4. U.S. Census Bureau (2008), "American Community Survey," data on educational attainment, available at http://www.census.gov/acs/www/.
5. Swanson, Christopher B. (2009), "Cities in Crisis 2009: Closing the education gap." Editorial Projects in Education, available at http://www.edweek.org/media/cities_in_crisis_2009.pdf.
6. United Nations (2008), "United Nations population division: World urbanization prospects; Table A.2 (p.81)," available at http://www.un.org/esa/population/publications/wup2007/2007WUP_Highlights_web.pdf.
7. Miami Dade College (2010), Fact Book, Office of Institutional Research, available at http://www.mdc.edu/ir/Fact%20Book/undprp.pdf.
8. Association of American Colleges and Universities (2007), "Greater Expectations," National Panel Report, available at http://www.greaterexpectations.org/report/1b.html.
9. Miami Dade College (2002), "Economic impact," Office of Institutional Research, available at http://www.mdc.edu/ir/iremployees/RN2002_02.pdf.
10. Lyman, Peter and Hal, Varian (2003), "How much information," School of Information Management and Systems, University of California at Berkeley, available at http://www2.sims.berkeley.edu/research/projects/how-much-info-2003/printable_report.pdf.
11. Technorati (2008), "State of the Blogosphere," available at http://www.sifry.com/alerts/2008/09/technoratis-state-of-the-blogosphere-september-2008/.
12. Google (2008), The official Google Blog, available at http://googleblog.blogspot.com/2008/07/we-knew-web-was-big.html.
13. Technium (2006), "The Speed of Information," available at http://www.kk.org/thetechnium/archives/2006/02/the_speed_of_in.php

6. Southern Oregon University: a case study for change in the "new normal"

Mary Cullinan

CHALLENGES FACING US

When I googled "higher education challenges" recently, 124,000,000 results popped up. During the last century, experts inside and outside of universities wrote untold numbers of articles and gave untold numbers of talks on the myriad thorny issues confronting higher education: affirmative action, new technologies, remedial education, political unrest, tenure, curricular reform, intellectual property, global competition, legal pitfalls. The list of issues is immense.

However, this first decade of the twenty-first century is setting a standard for challenge that is unprecedented for higher education, and particularly for public higher education, in the United States. Among the most disturbing trends are the following:

State Disinvestment

Between 1980 and 2000, the share of university operating expenses paid by state tax dollars fell by 30 percent. In many states, decreases in funding for higher education have accelerated greatly since 2000, and some states now have structural financial problems that will not quickly be solved (Hurley, 2009, p. 4).

In Oregon, which has never richly funded higher education, state appropriations per student dropped from $4,292 in 1989 to $3,460 in 2009–10. If you adjust figures in line with the consumer price index, the drop is to $2,009 per student in 2009–10 (Frohnmayer, 2009, p. 5). At the same time, of course, costs for universities in areas such as health care benefits and utilities continue to rise.

Tuition Increases and Debt

In response to state cutbacks and cost increases, many universities have cut programming and services and increased tuition. "Measuring Up 2008: The National Report Card on Higher Education," published by the National Center for Public Policy and Higher Education, shows that the amount borrowed by students to meet the costs of college more than doubled between 1997–98 and 2007–08 (Figure 7, p. 9). All states except California received an F for affordability in that report. Responses to recent dramatic decreases in state funding by the University of California and California State University systems will undoubtedly lower California's grade in the next report.

Negative Perceptions

Universities are not valued to the degree they were earlier in America's history. Several presenters at the TIAA-CREF Institute, Smart Leadership in Difficult Times (November 2009), highlighted the attitudinal challenges faced by higher education in this new century. Charles Reed, Chancellor of the California State University system, discussed how public perceptions and priorities have changed in the last twenty years: public priorities are health care, crime, and K-12, not higher education.

Appreciation for the enormous social, cultural, and economic contributions of public universities has diminished. Instead, universities are frequently viewed as bloated bureaucracies that blatantly increase costs without regard for students. David Gergen argued in his keynote speech at the TIAA-CREF Institute that the incivility of public discourse in the United States and the cultural focus on entertainment rather than on education are also deeply affecting the situation of universities.

Less-Educated Populace

As Daniel Hurley points out in *Considerations for State Colleges and Universities in a Post-Recession America* (2009, p. 3), "Those with a college degree are one-half as likely to be unemployed compared with those with a high school diploma" (4.7 percent compared to 9.4 percent). Yet, as a result of both affordability and perceptual challenges, the United States has fallen behind in the proportion of population with a college degree.

A report from the American Association of State Colleges and Universities states that while the United States ranks second among all nations in the proportion of its population aged 35–64 with a college degree, it ranks tenth in the percentage of its population aged 25–34 who have earned an associate or baccalaureate degree. This trend is ominous both for the global competitiveness of the United States and the economic wellbeing of American individuals and families.

Echoing Gergen's sentiment, Carol Geary Schneider, President of the American Association of American Colleges and Universities, has stressed that we are "part of a democracy that is deeply divided." Not only do we need graduates who have "cross-cutting capacities" that enable them to survive and flourish in an "unscripted" world, but we also need graduates who will become leaders in our communities and help build back a productive, civil society.

Our nation has a tremendous need for increasing numbers of highly competent university graduates. However, in light of public perception and lack of interest, legislators have little incentive to increase state support for public universities and, in many cases, have chosen to limit tuition increases as well. Many public universities are making unprecedented budget cuts across all areas.

It is an ugly situation – and a frustrating one. For those who recognize the pivotal role of public universities in the economic and social development of this country as well as in the lives of millions of graduates, the diminution of public trust and understanding is as painful as the disinvestment of state funding.

THE "NEW NORMAL"

As David Gergen stressed at the 2009 Higher Education Leadership Conference, this sorry state of affairs will probably be with us for a long time: it is the "new normal." The United States is not going to experience an immediate return to its former prosperity or a radical turnaround in culture or attitude.

Nonetheless, we cannot – must not – sit paralyzed. Whining may feel slightly therapeutic, but it is not terribly useful. We understand the consequences for our respective states and the nation as a whole if public universities can no longer serve, at moderate cost, the vast numbers of individuals who will continue to look to us over the coming decades. As educators and leaders who esteem and teach creative thinking and problem solving, we should view this situation as a true life-or-death crisis that requires our boldest thinking.

No one solution will swiftly reverse the knotty problems we face. However, in examining individual stories of institutions around the country, we can glean insights that will help us as we inspire, create, and manage change in our respective situations.

In that spirit, I present here the case study of Southern Oregon University (SOU). We are not yet a success story; we are a work in progress. But a brief analysis of our journey so far may be useful as those of us in public higher education look to an uncertain future and align our institutions with the "new normal."

SOUTHERN OREGON UNIVERSITY: ONE INSTITUTION'S STORY

The institution that is now SOU was founded as Ashland Academy in 1872 as a normal school and has gone through a number of new starts and rebirths during its history. Southern Oregon College became a university in 1997 and now enrolls approximately 5,000 students. With a traditional campus located in Ashland, ten miles from the California border, SOU also serves significant numbers of students in nearby Medford.

For many years, the area of southern Oregon and northern California (sometimes known as the State of Jefferson) depended on a natural resources economy. However, as those businesses have diminished, the area increasingly attracts retirees and small companies. Thousands of visitors come to the area each year to participate in theatrical and other cultural activities as well as in the outdoor activities related to our mountains, rivers, and lakes.

SOU has long been a major catalyst for the arts in southern Oregon, including the Oregon Shakespeare Festival, the Rogue Opera, Chamber Music Concerts, and a wide variety of music, theatre, and film organizations and events. With strong professional programs in business, education, and other areas, SOU graduates also form the mainstay of the professional workforce in the area.

From its inception, this university, located in a rural, lightly populated section of the state, has struggled with financial issues. Oregon's lack of investment in public higher education pre-dates the recent recession. Measures passed in 1990 and 1994 drained revenue to the state through tax limitations and mandatory criminal sentencing and prison construction requirements (Frohnmayer report 2009, p. 5). As a result, tuition began to rise substantially at all seven Oregon state universities.

A small university located far from a major population area, Southern Oregon University experienced enrollment decreases in the early 2000s when tuition costs were increasing. While the institution did cut back expenses, it did not respond strategically. Like many businesses and households nationwide over the past decade, SOU was overly optimistic, assuming each year that enrollments would rise and the situation would improve.

As a result, costs and revenues became mis-aligned as state allocations continued to drop and student enrollments remained below projections.

When I arrived as president in fall 2006, SOU was in a precarious financial situation. Fall enrollments were once again below target. Our reserves had sunk below five percent. We were facing a crisis. Since revenues had dropped by ten percent, we needed to adjust our permanent expenses by at least that much. We needed to open the faculty union contract and go into financial retrenchment.

Through my first year as president, I worked with the SOU administrative team, as well as with faculty, staff, students, community constituencies, and union leadership, to make the process as consultative and inclusive as possible.

Shaving travel and reducing supplies and services costs would not be enough. We had to reorganize entire units. We had to think boldly. I asked each vice president to put together a restructuring plan. And, although we worked out a three-year plan involving retirements, it was clear we would have to lay off staff and faculty. My "honeymoon" period as president was spent analyzing data, conferring with groups and individuals on and off campus, handling questions from the media and legislature, and meeting endlessly with deans and vice presidents to think through how and where to cut.

We knew that the key to sustainability was to think long term rather than to cut across the board as had frequently been done in the past. The process was unimaginably painful. Nonetheless, two years later, as we began fall 2008, we had stabilized our finances. The reserves were increasing. Enrollments were growing again.

Then, of course, before our three-year retrenchment plan had been completed, the United States and Oregon economy experienced an almost unprecedented crash. Once again, we faced cuts in state support, and, in spring 2009, the legislature swept the fund balances of state agencies – including the reserves we had been laboriously building back through our retrenchment plan.

The remainder of 2009 was grim for SOU – as it was for universities, public schools, businesses, individuals, and families across the country.

Ironically, however, as I wrote in an article for *The Presidency* published in spring 2009, the efforts we had made to stabilize and re-position the university before the crash put us in a better situation to face the crushing economic woes of 2008–09. We had done the foundational work that Hurley outlines (2009, p. 13) in facing recession: we reviewed mission-critical priorities, implemented strategic cost reductions, and enhanced revenue drivers.

With a vision and plan in place, we were able to reallocate, to invest in "core programmatic strengths," as Hurley recommends. Most importantly, we had begun to create a campus culture that understands the need for change and the importance of thinking strategically.

KEY FACETS OF SUSTAINABLE CHANGE

The following key components of our processes are helping us through truly difficult times – and positioning SOU for the "new normal."

Listening and Communicating

As a new president in a difficult situation, I had to learn about SOU, its culture, history, and environment, as quickly as I could. I also had to help others understand our situation – and involve as many people as possible in the change processes.

The SOU administrative team members worked within their respective areas, listening and sharing information and ideas. I met with committees and groups, held open forums (which we videotaped and put on the Web), and organized Pizza with the President events (some of which are still on YouTube) for students. I put informational materials and updates on a website, began a blog, welcomed comments in person, in writing, and online, met with reporters, appeared on local television and radio stations, and spoke to local service groups. We reorganized the budget process to make it more transparent and consultative.

As Ronald A. Heifetz wrote in *Leadership Without Easy Answers*, "Each of us has blind spots that require the vision of others" (1994, p. 268). It was important for all of us involved in the process to free ourselves from the weight of our own biases and experiences and to think seriously and objectively about ideas that came forward.

Moreover, it was important to demonstrate we were listening. When we published an interim retrenchment plan in early 2007, we received serious pushback. We did more listening, more creative thinking – and made substantial changes to the plan. No plan involving such dramatic change (and budget cuts) could be without controversy and complaint – but the listening and information-sharing processes were crucial to overall acceptance of the final retrenchment plan.

Building a Team

In *Good to Great*, Jim Collins discusses the importance of getting key individuals in place – "on the bus." "If you begin with 'who,' rather than 'what,'" he writes, " you can more easily adapt to a changing world" (2001, p. 42). In a public university environment, such changes take time. The key leaders we needed had to think strategically and creatively, had to make incredibly difficult decisions, had to be committed to our university goals and vision – and had to help position the university for a future that was different from anything we had known. And the leadership needed to be willing to work collaboratively in an environment with very few resources.

The team-creation and team-building process at SOU took three years. We re-thought job descriptions and structures, and brought on a number of new vice presidents, deans, directors, and department heads. The process has been unsettling and, at times, painful. No one says change is easy. However, the growing capacity of effective and committed university leadership has been crucial to our process.

Planning and Branding

When they first arrive on a campus, new presidents frequently initiate a strategic planning process involving large committees and a complex set of processes. The work brings the campus together to form and ratify a unified vision while, at the same time, enabling a new leader to move the ship in ways consistent with a plan and with the needs of the institution.

In the case of SOU, major plans for reorganization were underway during the first year of my presidency in almost every area as we went through the retrenchment process. We were also finishing a significant academic building in Medford, in partnership with our local community college, that was due to open in fall 2008. Tremendous amounts of planning went into bringing that building to fruition.

At the same time, in 2007, the Oregon State Board of Higher Education (OSBHE) asked each Oregon state university to present to the Board a report on our mission and "portfolio" of programs. SOU, moreover, was also writing a self-study for reaccreditation, planning for a site visit from the Northwest Commission on Colleges and Universities in November 2007.

Despite – and even because of – all these planning activities, it was clear that SOU sorely needed a unified vision and sense of who we were as an institution. What was our vision for the arts and sciences? Were we emphasizing a traditional four-year campus experience or a transfer experience for non-traditional students? What was the role of our professional graduate programs? What was the role of distance education?

People on our campus were struggling with an identity crisis even while individual units were framing plans. In my interviews for the presidency, faculty and staff asked me whether I saw SOU as a liberal arts institution or as a regional comprehensive university. Who are we? Without an accepted sense of mission and goals, everything had become a "priority." Meanwhile, university-wide strategic plans from the past sat on dusty shelves.

Despite the pressures of retrenchment and administrative changes, we clearly needed to develop a mission statement and a forward-thinking strategic plan that would actually help guide us. We also agreed to undertake a branding initiative, starting in spring 2008, to help us understand how the university was perceived internally and externally and to position us as we re-thought our enrollment management and marketing processes.

With input from key constituencies on and off campus, we created a somewhat unconventional mission-development and planning process that drew on but also helped shape plans already being formed in Student Affairs, Academic Affairs, Enrollment Management, Development, and other areas. Through an iterative process, we developed a one-sentence mission followed by key commitments that the campus understood and believed in. In January 2008, the OSBHE approved our mission statement.

We also began developing a strategic plan with goals focused on strengthening and highlighting academic distinctiveness and quality, on our commitment to the arts and the region, on our role as community partner and catalyst, and on financial sustainability. These four goals align with the powerful feedback we received through our branding process. The components of our brand reflect the tremendous importance of our region, both the physical and the cultural environment; the intellectual creativity intrinsic to our curriculum and our campus culture; and the connected or applied learning that emphasizes student-faculty interaction, undergraduate research, and community service. SOU clearly fills a unique niche as the public liberal arts university of the West.

For the first time, beginning in fall 2009, we had in place a mission statement, five-year goals, year-long goals, and a deeper understanding of what the institution values and how it is perceived. This foundation is vital to everything else we are doing now. It is also crucial to the changes we make as we adjust to the "new normal."

Reorganizing for the Future

Retrenchment forced us into restructuring, redefining positions and decreasing the numbers of administrators and instructors – all in a matter of months. Despite the lack of resources, reduced numbers of managers, and excruciating short time-lines, we knew it was vital to create structures that reflected our values and positioned us for the future. The institution had ultimately suffered when, during former budget cuts, offices such as

Institutional Research and International Programs had been dissolved or decentralized with little thought as to the long-term effects of those changes.

One of our major commitments as an institution is to provide personalized support for students. Under the leadership of the Vice President for Student Affairs, we created a one-stop Enrollment Services Center, bringing together areas such as financial aid, admissions, registrar, and the student account functions of business services. Staff from Student Affairs and from Finance and Administration were cross-trained to serve students effectively. This was an enormous and stressful undertaking, but one that continues to bring benefits to students. Our Enrollment Services Center, which opened in September 2007, was immediately termed a model by a consulting group hired by the Oregon University System to examine structures in Student Affairs.

To help us meet our commitment to financial sustainability, we reorganized individuals in Student Affairs and in Finance and Administration to create an Office of Institutional Research under the Provost. We also moved Marketing and Communications away from the office of the Vice President for Development to enable development staff to focus intently on fundraising. As of early 2010, we are reviewing areas such as athletics, human resources, and technology.

Reorganization in Academic Affairs reduced administrative costs but also underscored our commitment to interdisciplinary learning that connects students with the real world. With significant input and creative work by the deans and faculty, we reduced the number of Schools and created a College of Arts and Sciences composed of the former Schools of Science, Social Science, and Arts and Letters. We also decreased the number of academic departments, creating departments such as History and Political Science; Language, Literature, and Philosophy; and Social Sciences, Policy, and Culture.

With our newly articulated focus on the arts and on the environment of our region, we merged the departments of Theatre and Music to highlight performing arts and also created a Department of Environmental Studies, with faculty from areas in the sciences and social sciences. Both of these areas of distinctiveness attract students from beyond our state borders and will increasingly become leading programs for SOU. For both the performing arts and environmental sciences, despite our serious budgetary constraints, we agreed to hire external chairs to provide leadership for these strategic areas of academic emphasis.

The new Colleges of Arts and Sciences opened in July 2007. With a strong sense of our mission and commitments to what we value as an institution, we were able to gain buy-in for decisions that moved scarce resources and put them into operations considered vital to our long-term success. It was increasingly clear to the campus, as John Moore of Penson Associates likes to say, that we should not shut down our engines during a storm.

We are still sadly under-staffed in many areas. But now the "bones" of our institution are more effectively organized. As we build back, we can work within a plan and within priorities keyed to our mission.

Addressing Revenue

SOU had historically tackled reductions in state allocations by cutting costs rather than looking seriously at revenues. Now, in reorganizing fundraising under a Vice President for Development (no longer termed "Vice President for Advancement"), we created a more powerful and focused charge for this area of the university. The new vice president, who arrived at SOU in summer 2008, has worked with the university's Foundation Board to develop a short- and long-term fundraising plan that is tightly connected to SOU's mission and strategic goals. We are already seeing significant progress in this area.

Addressing our second and even more crucial revenue stream, tuition, was more complicated. We were still not at the enrollment levels of the early 2000s. SOU had to attract more students and retain them more effectively.

The newly formed Enrollment Services Center immediately proved helpful by reducing the frustrations of students who formerly shuttled among buildings and offices to get their questions answered and problems solved. However, we are still addressing retention and recruitment issues on all fronts. This work, which involves deans, department chairs, and faculty as well as staff in all the vice presidential areas, is being organized around the strengths of our brand. We are revamping our website as well as online and hard copy materials, creating new messages and visuals, and developing plans to have a more prominent physical presence in southern Oregon communities.

The reorganization of the College of Arts and Sciences and the firm focus on our academic areas of excellence are proving essential to our enrollment initiatives. Increasingly, our prospective students understand the value of a small institution that offers opportunities for undergraduate research, hands-on experience in the arts and sciences, courses that connect their classroom learning with the region, and interdisciplinary approaches that allow them to move easily among areas – such as our new program combining art, digital media, and communications.

Through participation in a consortium funded by the Sloan Foundation, we are also significantly expanding our online programming and providing more support to faculty who put their classes and materials online. Our new building in Medford, which opened in fall 2008, offers increased access to working and non-traditional students, many of whom either transfer from or are co-enrolled in the community college. And our newly organized Office of International Programs is actively working to increase international student enrollment rather than focusing almost exclusively on student exchanges as it had in the past.

Faculty and staff are working on retention issues through our freshman seminar, improved advising, programs in the residence halls, and a new Learning Commons in the University Library. Retention is increasing incrementally, although we still do not retain students, particularly freshmen, in the numbers we would like.

Part of our enrollment challenge results from the economic stress of our students and prospective students. This stress is undoubtedly also part of the "new normal." Through our new Institutional Research office, we are developing more sophisticated tools that facilitate decision-making with regard to in-state, out-of-state, and graduate tuition along with a more strategic approach to financial aid. And, once again, a personalized approach to each student is helping to forestall the financial crises that historically have led SOU students to drop out rather than re-think their finances and remain enrolled.

Developing and Deepening Partnerships

Almost all state institutions across the country realize they are not standalone institutions: they must reach out in partnership with K-12, with state and federal agencies, with other universities around the state and around the world, and with businesses. The "new normal" now makes partnership an essential component for sustainable growth and even survival of public universities. Moreover, partnerships are key to turning around the uninterested or negative attitudes communities may hold toward their local universities.

SOU has long had powerful partnerships with regional arts organizations – our faculty actually founded many of them – and with universities in Mexico, Korea, and other countries. Many of these partnerships go back over forty years. Our School of Business has always worked closely with local businesses, and our School of Education works hand in hand with schools. Our new building in Medford was created and built in a deep, far-reaching partnership with Rogue Community College that has garnered attention from around the country.

Now, however, SOU's mission and strategic plan highlight partnerships as a major, conscious, university commitment. We now intentionally pursue and think creatively about collaboration. Our first-year students go out every fall to participate in civic engagement. We work with local agencies and the City of Ashland with regard to sustainability projects. We are considering public-private partnerships to develop new campus housing. We created a program in the Management of Aging Services, in partnership with Pacific Retirement Services, to prepare business students for working in a field that is growing rapidly in our region.

Understanding the power of connected learning, our faculty link their classes and their students more closely with local agencies, businesses, and community initiatives.

Deans and faculty now work with advisory groups as they develop and refine curriculum – ensuring that student outcomes are connected to the needs of employers. We have partnered with the University of Oregon on a program for first-year students who are admissible to both of our institutions. We have developed a program for students at Ashland High School to complete their first year at SOU by the time they graduate from high school. We have initiated a bachelor of applied science degree that enables students with an associate's degree in a vocational field to receive credit for their technical education.

In the "new normal," we are living our commitment to powerful partnerships.

Maintaining Campus Morale

A campus cannot go through significant upheaval and change without faculty, staff, and students being affected. Yes, a transparent, inclusive, thoughtful change process helps to keep people positively engaged. However, no amount of transparency can eliminate people's fears and uncertainties, especially when families and businesses everywhere are suffering. To help raise morale, the SOU administrative team designed a number of approaches to bring people together in positive ways. These approaches were a crucial component of our whole planning process.

- In my first year as president, as we faced financial retrenchment, I formed a Sustainability Council, composed of students, faculty, and staff. The Council was charged with coordinating and planning "green" initiatives. In its first year, the Council worked with students to pass a student initiative that made SOU the first Oregon campus to offset all its electricity and natural gas with renewable energy added to the grid. Through supporting sustainable practices, the Sustainability Council helped SOU meet budget reduction goals, but it also helped bring the campus together to do positive work in difficult times.

- We designed an annual recognition and retirement event, now in its fourth year, for faculty and staff.
- We asked a faculty team to create a two-day event that would highlight undergraduate and graduate research. The group designed SOAR, Southern Oregon Arts and Research, a grand celebration of faculty and students also now in its fourth year.
- With a small amount of discretionary funds, I initiated a President's Mini-Grant Program to support faculty-student collaborative projects.
- We began *Campus Connections*, monthly brown bag events for all faculty and staff that are hosted in rotation by the president, vice presidents, and deans. Every host develops an interactive theme for these events. Attendees are urged to introduce new people on campus and thank individuals who have done something special during the previous weeks.
- We developed surprise "thank you" events for people who have done outstanding work. Every month or so, the president and vice presidents, and others show up at someone's office with noisemakers and a t-shirt to thank the individual for his or her significant contributions.
- Toward the beginning of each term, I present a brief state-of-the-university speech to the campus that is followed by a wine-and-cheese reception.

These types of events lessen a sense of isolation and helplessness on campus and help create a more closely knit community. They are events we will continue to do – even when we are not facing fiscal uncertainties.

RECOMMENDATIONS FOR SUCCESS IN AN UNSTABLE WORLD

Ronald Heifetz's book *Leadership Without Easy Answers* reminds us that there is no simple recipe for success. However, the following elements have been key to our work at Southern Oregon University:

- *Remember to serve students.* Maintaining a strong sense of mission and powerful commitment to students is crucial to success. Every decision needs to reflect the fundamental values of the university.
- *Engage the campus* in seriously reviewing the mission of the campus and setting long- and short-term goals.

- *Adjust budgets in a strategic way.* As Hurley writes, "Cuts should be made . . . with a scalpel – not a machete" (2009, p. 13). Look seriously at revenue streams as well as at ways to reduce expenditures.
- *Create a sense of urgency without creating panic.* Develop multiple modes of communication. Create messages that are honest but also provide positive steps to ensure successful outcomes.
- *Develop inclusive leadership.* No one person can do it all. Involve faculty, students, and staff in decision-making processes.
- *Develop and nurture powerful partnerships.* Universities cannot work alone. We all need to connect meaningfully with K-12, other universities, businesses, state and local government, alumni and other key individuals throughout the region.
- *Create a climate welcoming of change.* Even the "new normal" is not static. To flourish in this new decade of the twenty-first century, universities must be nimble. We need to constantly assess how to continue successfully preparing students within this unpredictable new social and economic environment.
- *Help people remember the crucial nature of what we do.* Everyone on and off campus must understand why universities, *public* universities, are so vital to the economic, social, and cultural health of the region, the state – and the country as a whole. No one else can effectively carry the message for us. We ourselves, in today's "new universities," must promote and help craft a world that values higher education.

THE FUTURE FOR SOUTHERN OREGON UNIVERSITY

The components of SOU's change process, of course, have not been sequential. Almost all of them are occurring simultaneously. We have been "building the bicycle while riding it" (or, more frighteningly, "redesigning the airplane while flying it"). However, each component has been essential to our progress.

We have experienced a number of successes. Our reaccreditation process was successful. Our enrollment and retention numbers are increasing. In fall 2009, we had the largest percentage of diverse students than any previous fall in our history. Our new building in Medford is a spectacular success. For two years, the Environmental Protection Agency has included SOU on the list of the top 20 Green Colleges and Universities. Data on student learning and satisfaction are strong. Our reserves are slowly coming back.

As we have made significant and sometimes difficult changes, we have kept students' needs and interests in the forefront. We constantly check students' satisfaction levels with the Enrollment Services Center, making modifications as needed. We revise curriculum to highlight high impact learning strategies such as capstones, internships, and service learning. We emphasize interdisciplinary curricula and civic engagement, enhancing connections between students and faculty, between students and our communities. We support undergraduate research and improved advising. We stress personalized approaches in Student Affairs and in academic departments.

Knowing that we share a strong commitment to our students, faculty and staff have understood more fully the need for change during these very difficult times.

We are not out of the woods even yet – and we still do not know how the United States or the Oregon economic situation will fare in the next few years. Nonetheless, the steps we have taken during difficult times are creating a more stable situation for SOU – and providing hope and excitement amid the stress of economic crisis.

Perhaps most importantly, our processes have enabled the campus and the community to envision an exciting and exhilarating future, even though it is almost certainly a future in which traditional revenue sources are decreased and many traditional roles have changed.

As the public liberal arts university of the West, SOU is poised both to survive and to help design tomorrow's "new normal."

REFERENCES

Collins, Jim (2001), *Good to Great*, New York City: HarperBusiness.

Commission on Presidential Leadership and Global Competitiveness (2009), *Leadership in Challenging Times*, Washington, DC: American Association of State Colleges and Universities.

Cullinan, Mary (2009), "Lemonade from Lemons: Gaining strength from financial crisis." *The Presidency*, Washington, DC: American Council on Education, Spring.

Frohnmayer, David (2009) "The coming crisis in college completion: Oregon's challenge and a proposal for first steps," Portland, OR: Paper commissioned by the Oregon University System, Office of the Chancellor.

Heifetz, Ronald A. (1994), *Leadership Without Easy Answers*, Cambridge, MA: Belknap Press.

Hurley, Daniel J. (2009), *Considerations for State Colleges and Universities in a Post-Recession America*, Washington, DC: American Association of State Colleges and Universities.

"Measuring Up 2008: The National Report Card on higher education," Washington, DC: National Center for Public Policy and Higher Education.

Schneider, Carol Geary (2010), "The world is changing: The economic and civic value of contemporary liberal education outcomes." Portland, OR: Keynote speech: College Learning and Oregon's future: Return on investment for students, the economy, and our communities (Business-Education Forum).

7.   Don't mourn, reorganize!

Robert C. Holub

I became chancellor at the University of Massachusetts, Amherst in August 2008; at the time when the offer of the chancellorship was extended to me in May 2008 there were propitious signs in the economy and politics of the state. The governor was an outspoken advocate of public higher education, which bode well for the University of Massachusetts and the future. In the spring of 2008 the University had received a modest, but significant increase in operating funds, and the recently passed bills for capital expenditures in higher education and for the governor's life science initiative both promised increased state participation in funding repairs and new construction on the campus, which had been insufficiently supported by the state for many decades.

The financial wheels began to fall off the national and Massachusetts economy one month into my first year on the campus. The capital bills still contain provisions for supporting multiple construction projects; but when we will receive this funding is now uncertain and pushed into future years after the economy recovers and revenues return. More disturbing is that we have already suffered a series of large reductions to our base budget. To this point we have lost approximately $71 million of state funding, falling from the $231 million that was in our operating budget for state appropriations at the start of fiscal year 2009. The federal stimulus legislation has given us a "grace year" in fiscal year 2010, but the future looks bleak. What we will retain in our base budget by the time we get to fiscal year 2011 is anyone's guess right now, but no one is predicting that it will be higher than what we are receiving this fiscal year.

The severity and continued decline of the economy was still an unknown in October of 2008, when I began to contemplate reorganization. In the face of the severe budget downturn I developed a plan to meet what at the time was projected to be a $46 million budget deficit. A fee increase would close the gap by about half, and two reductions of $10 million in years 2010 and 2011 would bring us to an almost break-even point in fiscal year 2012. Now that the deficit has gone up to $71 million, that original plan has been revised, but it was in the context of a $10 million reduction for 2010 that I suggested an administrative restructuring of the colleges on campus that would save us a large chunk of the $10 million we needed for that year.

The thought of reorganization occurred to me because, as a long-time faculty member, I reasoned that I should look in areas of administration before turning to instruction and research. Accordingly I sought to eliminate costs in non-core areas, that is, in non-academic areas and in administrative areas in the academic realm in order to protect essential obligations of the flagship institution. It so happened that the campus was scheduled to recruit three deans in the fall of 2008: one in nursing, one in the social and behavioral sciences, and one in the school of management. I felt compelled to continue the search for the dean in management since the school had been without a permanent dean for four years. But the absence of deans in the other two colleges gave me the opportunity to cancel the searches and seek administrative savings through restructuring at the level of schools and colleges.

Restructuring of colleges to save money was not the only initiative I undertook starting in the fall of 2008. I implemented various cost-saving measures that are familiar to college campuses: freezing searches for positions, restricting travel, savings in energy, and so on. I returned most of the base budget increase we had received in the original fiscal year 2009 budget to the state and satisfied a large part of the targeted $10 million by doing so. I was also able to eliminate certain replacement positions on the campus, both faculty and staff. Eventually the campus achieved its goal of a $10 million reduction in base budget. But the most controversial and time-consuming measure was the reorganization of colleges, and it remains today an incomplete process.

The absence of sitting deans in two colleges presented me with an opportunity in two areas of the campus, but at the same time I contemplated reorganizing the sciences on the campus to achieve administrative efficiencies. Massachusetts, like most land grant institutions, was originally devoted to agriculture. In fact the campus became a university only in 1947, existing for almost seven decades as Massachusetts Agricultural College (MAC) before becoming Massachusetts State College in 1931. Agriculture, however, was much less important to the state now than it was when MAC was founded in 1863, and most departments in the College of Natural Resources and the Environment (NRE), which had evolved out of the agricultural emphasis, were engaged in science teaching and research when I arrived on campus that did not differ significantly from what was done in the College of Natural Sciences and Mathematics (NSM), a college that contained the more traditional natural sciences departments.

Moreover, some years before I came to UMass a report had urged the unification of the various life science departments, most of which were contained in NRE and NSM. Since the dean for NSM had resigned shortly before I became chancellor and his position was held by an interim dean, it seemed to be a favorable time to renew the plan to unite the life sciences and to seek the formation of a larger college that would encompass most of the scientific enterprise on the campus. My thought was to move the organizational structure of the campus from the nineteenth to the twenty-first century.

The overall plan for administrative reorganization consisted of the following elements:

- I proposed to combine several functions and eliminate several positions in the office of the chancellor and the office of the provost, producing a savings of $0.5 million. The provost's office and the chancellor's office are located in the same administrative suite in the Whitmore Administrative Building. The resignation of the provost and several of her staff, effective at the end of the 2008–09 academic year, gave me the opportunity to restructure our operations and still retain an efficient office.
- I suggested a unification of the science departments on campus in a new College of Natural Sciences (CNS). This college would contain most of the departments in NRE and NSM. At the same time I proposed a transfer of two units from NRE to other colleges: Resource Economics would go to the Isenberg School of Management (ISOM); Landscape Architecture and Planning would go to the new college I was proposing from a merger of the Humanities and Fine Arts (HFA) and the Social and Behavioral Sciences (SBS). I also favored the relocation of two units formerly in NSM, Computer Science (CS) and Polymer Science and Engineering (PSE), in our College of Engineering.
- I proposed to combine HFA and SBS into a College of Humanities, Arts, and Social Sciences (CHASS), a liberal arts college that is a familiar structure in several institutions across the country. The Department of Psychology, however, which has many individuals conducting research in neuroscience, would be relocated in the newly formed College of Natural Sciences. I proposed moving the Department of Psychology only after the department itself petitioned me to move it into the new science college. As far as I know, there are few examples of psychology departments located outside of the social sciences, although those psychology departments that have greater strength in bench sciences have reason to belong to units containing natural scientists.

- The School of Public Health and Health Sciences and the School of Nursing were to be united under one dean and one administrative structure.

The nine colleges and schools on campus would therefore be reduced by three. The end result would be two large colleges, one containing most of the science departments on the campus, the other containing all other units traditionally associated with the liberal arts; and four smaller professional schools: Engineering, Management, Public Health and Health Sciences, and Education. The College of Engineering would be strengthened by the addition of two traditionally strong departments from the former NSM; the School of Management would profit from having its own economics department. (There would also continue to be an economics department in the new College of Humanities, Arts, and Social Sciences. The economics department, when consulted, did not want to move into the School of Management or join forces with Resource Economics; it preferred to remain with the other social science departments in SBS.) The proximity of landscape architects and architecture would provide new possibilities for cooperation. And the integration of nursing into public health appeared to be a natural alliance between units concerned with more applied biomedical activities.

I estimated the reduction in costs resulting from the proposed college reorganization to be approximately $1.5 million. I figured the various mergers and consolidations would save the campus the salaries of three deans (approximately $700k) and would eliminate duplication of back office operations in the new units ($800k). The relocations of departments that I was suggesting would not cost the campus any money since they involved the movement of a unit into another college. The costs of renovation would be relatively small since departments would retain the space they currently occupied; there would be some allocation of capital funds needed for reconfiguration of college offices and advising centers, perhaps, but the amounts should have been small. If we add to the savings for college reorganization the reductions in my office and the provost's office, we would save $2 million, or about 20 percent of the amount we targeted for fiscal year 2010.

At that point we anticipated receiving stimulus funding for a period of two years. We could therefore phase in the restructuring over a two-year period to minimize lay-offs and the disruption that inevitably accompanies these sorts of changes. Many matters require attention in such a reorganization, from advising to requirements to the constitution of college committees for tenure and promotion. But the two-year period should have provided sufficient time to transition into the new structures.

There was an academic rationale for the reorganization in addition to the financial motivation. We were in the process of opening a new Integrated Sciences Building on campus, and one of our donors was funding a pilot program to investigate and promote a new type of science curriculum. Having all sciences under one administrative roof would help foster this new curriculum and perhaps also lead to further curricular innovations on the campus. Cooperation would be encouraged in research; since chairs from all science departments would meet on a regular basis, there was the opportunity for discussion of projects that crossed departmental boundaries. The same appeared to hold true for the liberal arts, where curricular creativity would be encouraged and new research projects could flourish. The health sciences, which were a special initiative in the state, could join forces and seek common strategies on how to best position themselves for funding. Nursing would profit from a partnership with Public Health, and the health sciences could become a larger and more diversified unit on campus.

In addition, the relocation of individual departments into different colleges appeared to have academic advantage for the units and the colleges involved. The College of Engineering would be strengthened by the addition of two units that are already counted with the college in standard evaluations, such as the *U.S. News and World Report*. CS and PSE could retain ties to their old colleagues in NSM, but gain new collaborations in applied areas. The School of Management would acquire an economics department with which it had had previous contact and good relations, while Resource Economics could profit from the business orientation of students and working conditions in ISOM. Landscape Architecture and Planning would be in the proximity of practitioners of architecture, design, and art. I suggested that there would be the possibility for developing a separate school or program inside of CHASS from the efforts of these faculty members, and encouraged them to be creative and look for new possibilities for cooperation.

The plan was a rational one, and I still believe it represents the best structure for the campus given its current resources and strengths. It reduces administrative costs for the campus, but it has a minimal detrimental impact on the functioning of the colleges, the departments, and the faculty. It opens up new and exciting possibilities. Student life would be disrupted to a small degree while the reorganization sorted itself out, but I predicted that the new structures would soon normalize. The downside in terms of one-time costs and the inconvenience of revising such things as college requirements seemed manageable and well worth the time and effort.

When I floated the plan, however, it did not receive universal acclaim, but was met, rather, with a series of objections that in part were baffling to me. First, I should relate that the only part of the plan that elicited no negative comments concerned the administrative savings in the provost's and chancellor's office. Although these cuts were painful and reduced somewhat our effectiveness in the central administration, faculty members were exclusively concerned with their old and new units, and how they felt they would be advantaged or disadvantaged. I shouldn't have been surprised, but I was somewhat disappointed that only a very small group of faculty members thought in terms of the whole campus and what would be best for UMass Amherst as a campus. Most faculty members were concerned only with local effects, not with campus impacts and effectiveness.

It rapidly became apparent that faculty in the humanities and social sciences were more resistant to the changes I had suggested than faculty in the sciences. Although faculty in HFA and SBS consider themselves more progressive and more attuned to social and political change, they showed themselves to be institutionally conservative. Faculty members in the natural sciences, by contrast, were open to different structures and experimentation with changes in their administrative units. They appeared to be more excited about collaboration and genuinely interested in making the most out of new connections and possibilities. Nursing and public health, however, for reasons detailed below, were just as resistant as faculty in SBS and HFA.

In order to make progress on the reorganization issues, I developed a presentation that I delivered on about two dozen occasions. I spoke with the assembled department chairs in each of the colleges that would be affected by the changes. I also presented to groups of senior and distinguished faculty drawn from each of the colleges. And, as I relate below, I held a town meeting at a faculty senate forum and made several presentations to the executive committee of the senate. The presentation explained the details of the budget crisis and its severity, and presented the proposed reorganization as a partial solution. When asked how I knew that the reorganization would save money, which was a frequent question at these gatherings, I replied that the central administration would give the new colleges less funding for administration, thereby forcing them to economize in the ways we wanted them to. I also argued that reducing administrative costs in this fashion was preferable to eliminating faculty positions, that saving $2 million meant we would retain – conservatively – 20 faculty lines. The discussion at these sessions was civil, and I appreciated the chance to hear what faculty members were thinking, but it soon became obvious that there was a great deal of skepticism about the necessity for the changes I was proposing. It was also obvious that feelings about these sorts of issues were a matter of great sensitivity for at least a portion of the faculty, and that the administration did not have the full trust of the faculty.

Many of the objections I heard at these meetings and many more that I received in scores of emails struck me as either illogical or pretexts for other, unstated objections. Since the bulk of my time was spent with CHASS, I will relate here what the most frequent comments were to that part of the reorganization.

- I was frequently accused of having already made up my mind. This objection was strange to me. Certainly I favored what I had proposed – otherwise I wouldn't have proposed it. But if I was simply intent on establishing CHASS without any regard for the faculty and without hearing what they might want, and what they might suggest as alternatives, then I wouldn't have promulgated the proposal and requested input.

- I was also told on a couple of occasions that I was merging colleges at the behest of the President's Office, which was completely inaccurate. Each campus of the University of Massachusetts was encouraged to develop its own strategy for coping with the financial crisis. At no point did the President intervene with me or with any of the other chancellors. This objection obviously stemmed from deep-seated suspicions about campus-system relations and how I understood my role as chancellor: in short, was I an agent of the president or a champion of Amherst? In my view I was simply the campus CEO trying to meet a very difficult budget.

- On a couple of occasions I even heard that my "real" motivation for the reorganization was to position myself for another chancellorship or presidency at another institution. Coming barely six months into my assumption of the chancellorship in Amherst, this objection brought home to me very forcefully the distrust that existed among at least a small circle of faculty on the campus.

- Many individuals stated that research in the social and behavioral sciences was so different from research in the humanities and fine arts that the two units were incompatible. These objections were also strange to me since several departments in the humanities at UMass Amherst could just as well have been in the social sciences. Indeed, linguistics, history, and women's studies were located in the social sciences at Berkeley, where I was a faculty member for 27 years, while at UMass Amherst they are in HFA. Moreover, since I had been involved in German and the humanities as a faculty member for well over two decades, I knew first-hand of the many connections between social sciences and humanities. Indeed, when

I spoke of my plans to new faculty members, whom I entertained at a series of breakfasts in the spring of 2009, most of them thought the merger was a good idea, and many spoke of their connections, already established, across the two colleges. They welcomed the opportunity to establish more connections through CHASS.

- Other members of SBS pointed to the fact that many researchers were supported by National Science Foundation (NSF) grants, which made them completely different from faculty in HFA. But when I checked with the office of research, I found that only a handful of faculty in SBS actually received NSF funding. There was similarly a handful of faculty in HFA supported by NSF grants.
- There was a real concern over identity and the loss of identity. SBS in particular felt that it had spent many years trying to foster a college identity, and that just as it was succeeding, it was being asked to discard the identity for a new one that was being forced on it. I argued that it was possible to retain the identity within the new college, and I believe that a skillful dean can foster and enhance this identity while establishing and promoting new connections. But my arguments fell on deaf ears for the most part.
- The most mysterious objection concerned the potential loss of research productivity. I was told on several occasions that combining the colleges in the manner I was suggesting would have a deleterious effect on research, and some members of SBS even argued that having to identify themselves as members of CHASS would have a negative impact on granting agencies. I am still trying to figure out what is really behind this objection. It may involve the fear of a loss of funding from overhead recovery. Indirect cost recoveries on the UMass campus are returned by formula to the department (10 percent), the college (10 percent), and the PI (10 percent), the rest going to the central campus. If research support were spread among more units in the new college, then it is possible to argue that departments in SBS would lose funding that they had formerly enjoyed in the new college arrangement. The only catch here was that a few departments in HFA were fairly strong in research as well. In fact, if we were to rank the top four departments in the new college (and exclude Psychology, which was going to CNS) in terms of per capita grants, then two of the top four were in HFA. I didn't bother to counter the odd notion that a granting agency would be less likely to fund a PI because they were in CHASS rather than in SBS.
- I was also told that faculty would have less access to the dean, and that a staff serving more departments might mean a longer waiting

time for service. I conceded that this outcome might occur, indeed, that it probably would occur, but did not and do not regard it as decisive. In times of budgetary shortfalls service across the campus suffers because of staff reductions. SBS and HFA would not be unusual in this regard.

Because these objections were so vociferous and came from leadership positions, either department chairs or some senior members of the departments, particularly in SBS, I decided to discuss the issues at a general faculty senate meeting. At the same time members of the faculty petitioned for a general meeting, so that we were able to co-endorse this gathering. At the meeting I delivered my usual budget presentation and gave the reasons I felt that the changes I was proposing would be advantageous to the campus. I received very little public comment from faculty in the natural sciences; there were a few objections regarding the proposal for nursing and public health; the overwhelming majority of the discussion focused on the SBS–HFA merger into CHASS. I was not surprised.

Large, general meetings on controversial matters where the administration makes a proposal and part of the faculty objects follow a predictable pattern. Most individuals who attend and speak are opposed to what the administration is presenting, and comments tend to feed off one another. By the end of the meeting it seems to the uninformed observer as if no one is in favor of the proposal, that the administration is pursuing interests antithetical to those of the faculty, and that it was folly to develop the proposal in the first place. Although I heard nothing I hadn't read in the scores of emails sent to me during the previous weeks, and although I felt many of the arguments were just as weak orally as they were in written form, I didn't think it would be wise to proceed as I had suggested in my proposal and ignore the faculty will. A group of vocal and insistent faculty members corralled me after the meeting and asked me to form a committee to study the issue. It seems that there was a growing sentiment on parts of the campus that reorganization should follow an alternative path, one that involved the formation of a college of arts and sciences. (A college of arts and sciences had existed at UMass Amherst, but had been dissolved about 15 years before I arrived.) Although I knew that a committee consisting of department chairs would not be likely to endorse anything I had proposed for SBS and HFA, and although I was convinced that an arts-and-science (A&S) structure was not propitious for the campus, I consented to have a committee meet and make recommendations to me.

Since the main purpose of those faculty members working against CHASS was to blunt the merger, and since many members of SBS were truly convinced that their work resembled the work in the natural sciences, it was not surprising that the report I received advocated for the formation of a college of arts and sciences as the first alternative, while recommending that SBS and HFA be left separate colleges as the second choice. The alternative of a liberal arts college with the merger of units from SBS and HFA was rejected. Again I was not surprised at this outcome.

But I now found myself having to give a cogent rationale for not moving forward with the formation of a college of arts and sciences. If my goal was to reduce the number of colleges on the campus (one translation of my goal by some members of the faculty), then combining HFA, SBS, and NSM into A&S would do the trick. Obviously one reason for not proceeding was that it would have made the formation of a College of Natural Sciences almost impossible. An A&S unit with all science departments and all departments in SBS and HFA would encompass three-quarters of the campus, making the new college and the campus administration almost indistinguishable. Even if we formed a college of arts and sciences without NRE, it would have encompassed approximately two-thirds of the faculty on campus. In my view such a dominating college would make campus administration harder, not easier, and it would not save the campus any money. It would be unclear, for example, what role a provost would have, and I argued from experience that there would be inherent administrative conflict between the dean of the large college and central administrative offices in such a structure. If NRE departments were excluded, it would negate the significant positive impact of uniting the life sciences and would mix instead units that really do have a very different research culture. Because there would be over forty department chairs in the new unit, the proposed structure would effectively negate the interdisciplinary potentials of discussions at chairs meetings; indeed, it is difficult to see how such a meeting could be anything but administrative in function. Finally, I doubted that this structure would be economical since the college would require divisional deans, which would function much like the current deans of the colleges that existed in 2008 when I arrived on campus. It would require a dean of the college of arts and science and an attendant staff, but that would only add another layer of administration, eliminating the savings the campus needed to achieve.

In contrast to the College of Humanities, Arts, and Social Sciences, the formation of the College of Natural Sciences (CNS) proceeded relatively smoothly. It had the support of the deans of NRE and NSM as well as the majority of the faculty in the two colleges. I received many emails endorsing the unification of the sciences, and the faculty members in the life sciences were especially enthusiastic about the change. Committees began working to deal with details almost immediately; at the time of writing in early 2010 everything has not yet been settled completely, but there is a generally constructive attitude and an anticipation of better things to come with the new college structure.

The results of the individual department relocations were mixed. Resource Economics was content being integrated into the School of Management, and that transition proceeded uneventfully as well. The Department of Landscape Architecture and Regional Planning (LARP), however, had severe objections to its proposed new location and wanted to remain with the departments in the old college (NRE). I insisted that I would not place any department into the new CNS that was not primarily a bench science. Indeed, some members of the departments of anthropology and linguistics sought to convince me that they really belonged with the natural sciences as well. While I recognize that there are individuals in all three of these units that share research methods and practices with the natural sciences, I was not persuaded that any of them should be in CNS. Eventually LARP preferred to join SBS rather than HFA (after it was determined that we would not immediately combine these two colleges), and although I believe they have just as much or even more affinity with architecture in HFA, I felt their planning faculty had made a plausible case for a connection with the social sciences.

Finally, the departments of Computer Science (CS) and Polymer Science and Engineering (PSE) were reluctant to move into the College of Engineering. Polymer Science is really akin to material sciences departments on most other campuses, and I know of no other instance where these departments are not located in the College of Engineering. Indeed, PSE even has "engineering" in its name and trained engineers on its faculty. CS argued that it belongs with the other science departments and not in engineering, and the reasoning they used had much merit. However, most of the top computer science departments in the country are in fact located in a college of engineering, and many solve their dual identity by developing programs that can be taken by students outside of engineering. The arguments offered by CS and PSE for remaining with the other departments in CNS were therefore not always convincing, and as of early 2010 we are working with these departments on the notion of dual membership in CNS and engineering, an idea that our new provost, James Staros, brought with him from one of his old institutions. Since the Psychology Department also has many faculty more suited for membership in SBS, we will pursue this option for that department as well. Although we are not yet finished with CNS and the final location of departments, we are proceeding in an orderly fashion and receiving cooperation and support from almost all quarters.

The merger of Nursing into the School of Public Health and Health Sciences (PHHS) also did not go well. Both PHHS and the School of Nursing claimed that the proposed new construct would endanger their accreditation. Nursing objected to losing its autonomy and insisted that autonomy in governance and budget was essential for their accrediting body. Public Health claimed that having non-public health units in the same administrative structure with public health would raise questions for their accrediting body, especially since they currently have three non-public-health units in the college (Communication Disorders, Kinesiology, and Nutrition). Nursing, to my amazement, for the purposes of the accrediting body, is not a unit officially recognized by schools of public health; just as astounding for me, neither are communication disorders, kinesiology, or nutrition. The claims of Nursing and Public Health were based in part on accurate information about accreditation. I left discussions with these two units with some rather negative feelings about accrediting bodies and how they attempt to extort campuses into doing things that are not fiscally sound or advantageous for the general welfare of faculty and students. I also believe their definitions of their fields are restrictive and do not take into account interdisciplinary imperatives in modern health sciences. However, for the time being, rather than merge the two units immediately, we decided to combine back-office functions, which is made easier by the fact that nursing has very few faculty, and to continue to explore reorganization possibilities with the accrediting agencies.

After several months of intense debate and consultation, I arrived at a plan of action for fiscal year 2010. My compromise was promulgated in a memorandum that can be found at http://www.umass.edu/chancellor/budget_reorg_031209.html. I decided to move forward with the formation of the College of Natural Sciences, but to call for further study of many of the other issues. HFA and SBS are supposed to be looking at the possibilities of merger with an eye toward a merger within a year. I appointed an interim dean of SBS, who was a former associate dean, but did not give permission to hire a replacement of him as associate dean. I bequeathed this issue to the new provost, and as of early 2010 he is pursuing it with some hope of success. Nursing retained its interim dean, and its back-office functions were combined with the back office of the School of Public Health and Health Sciences. The provost may pursue with accrediting bodies the possibility of bringing the units closer together. The total savings were thus far a bit less than I had anticipated, but still amounted to around $1.5 million. I believe we will achieve additional savings as the process continues and will eventually reach the goal of $2 million for the administrative reorganization.

Perhaps the most disappointing part of this process was not the faculty objections, which I sometimes felt were not very compelling, but the actions of a very few faculty members who sought to pressure me through alumni and donors. In doing so, however, they only end up hurting their units. Donors and alumni, in my experience, do not want to invest time and money in operations that are surrounded by conflict. Having individuals who do not understand the issues very well intervene in academic processes does not raise the level of discourse, and it usually detracts from the units soliciting outside intervention as much as it does from the central campus administration. Donations, after all, more frequently go to support programs in the units themselves. By presenting a negative situation to donors and potential donors, faculty members end up shooting themselves in the foot.

The other great disappointment and discovery in this process was that there exists a deep-seated and long-standing distrust on the part of some faculties toward the central administration. I have been trying to understand this distrust and to address it with both talk and action. If the campus is going to move forward, especially in these difficult financial times, it must realize a unity of purpose it has not formerly enjoyed.

From the intense activity around this reorganization, I believe I learned several other things about academic administration and reorganization. Some are more general; others relate specifically to reorganization, and some are perhaps only valid for my campus. For what it's worth, I pass them on here:

- Rational arguments are not always successful arguments, even when you are dealing with people who are supposed to be rational. Personal contact is just as important in making your case for change, and it's more appreciated than less immediate forms of communication.
- For faculty buy-in reorganization must involve more than administrative efficiencies and more than financial savings. It must also offer research, curricular, or outreach possibilities for the faculty and students of the units involved.
- While faculty will support change in the abstract, many will not support it when it involves change for them. Make sure you try to put yourself in their position and see what the change looks like to them. Don't put your trust in abstract statements about change; rather, examine real connections and their effects.
- Saving money is something the administration has to do in times of financial crisis, but faculty members are often unconcerned about savings, especially if these savings affect something they hold dear. By and large faculty want money saved in areas in which they believe they are not involved (physical plant, athletics, the offices of the upper administration, and so on).
- Institutional history has an enormous hold on faculty and their judgment. As a new chancellor unfamiliar with the nuances of the

campus, I was unprepared for the objections I faced, many of which had more to do with past treatment and grievances than actual propositions and future directions.

- The more lead time you allow for changes, the better are the chances that changes can be implemented. Some units and individuals will have a knee-jerk negative reaction against administrative proposals that can be overcome with persuasion, resources, and time. Don't try to convince everyone, however, since that task is impossible.

- Work as much as possible with leaders of the faculty who share your vision for the campus and the future. Share your vision often and obtain buy-in for it. Remember that it is better to get something done and work on other things as long-range projects, than it is to accomplish nothing. Getting part of the way to your goal is preferable to the status quo.

- Make sure the financial incentives are clear and that the budget process and budget documents are transparent for everyone.

- Especially if you are new, as I was, engage the faculty as much as possible and parry objections with real actions. If faculty in the social sciences and humanities feel that they will be disadvantaged in research, for example, set up a special research fund and competition for non-scientists.

- Try to create excitement around reorganization by implementing reforms in other areas. On my campus I let faculty know that we would provide better support for their research and develop fundraising around faculty positions and initiatives. I also developed a Request for Proposal to compete for the few new faculty positions we could afford and located these positions in the sort of cross-disciplinary collaborations fostered by the reorganization.

The elimination of administrative costs through reorganization is a worthwhile, albeit difficult task. It is most effective when faculty members are actively engaged in the process, and when academic rationales dovetail with financial savings. It can save faculty positions and base budget without impairing the core functions of the campus. Unless administrators are willing to ignore and possibly alienate their faculty, it will probably entail a great investment of time and energy. But in periods of extreme fiscal duress, such as we have encountered this past year, we must be willing to do whatever we can to preserve the character and integrity of our institutions of higher education.

8.   Opportunities and obstacles: the imperative of global citizenship

J. Michael Adams

Large systems are inherently stable. They resist change. They do not readily incorporate new ideas, particularly those that threaten current operations, which may seem to be working well. Interestingly, opposition often increases in environments of obvious threat, chaos and attack.

In a study of American colleges, noted historian Frederick Rudolph concluded that "resistance to fundamental reform was ingrained in the American collegiate and university tradition." (Kerr 2001, p. 72) This is not unique to American colleges, though. Clark Kerr, the renowned higher education leader, once wrote,

> *Universities are among the most conservative of all institutions in their methods of governance and conduct and are likely to remain so. (Kerr 2001, p. 220)*

But wait a minute. Aren't universities beacons of change, full of radicals and revolutionaries eager to throw out the old and beckon the new? That's a popular perception. I went to college in the 1960s when the media convinced America that a revolution was brewing on college campuses around the country. And that reputation continues among the general public.

Assuredly, with all the intellectual activity running rampant on campuses, there's always someone somewhere looking to turn things upside down. But the broad picture today actually reveals a group of educators and administrators wedded to the familiar and a group of students searching for their place in the status quo.

The world spins rapidly, driven by one change after another, and yet universities remain grounded in tradition and routine, with structures similar to centuries gone by. In fact, Kerr suggested it was possible to identify 85 institutions in the Western world established around 1520 that still exist today with similar form and roles. These include the Catholic Church, the Parliaments of the Isle of Man, Iceland and Great Britain and several Swiss cantons. Also, he reports that 70 out of the list of 85 are universities! (Kerr 2001, p. 115) These institutions are not agents of change.

Traditions are wonderful to cherish and enduring for centuries is not a bad thing, provided that one can adapt and innovate in line with the times. Have universities been successful in this regard? At best, the record is mixed, but why?

Why is resistance to change so prevalent in higher education? How does this resistance relate to the need for and growing recognition that we must internationalize our campuses? Even in the midst of resistance, what are some measures educators can take to acknowledge external changes produced by globalization and help prepare world citizens?

THE SABER-TOOTH CURRICULUM

After my first year as president at Fairleigh Dickinson University, I discovered a fundamental academic axiom:

> *There are always at least three perfectly valid reasons why we cannot do something – even when everyone agrees such action is desirable.*

Indeed, most individuals instantly react to new ideas with a long list of reasons why things should stay just as they are. We know the tenacity with which academic turfs are guarded. We understand the determination to defend resources when funds are scarce, and we understand the critical suspicion of the new kid on the block.

There are sometimes compelling reasons for maintaining the status quo. But often, the skeptic is simply lacking the imagination to envision something better or is fearfully clinging to the comfortable. Fear and uncertainty are powerful deterrents. Despite all the well-rationalized motivators for maintaining the status quo, fear of an unknown future is the primary reason why adaptation and innovation often remain sidelined. However, if the purpose of higher education is to prepare tomorrow's leaders, then the past must sometimes be left behind.

I think all educators should be required to read *The Saber-Tooth Curriculum* by J. Abner Peddiwell (a.k.a Harold Benjamin). Published in 1939, this wonderfully satirical look at education is even more painfully accurate and relevant today.

In the plot, Peddiwell reveals groundbreaking "research" on the educational system of the Paleolithic era. His amazing discovery is that the original purpose of schools was to provide basic life skills:

- saber-toothed tiger scaring,
- fish-grabbing and
- clubbing woolly horses.

But then the ice age passed and the saber-toothed tigers fell to pneumonia, streams became too murky to catch fish because of the silt from the receding glaciers and the small horses went east to the dry plains. Despite these revolutionary developments, schools persisted in teaching the same life skills.

Those who suggested that there was no correlation between real life and fish grabbing were labeled heretics! (Benjamin 1939).

The lesson is clear. We must become more flexible. We must adapt to the changes around us and prepare students for a new world. This means that we must have the courage to face our fears, to rethink traditional lessons and methods and to update the saber-tooth curriculum.

REACTING TO NEW REALITIES

But the question is how do we respond to inherent institutional inertia? How do we initiate and accelerate the process of change when resistance is so strong? History, in fact, tells us that change most often comes not from within organizations, but from external forces. Pressure from the outside forces the issue, increases the recognition of the need for change and eventually triggers a response.

In a previous life I was active in the print-and-publishing industry. As an author and consultant, I used to speak about this very point with my colleagues in distribution. I would ask them to identify the greatest innovation or change that had influenced their business. The responses were typically technology-centered: "print-on-demand," "direct-to-plate," or "green inks and paper products."

I disagreed, saying that Federal Express had more influence on their business than anything going on within the field. "FedEx allows me to call an 800 number, 24-7, and find out where my package is anywhere in the world," I told them. "Yet I can call my print supplier only between 9 a.m. and 5 p.m., only during the traditional workweek, only to be put on hold while someone goes to a paper file to try to find my order."

And so book publishers and everyone else were forced to offer a similar service. And wherever there is a void of expectation, new players who can respond enter the arena – players like FedEx and Amazon.com.

The same thing happens in the midst of an emergency or crisis situation. We're awakened with a sense of urgency when something significantly bad jolts us out of our daily regimen. And then we'll consider a new way. We sometimes need armies of change pounding at our walls before we rethink the old methods.

It shouldn't be this way. We should not be dependent upon outside forces or dire crises to devise new and better operations. In higher education, the stakes are too high for this reactive form of thinking. We must be more agile than that.

I believe the key is empowering faculty. The key is to motivate faculty to take the lead. Presidents and higher education administrators cannot dictate change. But they can authorize, direct and empower others to enact change.

I was once accused of allowing a colleague to build an academic empire. Apparently, empire building in academia is a mortal sin, and I was equally guilty, as dean of the school, for allowing it to happen. My response was that not only did I allow it to happen, but I encouraged it.

Paul Hirshorn (head of the Department of Architecture at Drexel University) led the most selective program of its kind in the United States, which enjoyed, as I recall, a 23 percent acceptance rate, a 97 percent retention rate and a 100 percent employment rate for his graduates. Paul worked six days a week, knew the name of every student, funded laboratories through gifts and, whenever there was a faculty opening, received more than 200 applications. Why wouldn't I want Paul and others to build academic empires?

As long as they fit within the overall mission and direction of an institution, I suggest that academic empires are characteristic of the strongest universities. It's the local empires and faculty entrepreneurial thinkers who can best adapt to the particular needs of their constituents and their times while remaining true to the institutional goals. It's the innovators and empire builders who build institutional reputation, ensuring their students' success and their institution's survival. Indeed, that is the only way meaningful innovation has occurred in the academy.

The challenge of change – and the challenge of leadership in higher education – is to identify those individuals who can build empires. We must give dynamic faculty the tools, the authority and the autonomy to create lasting and powerful changes.

NO ETERNAL MODEL

There is a tendency for us to assume that because a structure has been in place for many decades, that it was always that way. The model and organization of higher education in America today is pretty much the same as it was when I was an undergraduate. If it has been in place for so long, then certainly it must be the right model?

I recently began reading a book on the influenza pandemic of 1918–19, with the hope of perhaps better understanding the H1N1 virus threat. *The Great Influenza: The Epic Story of the Deadliest Plague in History*, by John Barry, begins Chapter 1 with a surprising approach:

> *ON SEPTEMBER 12, 1876, the crowd overflowing the auditorium of Baltimore's Academy of Music was in a mood of hopeful excitement, but excitement without frivolity. Indeed, despite an unusual number of women in attendance, many of them from the uppermost reaches of local society, a reporter noted, "There is no display of dress or fashion." For this occasion had serious purpose. It was to mark the launching of The Johns Hopkins University, an institution whose leaders intended not simply to found a new university but to change all of American education . . . (Barry 2004)*

And the entire chapter proceeds without mention of influenza, epidemics or plagues. I wondered if I purchased a rare misprint, where chapters had been incorrectly collated? But no, it was exactly correct and appropriate. The formation of "The Hopkins" was a landmark decision that ultimately prepared a new generation of scientists to analyze and begin to understand the terrible influenza epidemic in 1918.

How so? The founders of Johns Hopkins took higher education in a new direction and rejected the traditional education model of Harvard. That model, used not only by Harvard, but by all American institutions at the time, involved enrolling undergraduate students in classes that were largely what faculty wanted to teach at the moment. There were no such things as academic majors. And at the end of the four years, if the faculty agreed, students were given degrees.

Then, on September 12, 1876, The Johns Hopkins University adopted the German model of higher education in which faculty would do research, publish their findings and focus on real-life issues. In fact, they would work to solve problems that existed in society.

Now, the reason the book started with this point is that medical education in America was particularly horrid at the time. You could go to a medical school that had no requirement for a science background – and many medical schools didn't even have an anatomy course. So the formation of Johns Hopkins and the adoption of the German model set the foundation to prepare the students who in 1918 were able to research, understand and diagnose the circumstances and indicators of the influenza epidemic.

By 1920, this new model resulted in acceptance of the germ theory, creation of the new field of public health and transformation of medical education in this country. It also became the standard for all fields and areas of American higher education.

What dawned on me was that the current academic model in our colleges and universities really only became the norm around 1920. The model many faculty and administrators may assume is eternal is a relatively recent creation.

Innovators change and external circumstances can change assumptions, approaches and models. What we have today is not eternal or an unchanging given. In fact, the case can be made that the current model is dysfunctional, unsustainable and destined to change. We prefer that the model morph into a new form, rather than collapse because armies of change are at the walls.

GLOBAL FORCES AT THE GATES

When one speaks of trends that demand a response in higher education, no army is approaching our walls faster and in greater strength than the forces of globalization. But colleges have been very slow to respond to globalization. For example, a study by the American Council on Education found that less than 40 percent of US institutions make reference to international or global education in their mission statements, and that the percentage of colleges that require a course with an international focus has dropped during the past decade. (ACE Press Release 2008)

Many prominent educators believe that schools should first and foremost develop loyal citizens with a strong sense of national identity. In fact, the contemporary elementary and secondary educational system was founded to develop children into faithful citizens of the emerging industrial nation-states. It remains important to celebrate national customs and stories. But in an increasingly interconnected world where opportunities and dangers flow across borders, education must cultivate greater awareness of other countries and help students make connections with other cultures.

In the global economy, professional careers depend upon networks of production and communication that synchronize individuals and teams from across the globe. In a world where diseases, environmental crises and violence migrate across borders at will, the need for collaboration becomes fundamental for our collective destiny.

It's quite telling that most in the business community recognize the importance of thinking and acting globally. They understand the need to adapt to the global playing field. They know that events around the world influence their business. They cross the globe in search of profits and develop relationships and bonds everywhere. It is up to us in education to follow this path.

The challenge is great but there is no other choice. We must expand our programs and expand our students' horizons. We must prepare our students for careers and challenges in a global age. Education must be global, or we risk being irrelevant.

WHAT IS A WORLD CITIZEN?

What should we do to better prepare students for tomorrow? Simply put, we must help them to understand they are part of a complex, intimately connected global community. We must prepare them to be world citizens; world citizens who understand global issues, who are comfortable in diverse environments and who can embrace different identities and work together with those near and far to solve global challenges.

"Hold on there," some object at this point. "What is this notion of world citizenship?"

I was struck recently by the news that professors at the Thunderbird School of Global Management had developed the world's first psychometric assessment tool to measure a global mindset. And they indicate that the nucleus of this global mindset includes intellectual capital, psychological capital and social capital. And each category features a list of information or attributes that define the degree of your global mindset. (Swain 2007)

As an academic I'm drawn to this precise evaluation, however, I also recognize that if we reduce our goal for world citizenship to a formula equation, we will never inspire our students.

So I define world citizenship a little bit less formally. I frequently cite the Ghanaian philosopher Kwame Anthony Appiah, who suggests that the two main strands in world citizenship, or cosmopolitanism as he calls it, are

1. *universal concern and obligations to others and*
2. *respect for legitimate differences. (Appiah 2006, p. XV)*

At the fundamental level, a world citizen recognizes all humans have common rights and interests, has the ability to look at the world through the eyes of others and is able to act on behalf of humanity everywhere.

Ultimately, though, how we define this isn't critical. There isn't going to be a set list of qualities or skills that we can all identify. But we can agree on the goal, and we can agree on the commitment. We know there is a compelling need to work outside borders and relate to others around the world, and so we all must prepare our students to do so.

There is no specific test or list of credentials to qualify oneself as a world citizen. But, by virtue of living in an increasingly interconnected world, with a global economy and with global challenges, it is up to educated citizens to extend their reach and embrace their responsibilities as members of a global community. It is up to universities to make sure their graduates understand they are world citizens.

Three years ago, I co-designed and co-taught, with my friend and colleague Angelo Carfagna, a course titled Globalization and World Citizenship. Throughout the semester, we acknowledged there is no passport or license or official checklist for world citizenship qualification. It is an issue of self-awareness and priority. At the end of the semester, we issued each student in the class a certificate of world citizenship. It was a symbolic gesture. Like in *The Wizard of Oz*, when the cowardly lion asked for courage and was issued a medal. Suddenly he saw himself differently.

The next generation of American leaders must see themselves and their world differently. That is the educational imperative for the twenty-first century.

THE FDU MODEL

There are many ways to provide a global education. We've done some exciting things at Fairleigh Dickinson University (FDU), particularly since the development of a new mission in 2000: to prepare world citizens through global education. And we've brought the mission to life in many ways.

But as I mentioned before, the key to make these necessary adaptations is to empower faculty. Our faculty have spearheaded our changes and led the formation of a number of breathtaking initiatives.

Some of our changes have been extraordinary, particularly our use of technology to foster greater connections with other cultures. In 2001, we became the first traditional university to require that all undergraduates take one online course per year. We not only believe the Internet is a fundamental learning tool that all students need to understand, but we also believe that the Internet can bring the world to campus in a form and substance not available until this century. The first course for freshmen, The Global Challenge, explores critical global issues and has been nationally cited for excellence.

At the heart of this mission-driven program is an important innovation: Global Virtual Faculty™ (GVF). The GVF are a group of first-rate scholars and professionals from around the world who contribute global perspectives via the Internet. Through e-mail discussions and guided by the campus faculty, they present important insights and put a human face on the global topics being studied. The Internet not only provides information from afar but it can facilitate collaborations across cultures.

Among the more than 60 GVF are the senior political columnist for the *Times of India*, a Hungarian environmentalist, a former head homicide detective from Scotland Yard, an Arabic literature professor from Egypt, a political scientist from Chile and an economist from Malaysia.

The GVF program has gained special recognition from the American Council on Education and AT&T for its use of technology as a tool to internationalize the curriculum. And, in 2009, FDU received the Senator Paul Simon Spotlight Award from NAFSA: Association of International Educators for our use of technology to foster global lessons.

With a strong digital infrastructure in place, we were able to build many online offerings, including programs for specific populations like the National Guard (made possible through significant funding by the United States Defense Department). And we're the only university in New Jersey that has both Internet access and an overhead data projector in every classroom. Education cannot be kept within walls, and new technologies enable us to cross barriers and transform lives.

Strong partnerships also enable us to extend our influence. FDU has developed affiliations with universities around the world. These agreements facilitate student-and-faculty exchanges, joint research projects and other cooperative educational ventures. In the last decade alone, agreements have been forged with institutions in more than 20 countries. In many cases, students can begin studying at their home institutions and then journey to FDU to complete the degree requirements. In these dual degree programs, graduates receive two degrees: one from their home school and one from FDU.

While we have a global focus, we don't lose sight of what's local. I remembered Gordon Bethune (former CEO of Continental Airlines), talking about the resurrection of Continental Airlines. He said, "One of the early decisions we made was quite revolutionary for the airline industry." He asked, "Why don't we fly to where the customers want to go?"

Following the same logic, I asked, "Where are there populations of students who cannot come to our campuses for degree work?" We established partnerships with eight community colleges and now deliver the last two years of a baccalaureate degree directly on the community college campuses.

You have to take advantage of your surroundings and provide students access to the unique resources within your reach. We are located near the United Nations and have long enjoyed a close partnership with the world body. Our UN Pathways Forum and Video Conference Series regularly brings ambassadors to campus for lectures and dinners. In 2008, we had the honor of welcoming UN Secretary-General Ban Ki-moon. Overall, more than 70 ambassadors, diplomats and heads of state have met and spoken with our students. In our videoconferences, several times each semester we broadcast panel discussions from the UN media room to our campuses and to other universities.

In addition, FDU students and faculty enjoy special access to UN facilities and briefings because we are one of the few universities in the world to have earned nongovernmental organization (NGO) status with the UN Department of Public Information, based upon our mission and commitment to global education. And, in 2009, we became the first comprehensive university to earn special consultative status as an NGO with the UN Economic and Social Council (ECOSOC). New opportunities for students include access to internships with ECOSOC agencies and participation in global conferences, while faculty and staff may be designated to serve as consultants or participants in ECOSOC forums and committees.

At FDU, we have introduced many other global initiatives – we expanded our study-abroad programs; we created Global Scholars programs that bring global-minded students together for exciting academic and social experiences; we welcomed more international students; and we opened a new campus in Vancouver, British Columbia, Canada.

These are just some examples. There is no single path to a global education. Our community has responded in various ways, but the key is that everyone knows and values the mission. There is a shared sense of purpose. And the other pivotal factor is that all of these programs were conceived, nurtured and shaped by faculty and administrators interested in making a difference and empowered to act.

I'm often asked what advice do I have for colleges looking to build global programs. My answer is that it must begin with a change of mindset. *It's not what you do, but it's how you view what you are doing.*

I frequently ask my colleagues, "Do you view yourself as preparing global citizens? Do you believe it's critical for students to understand their interconnected world and connect with other countries and cultures?" If the answers are yes, then actions and innovations will follow the mindset.

As the French writer Victor Hugo so memorably stated,

> *Nothing else in the world . . . not all the armies . . . is so powerful as an idea whose time has come.*

The time has come for all institutions to educate world citizens.

BUILDING BRIDGES

In this effort to globalize our campuses, we might be tempted to look for help from our national governments, which have sometimes played influential roles in the development of higher education. But national governments have been slow to recognize the importance of international education. Perhaps understandably, they will not jump at the chance to prepare students to think beyond national borders. They will not be our best allies to prepare world citizens.

We do not have to rely on national governments, however. Just as globalization has given individuals and citizens' groups the capability to act outside borders, it enables us in education – and it compels us – to work across departments, disciplines and national divides. The solution is not within the government, it's within the leaders in our universities and colleges, and it's within all of our efforts to connect to each other. It's our call to arms.

In many realms, we have seen the rise of nongovernmental organizations and the development of a global civil society. We have seen environmental groups form beyond borders, human-rights advocates unite across cultures and labor activists reach from country to country. We have seen the power of citizens' groups using technology and the tools of the information age to address the problems of globalization.

In education, these cross-border alliances do already exist. For example, since 1964, the International Association of University Presidents has brought leaders from different countries together to share ideas and combine forces. But we need to further strengthen our power and influence and form more connections that help us help our students.

We need an international militia of well-armed educators ready to prepare students for a globalized world. The power of the individual in today's age is greater than ever before.

Unfortunately, our world continues to be filled with barriers between countries and cultures. But I prefer bridges over barricades. So I challenge each of us to simply build a bridge. Reach out, make a connection, start a conversation and begin a collaboration with someone outside of the United States or someone outside your native land. And then use that connection to further your research or to provide an international lesson for your students. It is precisely the power of these connections – forged one at a time – that can help us change the future.

The sum of our efforts can indeed change the world. We do not need unified methods, but we do need a unified commitment; a shared purpose to build these bridges and prepare students who are capable of acting on the world stage.

UPDATING THE ARSENAL

The world is changing and all of higher education must adapt. In this chapter, I have focused on meeting the demands posed by globalization and the increasing permeability of national borders, but there are other important trends that require us to respond innovatively. These include:

- Rapid demographic changes, increasing diversity and the continuing rise of nontraditional students with nontraditional needs;
- Growing competition from for-profit education entities and international universities;
- Changing corporate expectations and the emergence of corporate universities; and
- Explosive growth of educational technology and online programs.

Some experts think that because of such trends the traditional campus is on the path to extinction. I don't share such a gloomy outlook. But I do believe that those institutions that do not adapt to the new realities and address the emerging competition will see their relevance disappear.

We need to inspire and channel the wonderful creativity of our faculty and staff. We need to provide strong leadership through example. We need to offer clear direction and a roadmap for individuals to respond with agility to new trends while still maintaining their core commitments.

It's trite but true: the only constant is change. But acknowledging this doesn't make adaptation any easier, especially for institutions as infused with tradition – and some would add inertia – as universities.

H.G. Wells once declared,

> *The universities go out to meet the tremendous challenges of our social and political life like men who go out in armour with bows and arrows to meet a bombing aeorplane. (World Brain, 1938)*

It's time to put away the bows and arrows. It's not enough for academic institutions to survive, they must demonstrate relevancy, adaptability and value. All of higher education must update the academic arsenal and meet contemporary challenges with contemporary lessons.

If we do not, we will have failed the next generation. And they will inherit a world they do not understand.

REFERENCES

American Council on Education (ACE) Press Release. "Colleges and universities make uneven progress in internationalizing their campuses." May 22, 2008.

Appiah, Kwame Anthony (2006), *Cosmopolitanism: Ethics in a World of Strangers*, New York: W.W. Norton & Company.

Barry, John M. (2004), *The Great Influenza: The Epic Story of the Deadliest Plague in History*, New York: The Penguin Group.

Benjamin, Harold (1939), *The Saber-Tooth Curriculum*, New York: McGraw-Hill Book Company.

Kerr, Clark (2001), *The Uses of the University*, fifth edition, Cambridge, MA: Harvard University Press.

Swain, Glenn (2007), "Is a global mindset in your DNA?" *Thunderbird Magazine* (fall).

Wells, H.G. (1938), *World Brain: The Idea of a Permanent World Encyclopaedia*, London: Methuen.

9. Leading in a changing environment
Kent John Chabotar

FORESEEING THE FUTURE

Predicting the future for higher education is an enterprise loaded with danger and risk. In 2006, if someone had told you what we would face in 2009, you would have had that person put in a straightjacket immediately. But despite the uncertainty, I will venture some observations although they hardly qualify as forecasts. First, tuition and fees will continue to be the number one source of revenue for private colleges and universities (no surprise there). Tuition may in fact go up as a percent of total revenue, not because colleges and universities continue the six to ten percent increases of the past, but because other sources of revenue grow more slowly, as will budgets. Current downward pressure on higher education budgets are unprecedented. When the budget is basically staying the same, even small increases in tuition will start to increase the percentage being drawn from tuition and fees.

Second, we will see increased tuition discounting, particularly funded (as opposed to unfunded) discounting. When I arrived at Bowdoin College as chief financial officer in 1991, endowments funded 75 cents of every dollar granted in financial aid. Eleven years later, only 50 percent of Bowdoin's discounting was covered by endowment funds, with the rest unfunded except by the operating budget. At Guilford College, the unfunded figure is 88 percent. As noted by Jane Wellman (Chapter 12), there are highly selective medallion schools that discount to promote accessibility and non-medallion schools that discount to ensure a student body large enough to pay the bills. Discounting pressure is going to affect most of us in very different ways.

Third, as the Baby Boomer generation "matures," colleges and universities will see more funding from bequests, from planned giving, and from life income trusts. Higher education is also expecting more of those gifts to be directed to areas of greatest need. When raising money for Guilford, more of the donors with whom I meet are asking, "What are the priorities? What are the needs of the College?" I am also hearing more interest in funding student financial aid, which is very helpful because such gifts, even though restricted, provide direct budget relief. I will almost never turn down a restricted gift if it is for financial aid, faculty salaries or books. What I would turn down is a restricted gift for an engineering program or for a law school at Guilford. We are an undergraduate liberal arts college and intend to stay that way.

Fourth, the current recession is very different from those that preceded it in the 1980s, 1990s, and early 2000s, in that the rebound from those earlier recessions was relatively fast and steep, while the recovery from the current downturn appears likely to be slow and sluggish. This means that the forces that bailed-out higher education in the past – full pay students (or, more likely in non-medallion schools, mostly able to pay students), growth of endowments, increased federal support, increased state support for residents who attend a private school – are unlikely to increase to a degree that will really offset losses elsewhere.

Fifth, with regard to the impact of rising unemployment, the official rate was recently announced at 10.2 percent, higher than at any time since the early 1980s. The unofficial rate is probably closer to 17 percent. During a recent presentation at Guilford, economist and Nobel Laureate Paul Krugman made the point that in prior recoveries, if the economy grew at the rate of 3.5 percent, the unemployment rate, at best, dropped by half of one percent annually. This implies that if a five percent unemployment rate is considered full employment, then it could take ten years to get back to full employment. The point made earlier about unemployment making it harder for people to give and harder for people to afford college is a point well taken then.

REVENUE SOURCES

It is very tempting in private higher education – and public as well – to write off the small gifts since the cost per dollar raised from small gifts does not make pursuing such gifts worthwhile. Going forward, however, focusing on smaller donors may pay off if larger donors are not likely to be as supportive as in previous years. Annual giving programs are getting more attention and support because they can be the difference between balanced and unbalanced budgets. Colleges and universities should also not expect big boosts in endowment spending from either rising endowment market values or increased spending rates. I do not think there is a magic bullet in privatization of some of our functions through outsourcing, nor do I anticipate wholesale mergers or consolidations to be a significant source of revenue.

With regard to tuition, the price elasticity of demand will depend on the institution. The number one reason why students choose a particular college – at least most surveys show – is academic reputation. The second reason is – and maybe this is parents talking more than students – whether this college will help me get a job or gain entrance to a top graduate or professional school. Those schools that can make the case that tuition is an investment in gaining that academic reputation, an investment in getting a job or going to graduate school, will probably face more inelastic demand and will be able to raise tuition without driving away lots of students.

Outcome measures are currently being pushed very hard. Student outcomes measurement is no longer just rhetoric used at convocations and commencements. Accrediting bodies such as North Central, Southern Association of Colleges and Schools (SACS), New England, and Middle states are demanding evidence that claims about student outcomes are based in evidence, as are the federal government and media. Those institutions that can make the case will have an easier time.

That being said, 2009 saw very small increases at the national level in tuition and fees in both the private and public sectors, lower than in previous years. Average prices before financial aid increased by 4.4 percent at four-year privates, 6.5 percent at four-year publics, and 7.7 percent at two-year publics although the latter is still less than $3,000. I believe that trend will continue, not so much because of the pressure from parents and students – although there is some of that – but because the major budget driver of all higher education institutions, the amount of available revenue, is stagnant or dropping and thus costs are going to have to flatten out. The big pressure, as mentioned before, will be on financial aid and the need to secure endowment support for as much of that aid as possible.

There is also a growing willingness among families in private higher education to send their children to community colleges for their first two years. Many of these institutions are excellent and relatively inexpensive. At Guilford Technical Community College in our own area, 30 percent of the students are not going for technical training in Heating, Ventilating and Air Conditioning (HVAC) or flight instruction. Rather, they are going for academic purposes, deciding to complete their first two years in community college and the last two years at a four-year college or university. Such a strategy saves a bundle of money. Average prices at two-year colleges, based on 2009–10 data, are about one-third of what four-year publics charge and one-tenth of the price at a four-year private college or university, although the differences narrow when financial aid is considered.

As a consequence, four-year institutions have to be much more intentional at the junior year level of intake. Furthermore, colleges and universities cannot just have the junior level be, "Oh welcome. Go find your classes." It will have to be an orientation and an introduction to the school similar to that provided for first-year students. Institutions must also have honest articulation agreements that let students and families know how many credits will transfer to the four-year institution and how much more time will be needed to earn the degree.

One more comment on tuition, there will be more unbundling of tuition on at least two levels. One is a base tuition for instruction. The second will be additional charges for additional services, fees if you will, much as have been charged for years in public colleges and universities. In this way, a single charge is unbundled, giving the student opportunities to pick and choose among services like information technology, student activities, preferred parking, and personalized career counseling and job placement.

Secondly, higher education will see more use of differential price structures. We will see it by undergraduate major or degree with nuclear physics, for example, probably priced higher than history. This difference can be direct with varying "sticker" prices or indirect with higher or lower levels of financial aid availability. That already occurs in many graduate schools, with accompanying concerns about affordability playing too large a role in what students choose to study.

We will also see it by age. Approximately half of the undergraduate students in the United States are over 25 years of age and adult education is increasingly important as a source of untapped revenue, particularly in down economic times. When the economy is bad, adults go to college to gain new skills or a credential because they are anxious or have time due to unemployment. When the economy is good, employers often encourage and even pay for continued education for their employees. Many colleges do not charge the same price to adults as they charge to traditional students because adults get fewer services.

Consequently, the realization that one tuition price does not fit all students will open another area of price elasticity, at least on average for most institutions that are willing to consider it.

BUDGET CUTTING

In private higher education, the largest growth in the last 20 years has been in administration. This is not because colleges and universities are trying to feather their nests with oligarchies, but because a faculty member is like an aircraft carrier and increasingly needs picket ships and supply ships in terms of instructional support, computing centers, and counseling services. Consequently, budget pressure is on the administrative side. Therefore, when cutting back, the same advice given in the 1990s still applies – start with administration. Not with a broad sword, but selectively. Where institutions failed in the 1990s was not following through with planned cuts, restoring many positions as soon as the economy and revenues improved.

In fact, when I arrived at Bowdoin, Bob Edwards, who was the president, said, "Balance the budget in two years, but don't cut any faculty, don't touch the academic program. That is our core business. Do it on the administrative side." We trimmed 70 administrative and support staff positions, mostly from attrition and two early retirement programs. We were less successful in staying trim; eventually 120 positions were added back even though the student body grew by only 10 percent. The headwinds that the budget director and I encountered were fierce when we attempted to deny a new or replacement position, including claims that we were hurting morale, competitiveness and academic quality. The same scene has replayed at hundreds of colleges and universities then and now. It reminds me of the ruinously expensive arms race among European powers that led to World War I.

It appears that most of higher education, both public and private, is now reducing administration. In North Carolina there has been a huge uproar in the state legislature over the growth in the University of North Carolina (UNC) system of administration relative to academics. That system has been cutting administrative positions very aggressively.

One can also perceive, however, a willingness to consider cuts on the academic side, forcing changes in productivity. These changes are not necessarily just increased teaching loads, but larger class sizes, reductions in the number of courses offered and less released time for service duties. Colleges and universities are also using differential criteria for faculty, so that one teaching load is not applied to all, recognizing that some faculty are more active in research than others. Many institutions are engaged in formal or informal program prioritization that uses student demand, centrality to mission, cost, and other standards to influence where faculty positions and budgets are allocated. We are witnessing more consideration of these policies than has been true before, and that to me is the hope for more long-term cost containment than just reducing administrative jobs.

FOR-PROFIT SECTOR

Among the practices to be learned from the for-profit sector is to focus on a more demand driven curriculum – not to say institutions are giving up their core values, the focus on the liberal arts – but to not limit offerings to just the traditional areas of humanities and social and physical sciences, but also business, criminal justice and sports management, to name a few. Guilford College added forensic biology a few years back, and it has become so popular with students and government agencies that I joke we have become "CSI Greensboro." At Bowdoin, faculty held a narrower definition of liberal arts. Many opposed almost any program or course that might be labeled "pre-professional," including one that I taught in the government department with just enough finance and accounting that undergraduates aspiring to be investment bankers and corporate trainees considered it a required rite of passage. Despite huge enrollments over almost a decade, my colleagues reluctantly let me continue teaching the course – after all, I was the chief financial officer with the money – but no longer allowed it to count toward the major.

The second lesson is flexibility. The University of Phoenix will start a class every week all semester. The idea that every course starts in September or January, and then in summer school, is outmoded for adult students and higher education must respond to the needs they have for scheduling flexibility. This is not new for traditional higher education which has used block courses of two to four weeks to supplement regular courses that extend over a full quarter or semester. Another aspect of flexibility is the absence of faculty tenure so that for-profits' staffing patterns can respond more rapidly to changes in demand or disciplines. I am not advocating the same for the rest of higher education but only that avoidance of overspecialization in faculty appointments, robust post-tenure review, and fair economic exigency plans can achieve similar ends if there is the will to adopt them.

The third area where the for-profits save money is in standardizing courses. Particularly in lower division courses, many institutions are teaching essentially the same materials, but rather than have scores of faculty each prepare their own syllabi, there is no reason that these introductory courses should not be similar everywhere. Higher education could also have more widely available course templates and even exemplary syllabi for common courses that others could use with attribution.

Would this approach be right for all of higher education? Probably not, but it is right for more courses than presently being used. "We have never done it that way" is not going to cut it as an excuse for inaction.

RESPONSE TO GROWTH

Enrollment growth is no panacea. Unless the institution is 100 percent tuition-dependent, it loses money on every student enrolled, and gifts, state aid, endowment earnings, and other revenue is required to get it to break even. It is different when there is excess capacity in the same way that filling a seat on an airliner that is taking off anyway earns marginal revenue. At Guilford, we can enroll 2,800 students and not have to make another major capital investment in office space, in classrooms, or in dormitories. If we enroll many more than 2,800, we will incur capital costs that wipe out much of the financial gain from enrollment.

The extent to which an institution has a burgeoning adult program will make it easier to grow. Adults live off campus, and their evening class schedule allows greater use of existing academic facilities rather than having to build new ones. Still, adult students must be treated somewhat differently. For example, a veteran in his late-20s can not be treated the same way as an 18-year-old just out of high school. Moreover, having a relevant orientation for adult students will make it easier to do a good job for veterans than if there is the mindset that they are treated the same as an 18- or 20-year-old. We have an adult transitions course at Guilford that is patterned after our first-year experience course for traditional students, but with very different learning points.

Secondly, adult students do not need the same services in general. The costs will be different as well. Many of them are not going to be in the same kind of clubs and other organizations. Almost none of them will participate in intercollegiate athletics. They are not going to make the same use of facilities. Besides not needing residence halls for the most part, they are not going to be frequenting the student union, cafeteria, gym, or theatre. We tried one year at Guilford to allow adult students to join up to four clubs or organizations open to traditional students – including intramurals – for only a $20 activity fee but less than 1 percent of the adult students were interested.

FINAL THOUGHTS

There is a lot of talk about innovation, retrenchment, and cost-cutting being the "new normal" in higher education. I do not see that particularly in private colleges. Most boards and presidents figure that the crisis, like the business cycle, is temporary and while scrutiny of our costs and outcomes will be greater, the future will not be nearly as bad as the present. When I ask audiences at conferences and workshops to identify institutions that have actually accomplished large scale, breakthrough innovations in the academic program or administrative services, hardly a hand ever goes up. That needs to change if the colleges and universities of tomorrow, especially the less selective and lesser endowed, do not want to share the fates of the auto companies, banks, and mainframe computer giants of yesterday who failed to change and are now gone.

10. The "new normal": prospects for postsecondary education in the twenty-first century

Bobby Fong

Like the law, higher education is deeply conservative in its processes. Faced with a question, faculty and administrators recur to established procedures and precedents, whether they lie in disciplinary modes of inquiry or models of best practice. In the main, this is consistent with academia's role as a steward of knowledge established over time through inquiry and disputation.

In the current economic environment, it is natural to hope that as America has weathered previous recessions to emerge stronger and more competitive, that it will do so again. But history and precedent may not be the best guide this time around.

The Dow Jones went from a historic high of 14,164 on October 9, 2007, to a trough of 6,547 on March 9, 2009. More recently it has recovered enough to breach 10,500. However, the downturn was precipitated by the bursting of a bubble compounded of inflated real estate and credit markets. The market may be adjusting for a truer valuation of assets, but investment values may not recover for years to come. At colleges where programs had been funded extensively by draws from endowment which have lost as much as 30 percent of their value, the prospect of maintaining previous levels of operation becomes unrealistic.

State support for higher education was declining as a percentage of operating budgets even before the downturn. The downturn itself has reduced state revenues, and most states have slashed education appropriations. Even when the economy recovers, there will be increased state spending in mandated areas such as law enforcement and health care. So long as higher education is seen as a discretionary good, it will continue to lose in its percentage of state largesse, if not in real dollars.

To these financial constrictions, we can add concerns about higher education's affordability and access; the inadequate preparation of K-12 students for college, particularly minorities and those from economically-disadvantaged backgrounds; and increasing competition, economically and educationally, from other nations.

The upshot is that colleges and universities can't expect to go back to business as usual. They can't expect to ride out the economic storm and return to status quo. As educators, we find the world shifting beneath our feet, the rules changing, and old verities called into question. We are required to lead when what awaits us is uncertain and we can no longer presume on prior experience.

THE "NEW NORMAL"

By the same token, it is not helpful to speak in sweeping terms of a "new normal" for higher education, for it implies that all institutions are in the same boat. They are not, and in order to discuss constructively what the "new normal" may entail for a given institution, our task is to differentiate higher education by sectors, by kinds of institutions, and finally by individual institutional missions to gauge our prospects. Amid uncertainty, what we still possess is the capability to assess our present situations. What follows in this section is my sense of the emerging financial prospects for the public sector, the private sector, and the for-profit sector of postsecondary education.

PROSPECTS FOR THE PUBLIC SECTOR

Among public universities almost without exception, we are seeing a diminution of state funding. California State University Chancellor Charlie Reed noted that in terms of real dollars, the budget of the California State University system in 2009 was 50 percent of what they had to work with in 1990. As a consequence, the burden of the cost of education necessarily has shifted to the family. Higher education, once considered a public good, is now being treated as a private investment.

With the decline of state support as a percentage of operating budgets, flagship public universities increasingly have relied on out-of-state students, whose tuition may be comparable to those at private institutions. As a point of reference, 2009–10 University of Michigan undergraduate tuition and fees for out-of-state students were $34,230, higher than my institution Butler University, a private comprehensive which charged $29,246. However, because public institutions were created to serve the population of a state, many legislatures are capping the number of students from other states as well as in-state tuition rates. The intent is to reserve spaces for in-state students and to keep the cost of education affordable. The effect is to constrict the revenue potential from both these sources. The public sector thus finds itself caught between what it would like to be able to spend and what the economics may allow.

The situation is exacerbated for branch campuses of public universities and state two-year systems, where both traditional-age students and adult learners turn for career education, particularly during economic downturns. In Indiana, the legislature voted to increase need-based aid to higher education for the 2009–11 biennium, but enrollment increases at branch campuses and the two-year system have led to a decrease in the availability of need-based state aid per student. In many cases, the students most affected are those least able to turn to their families for financial support.

But the prospect already is worse elsewhere. California State University Chancellor Charlie Reed presides over 23 campuses and 450,000 students, 55 percent of whom are ethnic minority students. Dr. Mildred Garcia is president of California State University at Dominguez Hills, which has experienced a 25 percent reduction in state funding. Both have warned that if California is a harbinger of what is to come, then the public sector of higher education may be financially unable to provide either the programs or the access needed by economically-disadvantaged students, particularly those from ethnic minorities.

Since World War II, the road to the American Dream has run through the state public higher education systems. If the gates to those systems now are open only to those families who can afford to pay for college themselves, I fear our becoming two nations, divided by educational attainment, with those denied educational opportunity being relegated to intellectual and financial impoverishment.

It has been suggested that the future of public higher education may include federal intervention, not simply through increasing financial aid to students, but in the form of direct support to state institutions that serve minorities and the economically-disadvantaged. Such support, however, will be accompanied by increased regulation that could include standardization of curricula, required acceptance of transfer credits from federally-accredited schools, caps on tuition increases, and federal audits of institutional budgets. In a time when some flagship universities yearn to be more independent of state regulation, the prospect of federal support and supervision of public higher education could lead to an even greater loss of institutional and academic autonomy.

PROSPECTS FOR THE PRIVATE SECTOR

In the private sector, the financial consequences are similarly complex. Let me offer a taxonomy in the form of a graph. On the x-axis, there are well-endowed universities on one end and tuition-dependent institutions on the other. On the y-axis, you have schools that are selective versus ones with more open admissions. The axes create four quadrants. Let me discuss each in turn.

For the well-endowed private, selective institutions, the prevailing assumption had been that the larger the endowment, the better off the institution. Endowment was thought to be an unmitigated good. Unfortunately, one of the byproducts of such riches is that these institutions finance an inordinately large portion of their operating budgets from endowment. At Harvard, over 30 percent of the operating budget came from endowment; at Yale it was nearly half. So when an endowment drops by 30 percent, as happened in 2008, the school finds itself unable to sustain programs and personnel at previous levels. My alma mater Harvard has had to suspend capital construction, rein in hiring, offer early retirement incentives and other measures to reduce staffing, and even cut back on hot meal options in dining halls.

Going forward, institutions in this quadrant will undergo a fundamental recalculation of how they use endowments. As donor stipulations permit, they may reserve more draw from endowment for one-time uses and less for ongoing operations. In addition, they may narrow the scope of programs they offer and ask students to assume a greater share of the cost of education. They may accept more students. Some of these schools are still committed to need-blind grants to cover the cost of education, but if their endowments don't recover, they could pull back on grants and reinstitute loans. Institutions in this quadrant will persist and flourish, but the amplitude of their operations will be straitened.

By contrast, in a second quadrant are those institutions with large endowments but which are less selective in admissions. Typically small liberal arts colleges, they find their situations somewhat more precarious. Historically, they have used their endowments to underwrite both need-based and merit-based aid packages that help fill their classes. A significant drop in their endowments has taken away their competitive advantage of being able to offer more and larger scholarships. Without as much money to offer, they may have a harder time making their enrollment targets. Going forward, they may experience a diminution in the size, quality, and diversity of their entering classes.

Nonetheless, the focus on endowment loss has obscured a more hopeful story. A number of private schools don't have large endowments but are doing well in attracting students. This third quadrant has been the one least affected by the economic downturn. At Butler, where endowment only provides about six percent of our operating budget, we've been able to tighten our belts without having to amputate an arm. So long as these tuition-driven schools can maintain their enrollments, they will continue to flourish. In the long term, they may encounter resistance to ever-rising tuition costs, but this was a threat even before the economic downturn.

The last quadrant is comprised of tuition-driven, non-selective schools. Many of these institutions are hurting. They need tuition payments to make their budgets, but they're cutting back on programs and people because not enough students are coming to them or staying through graduation. If the economic stresses continue, some of those colleges are in danger of closing their doors.

The challenge for all four quadrants is whether sufficient students and families will continue to pay for a private higher education. In Indiana, the private sector enrolls 25 percent of the four-year undergraduates in the state but annually grants 35 percent of the baccalaureates. Some Indiana privates are selective, but all provide a personalized education in which retention to graduation is enhanced through systems whereby each student is known by name and face. Nonetheless, if more prospective students opt for cheaper alternatives, the privates will grow economically and culturally more homogeneous, and those that can't enroll students in sufficient numbers will suffer. Private higher education may be regarded increasingly as an opportunity reserved for the economic and intellectual elite.

PROSPECTS FOR THE FOR-PROFIT SECTOR

The current economic circumstances may represent a significant opportunity for online, for-profit institutions that can keep costs low while serving students who are working course by course toward vocational degrees and certifications. Such providers do not have the ongoing expenses of physical plants, tenured faculty, or co-curricular programs and personnel. They can adjust quickly to local demand for particular fields of study. The best have evolved assessments that assure rigor and relevance in the courses they offer. Online instruction has found a market among nomadic students, those who are compiling credits from multiple institutions in pursuit of degrees earned part-time because of ongoing job and family obligations. Such enterprises could thrive in the coming years.

At the same time, for-profit, online providers tend to be career-focused. While their offerings constitute postsecondary education, there is a lively debate as to whether all postsecondary education is higher education. How significant is the distinction between applied learning and liberal education? What is the difference between postsecondary education for job certification and higher education designed to produce lifelong learners by inculcating the abilities to think critically, communicate effectively, work cooperatively, and act ethically?

The Association of American Colleges & Universities calls for a liberal education for all college students, which includes introducing them to disciplinary modes of investigation, equipping them for social responsibility and leadership, and enabling them to adapt knowledge and skills to new settings. A third of college graduates will eventually work at jobs that don't yet exist. Preparing them for a life of change is a different kind of education from simple certification for a particular job skill.

However, in a time when the quality of education is equated with economic competitiveness, and universities are being urged to be more efficient and cost-effective while serving more students who are often underprepared for college, perhaps the for-profit sector has gauged its priorities correctly. It has realized efficiencies by being focused on creating qualified workers. If workers then need to retool for new responsibilities, the online solution is to offer particular courses of training for the next job.

Hitherto, for-profit, online enterprises largely have ceded liberal education to traditional colleges and universities. But what might happen if online providers decide to apply their resources and experience in assessment to offering liberal education? What would it mean to teach liberally online? Could this be the ultimate democratization of liberal learning? For online for-profits, liberal education could be a new growth area if they deem it sufficiently remunerative to expand in that direction. For the traditional liberal arts college, can its time-honored approach to education, with its small student-to-teacher ratio, personalized contact, and residential experience, remain sufficiently distinguishable and valued when held up against a prospectively cheaper online counterpart? Embedded in this question is the key to the "new normal," and that is the necessity of institutional differentiation.

THE NECESSITY OF DIFFERENTIATION

We are living in a volatile epoch for higher education. But this should not obscure the fact that in the United States, there has been no unitary model for how undergraduate education is conducted. Indeed, the hitherto perceived strength of American higher education has been its multiplicity of approaches. Unlike the countries of Europe or Asia, the United States education and professional preparation in the baccalaureate is a synthesis made more timely by the economic downturn and increased international competition.

The point is not to create new hierarchies of educational institutions but to proliferate models that best-serve students. Each institution must think deeply about what it means to educate. Each institution needs to define its mission and outcomes that demonstrate whether or not that mission is being fulfilled. Each institution should be able to provide evidence that its students are graduating with the educational attributes consistent with its mission.

A MATTER OF VALUES

Even though I have tried to be hardheaded and focused in assessing the financial challenges to higher education, I remain convinced that our solutions for the future must be mindful of the heart of what we do: to prepare the next generation of students for life by passing on the legacy of human achievement. It is a matter of values, and any "new normal" must take that to heart.

We live in a world where communications, commerce, and culture transcend national boundaries, and our students must learn to be citizens of that world. Their future is multicultural, and if higher education is to remain true to its mission to educate, then it must give all students exposure to diversity and the practical experience of negotiating differences.

We live in a nation where educational opportunity increasingly is dependent on economic class. We cannot just winnow high school seniors for qualified students to admit to our institutions. So many students of potential have already been lost. Going forward, colleges and universities must endeavor to partner with school systems to create opportunities for the disadvantaged. It is an obligation of our institutional citizenship to think globally but act locally.

We live our professional lives in institutions that should operate for love of the student. Our structures and reward systems should reflect that love. Liberal education traditionally has been the equivalent of custom-tailored clothes rather than off the rack, fitting educational options to the individual student. Whether in a seminar or at a computer terminal, teaching and learning must take place one student at a time. We necessarily think in terms of institutional structures, but we succeed or fail student by student. Somehow we need to be able to preserve that sense of personal rapport in the midst of serving the masses.

One fundamental indicator of how well we are educating is the

does not have a federally-regulated, unitary higher education
see no prospect of America abandoning this diversity of moc
of a state-run system. Going forward, the path to sustaining
excellence must lie in affirming the institutional distinctives
guish each one of our enterprises from one another.

We need to think in terms of claiming niches in the landsca
education. Rather than being all things to all students, our
futures depend on our careful definition of individual missi
identifying the things we do that are unique, or more compreh
a higher standard of quality as compared to other schools. W
an institutional mission and commitments robust enough to
separate good ideas from those good ideas that fit the mission

Arizona State University (ASU) has sought to eliminate t
a flagship campus and branch campuses. Each campus is cha
college with a particular mission, identity, and pedagogy, wi
and schools distinctive to that campus. The goal is to elimina
matic and administrative redundancy as well as a sense tha
campuses are more prestigious than others. In seeking to eve
100,000 students in the system, President Michael Crow en
college filling an intellectual niche rather than multiplying ca
the same offerings.

In the private sector, a different approach is embodied
American Colleges and Universities (NACU), a national co
twenty selective, small to mid-size independent colleges and
dedicated to the purposeful integration of liberal education,
studies, and civic engagement. Rather than seeing liberal and
studies as at odds with one another, the consortium subs
ideal that all its students benefit from liberal education, and
professions can be taught liberally. So in addition to colle
arts and sciences, member institutions also house schools (
law, engineering, health sciences, and business. At NACU m
University, our hope is that each graduate will not only be
make a living, but also to make a life of purpose, in which ind
ishing is intertwined with the welfare of others.

The NACU commitments embody an emerging sense that
artificially reserve liberal education for the baccalaureate and
preparation for graduate school. It is possible to provide
learning and undergraduate professional preparation, to offi
ties for both reflection and applied learning, to equip undergi
to do well and to do good. There are more comprehensive
universities in the United States than liberal arts colleges and
versities combined. The comprehensive enterprise to provid

percentage of the entering class that persists to graduation. Of four-year colleges and universities, fewer than 300 report six-year graduation rates of 70 percent or above. Compound this by the number of students who don't ever darken the doors of our institutions, and we have an inkling of the magnitude of the need for education in our nation.

That's why, in the end, we can't just have one model of a college degree or one model of higher education. There must be many different kinds of degrees, and different kinds of institutions. Let the differentiation of our missions lead to a greater respect for what each of our institutions do for particular students. That should be our "new normal."

11. Enhancing faculty vitality and institutional commitment: smart leadership in difficult times

Devorah Lieberman

SECURING AND SUSTAINING FACULTY COMMITMENT

As a living organism with its students serving as the lifeblood, the faculty as the soul, and the administration at the head, a college or university is constantly refining and shaping its values and its culture as it adapts to a rapidly changing environ for higher education. But, perhaps the most critical element within that organism for affecting such culture change is its soul: the faculty. It is that culture that that drives the reputation that attracts human, political, and economic capital and commitment on which the success of every institution rests. The better we invest in, protect and nurture our faculty, the better able we will be to meet our institutional missions and to reach beyond our strategic goals.

All institutions seek to recruit and retain permanent and adjunct faculty who are motivated to teach, to pursue scholarship and research, and to personally invest themselves in the life of the institution and its extended communities. The job of developing a faculty, though, does not end with a successful hire, or a promotion, or a tenure decision. It is the beginning of a process that needs to continue throughout each faculty member's career.

The effort to engage faculty in their own professional and personal growth should occur throughout the institution, at all levels, irrespective of good times or bad. This begins with assessment of academic needs, continues through the recruitment of an appropriately talented and diverse professoriate, and incorporates professional development that fosters their continuing renewal. Throughout this process, be mindful that all members of the faculty are individuals. The needs of their families and their personal and professional aspirations all dictate priorities in time and the choices they make. While this chapter is written in the context of the turbulent economy of the start of the second decade in the twenty-first century, also remember that periods of high prosperity can challenge faculty commitment to institutions. Increased philanthropy, heightened availability of public funding, and an expanding sense of opportunity, the greening grass of other pastures may seem more rewarding to faculty we hope to attract and to retain. Whether the market is bull or bear, the processes for securing and sustaining faculty commitment are much the same.

IN PURSUIT OF FACULTY COMMITMENT

To develop strategies to deepen faculty commitment, it is helpful to review the reasons faculty choose enter the professoriate. According to Paul J. Yakoboski, in *Do Great Minds Think Alike? Faculty Perspectives on Career and Retirement*, the findings from the 2007 TIAA-CREF Institute Faculty Generations Survey, faculty representing three generations (Early Boomers, 1946–54; Late Boomers, 1955–64; and Gen X, 1965–80) report very similar motivations for pursuing careers in higher education. Though these data may not be applicable to faculty perspectives clustered by institutional type, they are generalizable to the wider professoriate.

Additional studies, funded by the TIAA-CREF Institute, are similarly illuminating. In 2007, Jerry Berberet, founding executive director of the Associated New American Colleges (currently named New American Colleges and Universities – NACU) and vice president for academic affairs at Carroll College, conducted a poll of 450 "New Career" faculty of five or fewer years service and reported the findings in *Perceptions of Early Career Faculty: Managing the Transition from Graduate School to the Professorial Career* (2008, TIAA-CREF Institute). Their average age of newer career faculty was 39, which correlates approximately with Gen X. All were employed by NACU-member institutions. NACU schools enroll between 2,500 to 8,000 students and offer a number of professional programs integrated with a strong liberal arts core and a commitment to civic engagement. Early career respondents reported choosing the higher education profession because they "very much" enjoy:

- Teaching – 82 percent
- Working on a campus – 61 percent
- Serving society – 56 percent
- Living the faculty lifestyle – 47 percent
- Research – 35 percent

These data align reasonably well with motivations presented in the *Faculty Generations Survey*, as detailed in Table 11.1.

Table 11.1   Reasons for choosing an academic career

	All	Generation X	Late boomers	Early boomers
Wanted to teach	39%	43%	36%	41%
Wanted to do research	34	40	31	30
Enjoy college/academic environment	24	26	27	19
Wanted to pursue a particular discipline	14	4	21	15
Flexibility of schedule/lifestyle	8	11	6	8
Like learning, intellectual curiosity	8	5	10	8
Make a difference; contribute to society	5	2	9	2
Relatives had a career in academia	5	1	11	1
Encouraged by professor/mentor	4	8	4	2
It's my passion/interest	3	3	4	1
Best job option available	2	3	1	4
Fell into it by chance	2	0	1	4

Source: TIAA-CREF Institute, Faculty Generations Survey (2007).

Yet, striking in the Faculty Generations Survey data are the differences in motivations between faculty age groups. Gen X faculty seem much less interested in pursuing a specific discipline (4 percent vs. 21 percent for Late Boomers and 15 percent for Early Boomers). However, according to *Perceptions of Early Career Faculty*, 94 percent responded that "learning and intellectual stimulation from my field" was important or very important. Gen X faculty are more enamored with flexibility of schedule/lifestyle (11 percent versus 6 percent for Late Boomers and 8 percent for Early Boomers) and they also appear to be more enticed by the opportunity to conduct research (40 percent versus 31 percent for Late Boomers and 30 percent for Early Boomers) and slightly more motivated by teaching (43 percent versus 36 percent for Late Boomers and 41 percent for Early Boomers).

One might ask if our rising new cadre of senior faculty, Gen X, really has less allegiance to a specific academic field. And, if so, are they more apt to be excited by opportunities for interdisciplinary collaboration? In similar vein, is the opportunity to pursue research and scholarship a compelling motivation that secures and sustains faculty commitment? Finally, it seems clear that Gen X professors enter higher education because of the lifestyle that academe presents.

In *Perceptions of Early Career Faculty*, Berberet reports that early career faculty agree that:

- I enjoy the challenges of my job – 94 percent
- If I had it to do over, I would still choose a faculty career – 92 percent
- I agree with the institutional mission of my college – 88 percent
- Faculty rewards support the goals of my institution's mission – 66 percent
- My institution is well managed; administrator work supports the mission effectively – 64 percent
- Faculty work supports institutional mission effectively – 62 percent

Clearly, young faculty members report that they are highly satisfied with their career choice and are generally well aligned with the respective missions of their institutions. However, nearly four out of ten do not feel that faculty work supports the institutional mission. Approximately, one third do not feel strongly that the institution is well managed or that administrative work supports institutional mission, or that the faculty reward system supports the goals of their college or university. These data raise the question of whether young faculty are receiving ample reinforcement for the relationship between what they do on a day-to-day basis and the mission and strategic vision of their college or university.

Not only that, but responses to questions regarding how effectively early career faculty felt prepared by their graduate school experience to teach, research, advise, serve on committees, or obtain grants suggest that their graduate alma maters are not filling the bill in readying newly minted faculty for their responsibilities. Given the wide ranging taxonomy of American colleges and universities one wonders if, rather than placing blame on graduate programs for failing to prepare faculty for the specific realities of their initial professional practice – can a single doctoral program prepare a candidate to perform with equal success in the demographics and cultures that distinguish a flagship research university from a regional public university or from a selective private college of the arts and sciences. Further, it seems nearly impossible to prepare those in graduate school for what to expect when faced with institutional politics, competing pressures within the institution, and day-to-day institution specific pressures. Would it not seem that the acculturation of new faculty, regardless of institutional type, would be more appropriately placed with their initial institution of employment rather than only the university from which they received their terminal degree? The early career survey shows dramatic improvement between perceptions of being "very effectively prepared" and "working very effectively." Berberet states that the first few years of professional teaching seems to be a kind of apprenticeship, albeit with full-time responsibilities.

While much of the above addresses issues around faculty entering the

*Table 11.2   Late-career faculty perceptions of satisfaction and
institutional commitment*

	age 50 to 59	age 60 and over
% agreeing or strongly agreeing with each statement:		
Intellectual stimulation I receive from my academic field	98%	98%
My contributions have a positive impact at my institution	94	94
Faculty members have important civic responsibilities to society	94	94
I would choose an academic career, if beginning my career again	93	94
Having favorable peer evaluation of my professional performance	89	93
Having favorable student evaluations of my teaching	89	87
Receiving an appreciation award or special recognition by students	79	79
This is an especially creative and productive time in my field	76	75
High priority I place on service to my institution	60	60

Source: Berberet, Bland, Risbey and Brown, 2005.

profession, retention of those who have progressed beyond the first few years from an instructor or associate professor, it is equally critical for an institution to deepen and sustain faculty commitment. According to *Faculty Generations Survey*, 96 percent of faculty were either very satisfied or somewhat satisfied with their job overall in comparison to the aggregate of the general American workforce where 80 percent were very or somewhat satisfied. (Note that these data were gathered before the onset of the 2008 recession.)

Berberet, along with Carole J. Bland and Kelly R. Risbey from the University of Minnesota and Betsy E. Brown, University of North Carolina in *Late Career Faculty Perceptions: Implications for Retirement Planning and Policymaking* (*Research Dialogue*, TIAA-CREF Institute, 2005) present a similar view: "Our survey findings portray a highly productive, hardworking, and largely satisfied late career faculty cohort – an observation that holds up for both the age 50–59 (1,296 respondents) and age 60 and over (620 respondents) groups." (see Table 11.2.) This survey was not limited to faculty at The New American Colleges and Universities

Table 11.3   Job satisfaction in higher education

	All	Generation X	Late boomers	Early boomers
Job, Overall				
Very satisfied	53%	54%	54%	49%
Somewhat satisfied	43	42	43	43
Not too satisfied	3	3	3	3
Not at all satisfied	2	1	0	5
Relationship with colleagues				
Very satisfied	55	54	63	45
Somewhat satisfied	37	37	35	42
Not too satisfied	5	9	2	5
Not at all satisfied	1	0	0	2
Work/life balance				
Very satisfied	42	38	48	39
Somewhat satisfied	42	45	41	40
Not too satisfied	14	16	11	18
Not at all satisfied	1	2	1	2
Salary				
Very satisfied	23	14	30	22
Somewhat satisfied	52	58	49	48
Not too satisfied	19	20	14	25
Not at all satisfied	6	7	7	5

Source: TIAA-CREF Institute, Faculty Generations Survey (2007).

(formerly Associated New American Colleges or ANAC) institutions and may not represent the norm.

The last response is troubling. Four out of ten senior level faculty do not agree that they place a high priority on service to their institutions. When one considers data from *Faculty Generations* (see Table 11.3), it suggests that those who have served in the profession for the longest time tend to be the least satisfied with their jobs overall, their relationships with colleagues, their work/life balance, and salary. And those who are entering the middle period of their lives, with all the attendant social and economic stresses, report the greatest satisfaction. What, then, does this suggest in terms of defining the roles of senior faculty as mentors? I would posit that the older faculty have invaluable experiences to share with the junior and entering faculty, but they too need special professional development attention if they are to be perceived as role models.

The portrait painted by *Faculty Generations, Perceptions of Early Career Faculty,* and *Perceptions of Late Career Faculty* no doubt present

*Table 11.4   Selected perceptions of senior faculty vs. full-time
administrators with faculty appointments*

	Administrator	Faculty
% agreeing:		
Importance of service to larger community and society	90%	77%
Importance of service to my field and profession	85	69
Importance of service to my institution	88	58
Interest less focused on my institution than in earlier	15	40
Institution does not adequately use my leadership abilities	27	50

Source: Berberet, Bland, Risbey and Brown, 2005.

an incomplete portrait of faculty satisfaction with other salient aspects of their career. However, the message is clear. Colleges and universities that seek to recruit and retain highly qualified faculty committed to institutional mission must be strategic and intentional in the professional development. They must exhibit clarity in establishing and managing expectations during faculty recruitment. They must develop effective processes for reinforcing the value that each faculty member brings to the institution in terms of fulfilling its mission and vision. And they must become adept at reading and addressing the professional needs of faculty, particularly new and senior faculty if they are to ensure a culture of sustainable commitment.

Digging deeper into *Perceptions of Late Career Faculty* yields another very fascinating set of data. Senior administrators who hold full-time faculty appointments as well are much more committed to their institutions than their peers who serve only on the faculty (see Table 11.4).

These data suggest that senior faculty with full-time administrative appointments feel a much more direct involvement than other senior faculty (who do not have full-time administrative responsibilities) with the mission, vision and implementation of strategic planning of their institutions. Thus, they feel more deeply engaged, perhaps vitalized by their ability to make a difference and create a personal legacy. Rather than finding the differences between these two groups troubling, I see opportunities to expand administrative validation of the assets that senior faculty bring to the institution, to develop opportunities for them to share their accumulated wisdom with new and mid-career faculty, and to celebrate publicly their achievements among all campus constituencies.

COMMITMENT BEGINS WITH RECRUITMENT

The best admissions counselors not only think about recruiting and retaining students per se; they think of recruiting alumni. Whether recruiting tenure track position or an adjunct, the goal of every faculty search should ride on the same philosophical undercarriage: securing the commitment of a highly qualified and talented scholar who is well equipped to discharge required tasks, eager to participate actively in the culture of the institution, and dedicated to advancing its mission and vision. No reliable psychometric system allows us to test a candidate's potential for commitment. Rather the issue rests on a host of factors rooted equally in a candidate's personal and professional needs, the needs of the college or university and the needs of the hiring department. Just as in admissions, the goal is not to fill a seat but to engage the intellect and emotion of an individual who has the highest propensity to be retained because of good work and who is most likely to want to stay with the institution for a significant period.

Recruitment rests first and foremost on the assessment of the academic program's and the department's strategic needs. If the department's faculty and senior institutional leadership were to envision the program and department ten years down the road, what would they see? How would courses of study – majors, minors, graduate programs, certifications, and so on – evolve? How will changes in technology affect pedagogy? Will the economy or political developments lead to significant changes in the market for graduates? Will continuing shifts in demographics suggest that the department may be serving new clientele? How can a new hire help achieve diversity goals? Will budgets remain competitive with peer institutions? What must the department and the institution do to nurture new faculty commitment?

Virginia Commonwealth University (VCU), in Richmond, Va., offers insightful perspective on the entire hiring process and is especially articulate regarding the incorporation of activities designed to ensure that diversity goals are achieved. Regarding the latter, VCU presents the following on its excellent website vcu.edu/eeoaa:

- What is the stated mission of the program?
- What are the demographics of the institution and the community in which it resides?
- What are the demographics of prospective students who have applied or who have been admitted to the program?
- How many students of color are majors? How many graduate students?
- Are there strategies for recruiting ethnically diverse students?

- How many faculty/staff of color are in the program?
- How many courses address ethnic diversity issues? Is diversity part of the content of required courses?
- Are students exposed to experimental opportunities/field trips that focus on diversity as part of course requirements?
- Do guest speakers include people from diverse ethnic backgrounds addressing issues both of diversity and other topics within the field?
- How are students of color supported academically?
- Do students of color have ethnically diverse faculty to serve as role models on the campus?
- Do majority faculty have an interest in working with ethnically diverse students?
- Are there any tensions between white students/faculty and ethnically diverse students/faculty?
- Do students of color have difficulty finding faculty to chair their theses or dissertation committees or gaining acceptance of their topics when they address issues of diversity?
- Are funds set aside specifically for recruiting ethnic minority faculty?

Clearly, VCU is intentional from before the first description of a vacancy is drafted that it thoroughly investigate the setting in which the new hire is expected to perform professional responsibilities. Behind VCU's set of questions lies the terrain of the culture of the recruiting institution. How would one describe the ethos that pervades the college or university? Can one truly say that its primary constituencies are well united and committed to the vision and mission of the institution? Are faculty and staff dedicated in the main to advancing, say, a specific and clearly articulated view that integrates subject matter, pedagogy, scholarship, and civic engagement such as in my college's Wagner Plan for the Liberal Arts? While Carnegie classifications define the taxonomy of an institution, the way those sets of characteristics play out day-to-day as evidenced by the relationships among faculty, staff, students, and other constituencies creates the ethos that constitutes a college's culture.

Creation of a set of recruiting procedures that moves from the identification prospects to their acculturation is the first step in securing and sustaining faculty of commitment. The process is at once an assessment of professional and personal attributes. VCU's list addresses many of the professional issues. But often, personal considerations carry the day. How well do candidates see themselves collaborating with colleagues within the department that is considering them and with others on campus? Is employment available to prospects' spouses? Is the cost of living commensurate with anticipated compensation? Are schools and housing and health care of appropriate quality reasonably available? Does the region offer a portfolio of cultural amenities that satisfy avocational interests? All of the surveys on career satisfaction stress the importance of the balance between faculty work and life. Successful recruiting strategies address these issues forcefully, for in them reside seeds that sow retention as surely as explicit articulation of new responsibilities, and demonstration of the relationships is expressed largely through the interview process.

PROFESSIONAL DEVELOPMENT FOR COMMITMENT

Though the term "professional development" has been in vogue for more than a generation, it strikes me as unduly limiting. We are really talking about creation, implementation, and evaluation of an ongoing process that evolves the capacity of individuals to achieve their personal goals and intellectual passions while meeting (and we hope exceeding) institutional expectations set for performance of their duties. Writing in *The National Forum for Teaching and Learning* (vol. 13 no.3), Mary Deane Sorcinelli, associate provost and director, Office of Faculty Development at the University of Massachusetts, offered a list of *The Top Ten Things that New Faculty would Like to Hear from Colleagues*, "as they try to figure out how to live an academic life–that is, how to teach well, produce fruitful research, earn tenure, pay attention to a partner and children, lead an examined life, and make plans for the future." (The unabridged version is available at www.wfu.edu/tlc/pdfs/TLC Forum.pdf).

(1) Remember: you are great.

You were hired because we think you have high prospects for success and our goal is to have you succeed. But, despite your brightness you're not expected to figure out everything on your own. Reach out to all of us. Ask questions. Ask for help.

(2) You don't have to be superman or woman tomorrow.

Excellent faculty didn't become that way in a month or a year. It takes new faculty two or three years to get established; so, pace yourself for the long run. Things will take off more quickly than you think. Start by setting goals for yourself and reviewing them with your mentors. Break down big visions into small, manageable goals. Meeting them will motivate you toward success.

(3) To achieve tenure, figure out what matters.

Promotion and tenure requirements vary widely from institution to institution (and within their subordinate units). They'll seem confusing and contradictory. Talk to everyone – department chair, dean, recently tenured faculty, straight-shooters among the old guard, and colleagues in the same boat as you. Listen and form your own judgments. Meet annually with your dean, review your plan and accomplishments, and set new manageable goals for the next year.

(4) Decide what doesn't matter.

Balance teaching and scholarship with service that matters. Talk with wise senior colleagues about to deploy your departmental citizenship in ways that support your goal of making tenure. It might be fine to serve on the department website committee in that first or second year, but consider as well a role on recruitment, development, and research committees. Develop an on-campus seminar series that brings national leaders in your field to campus. Their input about your work will be valuable, and you will be expanding your network of colleagues beyond our campus. A positive, national reputation does not hurt in influencing tenure decisions.

(5) Teaching matters.

Teaching is primary to the missions of most colleges and universities, and early career faculty find great satisfaction in being valued as a teacher and advisor by students. Senior colleagues can help you improve. Take advantage of teaching and learning centers on campus, and offer to help others in pedagogy where you shine.

(6) Make a plan.

Consult with your department chair about the priorities you set. Play to your strengths. Think about what you know, what you are comfortable with, and what you are ready to teach. Cultivate a specialty that you enjoy and do well (first year program, civic engagement) as it will make your teaching more coherent and enjoyable. You were hired because your institution wants to capitalize on your strengths. Take a look at your department's planning documents. Think about how you fit into the scheme of things.

(7) Think "mentors," plural.

Those who are older are sometimes wise and can give you realistic and solid advice on a lot of issues. Mentors inside the department can help you with issues of teaching and scholarship and also on how to read the culture – who's who and what visions they have. Reach out to colleagues beyond the department for a broader view (and to develop interdisciplinary ties).

(8) Invite community.

Share a sense of excitement about your teaching and scholarship. Participate in co-curricular activities that interest you. Make informal connections and nurture them. Don't forget your own students.

Be sure to invite their feedback – they just might be your best
teachers.

(9) Don't work on 15 things equally all at once.

Remember figuring out what matters doesn't just apply to tenure. As
a new faculty member you'll be confronted with 15 things that seem
to need being done today. Pick one or two and do them well. Think
of the others as balls in the air. You'll get better at juggling multiple
roles and tasks – a skill necessary for a successful career in academe.

(10) Have a life.

Take care of yourself and your life outside of work. Fatigue, whether
emotional or physical, saps strength vital for effective teaching and
collegial friendships. Work out, make time for your family, see
a show, hike, and steal a long weekend. Share your joys and disappointments with friends. You'll keep yourself rejuvenated and
intellectually and emotionally engaged.

EFFECTIVE STRATEGIES FOR FACULTY PROFESSIONAL AND PERSONAL DEVELOPMENT

During the late 1990s, in an effort to revitalize the college after a long
period of severe financial stress, Wagner created a new and comprehensive
curriculum – The Wagner Plan for the Practical Liberal Arts. The new
curriculum was developed by existing faculty with no outside funding. Its
success resulted in a 50 percent increase in enrollment, significant gains
in retention, growth of endowment from $3 million to $50 million, and
establishment of a national reputation. The Wagner Plan is based on an
intensive series of first-year, intermediate, and senior seminars that are
often interdisciplinary and integrate theory with civically-engaged experiential education. Demands on faculty are much heavier than in traditional
curricula grounded in lecture and laboratory classes.

To sustain faculty engagement and to provide continuing opportunities for their professional and personal renewal, Wagner embarked on
an extensive and aggressive system of faculty development which was
designed to broaden and deepen their commitment to the students and to
each other. It must be said that, even though the college was recovering fiscally when the decision to implement the new program of faculty development was made, trustees and senior faculty and administrative leadership
made the financial investment. They knew that Wagner's primary assets
were the strength of its faculty and the faculty's willingness to devote the
additional time and energy required by The Wagner Plan.

Wagner's faculty development strategy is founded on four principles:

- Active learning requires continuing evolution of pedagogy. It is important to create opportunities for faculty to interact, teach one another, learn from one another, assess each others' work, respect one another, engage in civil discourse.
- Professional growth is a developmental process. Faculty responsibilities exist in a dynamic state of flux with more experienced faculty moving into leadership roles and new faculty coming aboard to fill vacancies, professional growth is a developmental process which passes along effective practices and which acculturates newer members of the faculty.
- Creating venues for social interaction to exchange information about the institution is a valid form of faculty development. Formal and informal faculty interactions lead to greater exchanges of ideas, greater self-reflection, and greater opportunities for personal and professional growth.
- Finding renewal and meaning in one's work is critical to continued growth and development. Activities which support faculty in their teaching, scholarship and service, created in a way that is meaningful supports this principle.

The following are a host of activities, now institutionalized, which seek to achieve these outcomes. During times of economic stress it is critical to maintain these activities and support. These provide a consistency, a constancy and a balance for faculty. Where there may be significant changes or a pause in some progress (for example, salaries and new faculty hires), it is important for the existing faculty to enjoy stability in the administration's ongoing support of their success inside and outside the classroom. Wagner College's faculty development activities take a multi-pronged approach. These prongs include: financial support, structural support, personal support, and intentional venues for promoting collegiality.

FINANCIAL SUPPORT

Maintaining faculty aid for scholarship and professional development. Faculty aid is a common pool of funds intended to support faculty scholarship and professional development. In 2007, these funds reached approximately $240,000. Funding faculty scholarship and professional development, especially during difficult economic times, helps to maintain vitality and confidence in the institution.

Providing *additional financial support for presenting scholarship at higher education organizations.* As the institution continues to increase national visibility among its peer institutions, the Provost's Office provides additional funds for faculty who are presenting their scholarship and research at national higher education meetings that are not discipline based (for example, Association of American Colleges and Universities (AAC&U), American Council on Education (ACE), Campus Compact).

Providing stipends for taking a leadership role in campus-wide initiatives. It is important to continue to maintain campus-wide commitment and excitement around overarching initiatives, those that distinguish the college and provide opportunities for faculty to stay interested and excited about supporting the mission of the institution through the curricula and co-curricula. External funds offer the flexibility to provide additional stipends, which supplement faculty income during periods when general increases in compensation may be stagnant or curtailed.

A perfect example of this at Wagner focuses on its initiatives in civic engagement. Experiential learning is one of the cornerstones of the Wagner Plan and learning communities. Civic engagement is one of the accepted experiential learning models at the college. Every first year and senior year learning community (in which all Wagner students must participate) is required to have an experiential component that is aligned with the student learning outcomes of each course. Wagner's civic engagement model is sustainable across the curriculum and developmental within a department. It increases student commitment to personal and social responsibility and enhances community organization, commitment and trust with the College.

Within the past four years, approximately $3 million, in external funds, have been raised to support these efforts and the college's Center for Leadership and Service which facilitates, coordinates, and expands civic engagement. Funds also underwrite stipends for the faculty, additional scholarship opportunities, and further commitment to the goals of the institution.

Maintaining financial support for faculty sabbaticals. Sabbaticals, though seen by some as a place to cut expenditures when times are tough, are crucially important to faculty. They not only provide substantial intellectual and personal renewal, but of perhaps greater importance they signify the institution's inviolate commitment to faculty.

STRUCTURAL SUPPORT

Sustaining the Professional Development Semester for all faculty in the first-year program. Every faculty member who participates for three years in the First Year Learning Community is eligible for a Professional

Development Semester (PDS), which provides full salary and benefits for a semester devoted to scholarship and professional development requiring no other college responsibilities. Most newly hired faculty participate in the First Year Program, a time consuming program which partners two faculty with a class of entering freshman. Each learning community is a combination of integrative learning, civic engagement, intensive writing, reflective practice, and strategic advising. The PDS provides an opportunity for faculty (especially junior faculty) to remain off campus for one semester to focus on their professional development and provides time for their own reflective practice. Faculty participating in a PDS are equally eligible for sabbaticals at the appropriate time.

Maintaining the reduced teaching load. In 2006, the college reduced the full-time teaching requirements from seven courses per year to six courses per year. This was approved by the Board of Trustees with the understanding that the reduced teaching requirements would provide more time for the faculty to devote to (1) scholarly activities, (2) pedagogical and professional development, and (3) student advising. Increasing teaching load as a response to recession threatens the quality of a student's academic experience, may accelerate attrition among students and faculty, and can lead to divisiveness between faculty and staff with the former feeling that the institutional budget is being unequally balanced on their backs.

PERSONAL SUPPORT

"Scholarship circles" to provide research mentors for faculty. Approximately ten faculty per year submit proposals to be part of the year-long "scholarship circles." These faculty meet together monthly with the Associate Dean of the Faculty or the Faculty Scholar for Teaching and Learning. (The faculty scholar is a full-time faculty member who receives an additional stipend for assisting faculty with individual needs, fostering campus dialogues on pedagogy, and encouraging faculty to conduct research that enhances their teaching, student learning and results in publications.) Additionally, a resource librarian joins each group meeting. Members of the group assist one another in scholarly projects. The assistance includes feedback writing and research design and time management and the identification of appropriate outlets for presentation and publication. Data indicate that junior faculty who participate fully in the Scholarship Circles are more productive researchers than those who do not participate.

"Grant Circles" that allow faculty to assist each other in identifying and pursuing project funding. "Grant Circles," similar to "scholarship circles," are led by the Faculty Grants Coordinator, a full-time faculty member

who receives an additional stipend to facilitate a year-long process during which those interested in pursuing external funding for their scholarship meet with other faculty to research, write and submit their proposals.

A Center for Teaching, Learning and Research to support new pedagogies, academic research, and assessment processes. In 2009, The Center for Teaching, Learning and Research was established with the help of donor funds. Creation of a physical space on campus, a place where faculty can go for professional development assistance is an important and tangible manifestation of the institution's commitment that teaching, learning, and scholarship are among the highest of college priorities. Opening the Center during the economic downturn was propitious in that it represented to the faculty that donor support for these activities is realistic.

Supporting an annual "Focus on Faculty" symposium addressing teaching, learning, and research. The annual "Focus on Faculty" is an opportunity for all full-time faculty, adjunct faculty, and interested staff to come together for an event that focuses on teaching and learning. This annual event, first instituted in 2007, occurs on a day during the week prior to the beginning of fall term. Themes have included: Pedagogy and Internationalization, Classroom Assessment Techniques, Meaning and Renewal in our Faculty Work; and, Teaching and Learning with Technology. The "Focus on Faculty" begins the academic year with a very public expression of commitment to teaching and learning, bringing all faculty together in common purpose, and providing new ideas that can be readily applied as classes open.

COLLEGIALITY SUPPORT

Open conversations with the provost. Each month during the academic year, different groups of faculty are invited to the provost's home for a 90 minute gathering with cheese, fruit, and wine. Each "conversation" is designed to be an unfettered discussion about any issues that are on their minds. I begin every "open conversation" with the same two questions: "What have you heard?" and "What do you want to know?" These are informal opportunities to address rumors and to calm anxieties. Here too we can step away from the business of the campus and to talk with one another as friends and colleagues. The "open conversation" ends with a final question from me, "Now, tell me something I don't know." These conversations help ensure that lines of communication remain open.

Open conversations for adjunct faculty. Every semester, the Associate Dean of the Faculty hosts an "open conversation" for adjunct faculty. Similar to the Provost's open conversations, these on-campus receptions bring together the adjunct faculty who serve an increasingly important and visible role on the campus and in the classroom. To more effectively engage and acculturate adjuncts, they are encouraged to use all campus resources including the library; physical fitness center and natatorium, theater, and special departmental facilities, and they are especially encouraged to take part in cultural and other co-curricular programming.

Learning Community for First-Year Faculty. What better vehicle for faculty teaching in Wagner's learning community-based First-Year program than a learning community expressly for the 21 teams of two faculty each in the program? Learning community partners usually commit to the First-Year program for at least three years. Relationships between the faculty partners become very deep. All First-Year faculty spend two days together in May at an off-campus retreat. They assess the year that just ended; explore improvements in pedagogy; and discuss strategies for enhancing internationalization, diversity, and civic engagement. Each year, approximately 40 percent of the faculty participate in the First-Year program and this retreat provides an extremely powerful opportunity for the kind of focused, yet informal, conversations that deepen commitment to each other and to the institution. Additionally, all learning community faculty meet in aggregate once a month throughout the year for conversations on similar topics.

Faculty Forum. Once a month, a single faculty member or perhaps a pair, share recent research or scholarship with colleagues during a late afternoon Faculty Forum. Not only do these presentations highlight the importance of research, but they also fertilize collaboration on teaching and scholarship. A reception with refreshments typically follows each forum.

CONCLUSION

Securing and sustaining faculty commitment, whether in difficult or expansive times requires an intrinsic dedication by an institution and especially by its senior administration and trustees. At Wagner, it is understood that this is an investment in continuous improvement of faculty, which produces a return on investment that allows the institution to remain competitive with its peers. Higher education is extremely dynamic and especially so during periods of economic and political uncertainty. This translates to activities where colleges become more aggressive in recruitment and students become more mobile and more eager to seek the best value. Short-sighted institutions that reduce funding for the professional and personal development of faculty before making significant reductions in other areas of activity risk alienating the constituency which delivers the core mission: teaching, learning, research and service to the campus and external communities. Such reductions communicate the unfortunate message to the faculty that they are not as highly valued as those elements of the college where budgets suffer less. Many of the tactics Wagner has instituted over the past few years cost very little in comparison to the college's overall budget. They do, however, require a commitment of staff and faculty time and the agreement of senior leadership that the expenditure of that time is critical to the future success of the college or university. Why is the commitment of time perceived as being so powerful? It is direct and tangible evidence that the organization truly cares for its members. If an institution demonstrates its commitment in real and meaningful ways to the members of its community, they will, in turn, reciprocate by demonstrating their commitment to the institution.

12. Where is the money? Leading in a changing environment

Jane Wellman

FINDINGS FROM THE DELTA PROJECT

"Where is the money?" The answer to this question is, for the most part, that the money which higher education is going to receive is the money that it already has. Higher education is an economically stratified industry with a relatively small cluster of institutions having access to significant resources that (both by levels and types) do not exist in other parts of higher education. Therefore, all generalizations about finance and higher education, except for this one, are wrong. What is true for one sector and one type of institution, is not true for much of the rest of higher education.

That said, the funding pattern for higher education in the 1990s was toward privatization. This translates, for the most part, into increases in tuition as a source of general revenues for colleges and universities. This has happened in all sectors of higher education, public as well as private non-profit institutions, with the possible exception of some of the leading private research universities and the nationally selective baccalaureate institutions. The biggest change in revenues is evident in the public sector, where since the late 1980s the pattern has been a slow erosion of state funds with a replacement by tuition revenues.   .

The majority of students enrolled in private colleges and universities are in institutions for which tuition revenue constitutes somewhere around 80 percent to 90 percent of net revenue. These are not institutions that have historically had access to substantial amounts of private gifts, or with endowments that have produced resources sufficient to relieve the pressure on tuition as a primary source of revenue.

A widespread misperception exists that private funding and endowment revenues have become a significant revenue source across much of higher education. In reality, the 1990s witnessed a growth in access to private resources through endowments and gifts that spiked considerably in a few of the wealthiest institutions. But again, it was only a relatively small handful of institutions, collectively enrolling less than ten percent of all college students, that experienced that upward wave. Endowment revenues grew so quickly in these institutions that by the early 2000s they had come to rely upon them for close to 40 percent of operating resources – a greatly increased level of funding dependency than had existed on these campuses before the mid 1990s. These resources began to dip considerably with the start of the recent recession, but it's important to realize that the declines being experienced by these institutions are from a relatively high base. After the recession, these institutions can be expected to return to spending levels closer to the historic norms experienced up to 1998.

The trajectory forward for state appropriations for the large majority of public institutions is negative. Near term, given the structural deficits existing in all states, there will be significant continuing erosion in virtually every state for public funding of higher education. The pressure will be on tuition revenues and on managing within the resources that colleges and universities already have.

PROSPECTS FOR REVENUE STREAMS

In response to these dire conditions, colleges and universities will have to structure costs differently; institutions cannot continuously look to increasing revenues without paying attention to their spending. Higher education will have to manage its resources in a way that supports the goal of increasing educational attainment. This can be done through prudent attention to cost management and through a better focus on institutional mission and core strengths. A decrease in funding relative to previous levels does not mean that colleges and universities can back away from the collective responsibility for serving public needs for higher education; this includes the private non-profit sector as well public universities.

Colleges and universities should also not make it a high priority to maintain the current level of resources by using tuition increases to continue backfilling for public funding cuts. Tuition levels at such a level will hurt the goal of access and increased degree attainment, and they will lead to public rebellion harmful for all of higher education. The flashpoint of public critique regarding higher education is over perceptions that costs are increasing without institutions increasing the value to students as a result. Higher education might not want to admit this, but the public is right: tuitions are rising without a commensurate rise in value because they're being increased to replace costs rather than to increase services. The costs of production in public higher education have actually been flat or declining, but the public does not know this because, not surprisingly, higher education is not particularly forthcoming about its cost and revenue structures. The public see tuitions continuing to increase and assumes it is because colleges and universities are bad managers of resources. Unless higher education reins in tuition increases and does a much better job of public transparency regarding fiscal stewardship, it is never going to turn around the tide of negative public policy perceptions that are the excuse as much as the reason for disinvestment of public resources.

That said, some amount of tuition restructuring probably has to happen in many states, particularly in the community college sector, recognizing that the tuition and fee are lower than they need to be and could increase. In this environment, maintaining the myth of open access by advocating no tuition is not sustainable, realistic, or necessary. California is a perfect example of this state of affairs. The community college sector in California is seriously underfunded, and as a result, thousands of students are being denied access to the higher education opportunities that they deserve. While the state is unlikely to significantly increase its investment, this is a sector that for political and historical reasons still charges only $100 a year in tuition. That policy should be changed. Tuition in these community colleges could be increased while not increasing net tuition to a single student in that sector, much less to just the poorest students, by appropriate structuring of federal and state financial aid. Sadly, the political allergy in California to having that conversation is so severe that the discussion is a non-starter.

FUTURE FEDERAL SUPPORT

Higher education faces a very tough public policy environment at the federal level as well. It is not realistic to assume that the federal government is going to play a significantly larger role in providing core operating revenues for the majority of institutions. The federal policy agenda is already extremely crowded. And to get a significant investment of federal resources in the higher education in the next five to ten years is a long shot.

A basic role for the federal government is to ensure greater income equality, however. And reducing the uneven access to higher education, which could turn into perpetual social inequality, is a legitimate federal responsibility and something for which higher education should advocate. This does produce an opportunity to increase federal resources, particularly for a sort of higher education equivalent of ESEA (Elementary and Secondary Education Act) Title I.

The single most important thing that the federal government could do to help higher education is to control the spiraling cost of health care. That cost explosion is chewing up state budgets and forcing resources away from higher education. For the most part, policy makers are not disinvesting in higher education because they think that is a good idea, but because the options are so limited and the revenue streams are so tight. If there is a single message higher education can and should mobilize around right now regarding federal resources, it is the issue of health care cost containment.

Beyond that, a selective investment agenda, including a small number of core capacities, would be a good approach. But it remains unrealistic to expect a long-term structural shift toward greater federal spending for core operating support for higher education.

COST CONTAINMENT AND GOAL ACHIEVEMENT

This commentary may sound negative, but higher education's goals are achievable and the resource challenge is manageable. To do so will require both strong leadership as well as solid management, even though the culture in higher education does not value management, and doesn't like to make choices such as those that are required to reduce costs. But with a little bit of luck, some favorable politics and good management, the goals of higher education can be met.

In addition to cutting costs, colleges and universities should be prepared to talk about increasing productivity, particularly what Bruce Johnstone has called learning productivity – which means paying attention to the production process and how courses and credits accumulate to degrees, and doing it in a more efficient manner. Delta Project studies indicate that about 40 percent of the cost of degree production at the baccalaureate level is attributable to either excess credits that are taken en route to the degree or attrition – the credits that are taken by students who never get any kind of a degree. Colleges and universities can increase performance and reduce costs by paying attention to that throughput, reducing attrition and, through improved counseling and course scheduling, making sure that excess credits are taken for an academic reason and not because of drift in the curriculum. If higher education can get more students through faster at less expense to them, at less expense to the institution, it will help meet attainment goals.

On the cost side, higher education needs to tackle the cost drivers, and not just by trimming the academic program or reducing program offerings. The savings from those kinds of reductions are not that significant, although they may be good academic policy. But to reduce costs one has to reduce the building blocks for the budgets, which mean things like employee benefits and the growing costs of benefits relative to shrinking salaries.

LESSONS FROM THE FOR-PROFITS

With regard to growth in the proprietary sector, much of it is a percentage growth from a very small base. The proprietary sector reports big numbers on growth, but the absolute gain is less than the growth percentages would suggest. It is an industry very much built around rapid growth, which produces some vulnerability for that reason. Having said that, the sector is very smart and strategic regarding their cost structures and revenue patterns. In addition, they maintain a very focused curriculum. They are smart about student counseling. The day a student enrolls, she is given a comprehensive package of where to be at every step in the curriculum. If the student strays from that plan, the institution is on them with counseling. The aggressive counseling and aggressive course scheduling – all designed to make sure that the courses are delivered on time and to get the students through – is attractive and definitely something that traditional colleges and universities ought to copy.

Another factor working in favor of for-profit colleges is that they do not have the same degree of internal cross-subsidization that exists in most public and non-profit institutions. In most colleges and universities, there are a handful of very expensive programs (for instance, in the health sciences, or in engineering, or business or nursing) that are supported through internal cross subsidies, or low cost programs that generate more in tuition and state appropriation revenue than is spent on them. The proprietary institutions don't have those courses unless the costs are covered by tuition revenue. They also do not have high cost graduate programs, they do not permit under enrolled courses, and they do not carry programs that don't pay for themselves. If revenues do not cover costs, with the right margin for profits, then the programs are eliminated. By comparison, public and non-profit colleges and universities maintain high-cost programs and low-demand programs in perpetuity for all kinds of reasons that are often not carefully considered. The for-profit colleges simply do not do that. The for-profit sector pays very close attention to its cost and revenue structures, something that really can't be said for many non-profit or public institutions.

In addition, if we are to increase attainment and get more students through to the degree, more spending, not less, should occur at the lower division level. Lower division education has historically been used as a source of revenues for graduate education. When state subsidies paid for the lion's share of the costs, that wasn't particularly troubling, but it is getting so as tuition revenues cover a higher and higher proportion of costs. This means that undergraduates are paying for services they never see since the funds go to pay for the more intensive investments at the graduate level.

Another way to increase performance is to open up more opportunities for students to receive credit for prior learning and experience. This would be particularly relevant to adult learners and returning veterans. It does not make sense to require somebody who has been a medic, for instance, to go back and take the entire health curriculum over again.

To open up new thinking about ways to reduce costs and increase performance, higher education must be prepared to get rid of old assumptions about resources that are getting in the way of change. One such assumption is that it is impossible to control costs without harming quality. Another is the long-held assumption that money equates with excellence. Examination of the data and research on spending in relation to all kinds of measures of performance reveals that there is not a great correlation. So to be sure, resources buy reputation – do they really buy performance? No. What really matters is how institutions use the money they have and produce results from those outlays.

13. Ten potential lessons from investor-owned higher education

Gregory M. St. L. O'Brien, Craig Swenson, and Geoffrey Bannister[1]

The theme of the 2009 Higher Education Leadership Conference was appropriately *Smart Leadership in Difficult Times*. Through the several panels we are seeking new models for our enterprise to survive and to thrive in unprecedented times. Unlike earlier downturns in higher education, particularly in state supported higher education, the challenges faced by colleges and universities today are unlike those ever encountered in the twentieth century. In many ways the "perfect storm" of difficulties is being encountered by our universities and colleges: state appropriations and available state resources are in sharp decline as state budgets plummet; investment portfolios are fractions of what they were merely 24 months ago; donors and benefactors have been shocked and frightened about their own financial security by these downturns and both new and planned gifts are necessarily put on hold or cancelled entirely. Even available federal support was briefly paralyzed by the financial uncertainties during the financial crisis of 2008 and has not recovered its responsiveness as new alternative forms of aid are being considered in a deadlocked Congress.

Nevertheless, students continue to find ways to attend college and graduate schools to enhance their skills and credentials to prepare for an increasingly competitive and challenging job market and slower economy. One of the sectors that have seen constant and dramatic growth in the past decade, even in these very draconian times is the investor-owned (or for-profit) sector of higher education. These institutions derive their resources and charter from publicly traded or privately held investment groups who are able to provide the capital to expand access and programs. From a minor player merely a decade ago, investor-owned higher (postsecondary) education now accounts for over seven percent of today's student population.[2] Why does this sector seem so able to withstand all of these vexing pressures? A simple answer is: they don't; but they perhaps address these pressures differently. From these differences, some lessons can be learned to help the broader higher education enterprise.

First, investor-owned higher education is subject to all of the same negative pressures on financial assistance, declining capital markets and uncertainty that public and independent universities and colleges face. The differences in investor-owned higher education's ability to cope and even thrive in these times rests with the mission, resources, governance models and investor/sponsor confidence that undergirds the operation of these institutions. Second, the agility of decision-making enables these institutions to adapt more quickly, and perhaps sometimes more effectively to changing circumstances and turbulent environments when compared with many more traditional institutions. Finally, the business model of investor-owned higher education strives for growth through increased access to higher education, which incents institutions and investors to respond to un-met needs and constrained capacities in the public and independent sectors.

While there are many differences among the public, independent and investor-owned sectors, the similarities far outweigh the differences. Unfortunately assumptions based on incomplete information, and presumptions about motivations of sponsors and leaders in each of these sectors too often prevents us from learning from one another to strengthen access and quality at a time when our nation must improve both to compete in a twenty-first century global economy. While there are "bad actors" and even scandals in all sectors of postsecondary education, too often the sins of the few are generalized; and what can be learned from another sector is often ignored or dismissed. A first task in learning what can be gleaned from investor-owned higher education may be to analyze and perhaps dispel some broadly held assumptions about the sector and its institutions. There is both some truth and some inaccuracy in each of these stereotypes. If we are to learn from the investor-owned sector, we need to parse fact from false presumptions.

SHORT-TERM VERSUS LONG-TERM FOCUS

For all institutions and their leaders, presenting an accurate, positive picture of their respective institution is desirable. Whether that presentation is to a board of trustees, a faculty senate, a legislative committee, or a group of donors, each of us wants truthfully to put our best foot forward. We all work diligently to have our institution "in shape" for the accreditation visit or other view by external constituents. Imagine the pressure is a public call with institutional investors, analysts, and stockholders every 90 days. That quarterly reporting pressure does put pressure on institutions to show themselves positively on a shorter-term basis. But it is the long-term success of these institutions that adds value to their firms. Decisions that make for long-term added value are typically what investors, especially institutional investors (insurance companies, pension funds, and so on) strive for in their higher education portfolios. Certainly some leaders make decisions to highlight short-term success. Perhaps they will slow longer-term investments to ensure a good profile at the quarterly or annual meeting or presentation. However, as these institutions are typically growth oriented and give little or no quarterly dividends, the long-term success of the institution is or should be the principal driver.

Yes, some people do cut corners to look good for that quarter or that legislative session or that accreditation visit; but, regardless of sector, both long-term institutional success and short-term triumphs count in all sectors of higher education. There are some who want to take advantage of the system and sacrifice the long term for short-term positive visibility, but these are the exception for those who seek leadership careers in these fields.

FACULTY ROLES IN CURRICULUM AND GOVERNANCE

It has sometimes been asserted that faculty members in investor-owned colleges and universities have no real role in governance or curriculum matters – that they are just cogs in a big corporate wheel. This is often compared to perhaps an idealized and unrealistic image of decision-making in public and independent colleges where faculties deliberate thoughtfully on important academic decisions in a selfless and collegial manner. Those of us who have served in all three sectors recognize that internal political pressures, departmental issues and self interest are as prominent in traditional academic governance as they are anywhere in society today.

Accreditation standards, which differ widely among institutional and programmatic accreditors, generally have guidelines that ensure the participation of faculty in development and approval of curriculum. How faculty involvement is achieved may vary widely, from an online or virtual faculty committee approving courses and curricula for implementation on multiple campuses and/or online delivery on behalf of vast institutions or systems to a face to face conversation among the faculty wide meetings at smaller institutions. While the modal time and roles of faculty involvement in decision-making may differ between investor-owned and more traditional institutional types, the variations within each sector are equally as great as between sectors. To capture these differences within sectors of higher education, consider the differences in governance between a large community college system compared with a small liberal arts campus or between a highly regulated and licensed program with required curricula compared with a more unstructured student self guided program in an unregulated field.

UNIFORMITY AND LACK OF INDIVIDUAL INNOVATION

In all sectors of higher education, the press toward uniformity in syllabus, format of offerings, learning outcomes and means of assessment is increasing. Online, multi-section or blended format courses have strong academic reasons to have the same learning outcomes sought, the same syllabus and texts and often the same supplemental materials. This is regardless of sector. The pressure for greater uniformity in online education is often seen as exemplary of a lost faculty role in curriculum and attributed to the for-profit, investor-owned sector. These pressures will be the same regardless of sector if faculty members share in the development of new courses with educational designers, online specialists and external subject matter experts, external to that faculty. The pressures toward uniformity are there in all sectors in multi-section and online course development. Where the difference may be is in how these pressures are addressed or ignored.

Accreditation requirements generally emphasize the role of the faculty in designing and approving curriculum in all accredited institutions, whether in the large multi-section university campus, in the community college system, in the state that requires common syllabi across all state institutions, or in the for-profit institution that develops a common course for implementation on all campuses and in online sections. How this is done is an institutional difference by mission or tradition. That it is done is a requirement.

Large, investor-owned institutions typically do have much greater uniformity in their offerings across campuses and programs. This allows for scaling of offerings, cost savings, consistency in offerings documentation, and so on. Such uniformity in syllabus and content may also facilitate assessment of student learning across a vast geographical area. In this sector perhaps the commitment to the result of more consistent and uniform offerings changes the latitude of the individual faculty member, but that does not mean that the faculty as a body has lost its central role in approving and ultimately determining the educational program.

The demands for consistency may be decreasing the sense of individual flexibility in all sectors of higher education, but the need for consistency in learning outcomes and student competencies and the need to ensure consistent knowledge and skills among our graduates outweighs this loss of flexibility.

TEN POTENTIAL LESSONS FOR US ALL

There are differences that have historically derived from the way investor-owned higher education has emerged, how it has been accredited, how it has been accountable and how it succeeds or fails when compared with other sectors of higher education. The question in these hard times is, "Are there some lessons to be learned from these differences that can help all leaders in higher education manage more effectively in what appears to be a difficult decade ahead?"

The answer, we believe, is a resounding, "Yes!" All of these lessons may not be appropriate to replicate in a wholesale way, while others may be easily translated from one sector to another. Even where direct translation may not be appropriate, there are insights as to why these lessons have served investor-owned institutions well that may help the leader of a non-profit college or state university to manage and sail through the turbulent fiscal and social seas of change. Here are ten that we recommend leaders consider.

1.   Operate with Agility and Just-in-time Decision-making

Where there does seem to be a typical difference among the sectors is the speed of decision-making. This is an area where non-investor-owned sectors may be able to glean some useful tips from investor-owned institutions and systems. Decision-making in investor-owned institutions, especially in larger or publicly traded institutions, is more time bound and often faster. Usually there is more information available to the decision makers (see items 4 and 5 below).

It is often the longer times, the more complicated, cumbersome processes and the felt need for consensus that slows the responsiveness of traditional institutions, with their bureaucratic and faculty governance mechanisms, that cause failure in responding to external forces or opportunities. Faculty consultation and, where needed, faculty approvals are typically given in a more time-sensitive manner in investor-owned institutions. Another key factor is to be clear where input and advice/reaction are being sought, versus where a required permission is being requested.

When a decision is needed about how to develop a new program within a month, or whether to permit launching or modifying a program, during the upcoming enrollment term, in the investor-owned sector, the deadline for the decision is far more likely to be met than ignored. In this sector one would rarely if ever hear comment, "We need more time to think about it. Ask us about this next fall."

2. Emphasize Scalability

When a new program is developed in the investor-owned sector, its planning is often premised upon the twin assumptions of:

- Scalability – the ability of a particular entity to grow to enjoy economies of scale, and
- Replicability – the ability to repeat the development at another time and place.

While a single campus non-profit model will normally value distinctiveness and uniqueness, the investor is looking for an efficient delivery system rather than a unique entity. While the system needs to be distinguished from its competition, the individual campus sites need to be closely standardized, so that they can be:

- Managed more efficiently,
- Assessed more effectively, and
- Continuously improved based on a wider pool of experience.

The stress on replication mirrors the philosophical approach of Michael Gerber to small business development.[3] Gerber's argument for small business development has strong relevance for branch campus development, no matter which ownership model is used. Developing a replicable model makes good business sense even if the goal is not initially to do so. The discipline of developing a franchise-like entity drives discipline and efficiency into the system design. Rather than relying on talent to find a way to create efficiencies, the "E-Myth" strategy derives efficiencies from the systemic management approach. The investor-owned sector's emphasis on growth, replication and consistency fosters an environment where first questions are "How well can this be replicated?" or, "How do we know this will work elsewhere with different faculty members and different students?"

The press for scalability drives issues of consistent quality, efficient cost, and reliable results, even if the course or program is only offered in one place. At the same time it permits more intense effort in developing the program right the first time so it can be consistently implemented successfully in other settings.

3. Make the Student Come First

We all care about the student, otherwise none of us would be involved in this enterprise. In many traditional universities, though, decision-making too often considers faculty priorities over student needs, wants, convenience, and so on. In investor-owned institutions the class schedule is targeted toward the times and places which students would prefer to use rather than scheduling those classes in deference to the faculty members' research, consulting or other schedule constraints. The faculty member who says "I don't teach on Mondays" (for whatever reason), may not teach if Monday is the day that the students need the class in an institution whose entire budget depends on student enrollment, rather than endowment, grants, and so on.

While as faculty members we all strive to ensure the student achieves the skills and competencies needed for their chosen field, often factors extraneous to student need creep into the dialog in more traditional ivy covered walls. General Education requirements may more accurately reflect the need for course enrollments in departments with declining student majors than the faculty's conviction that that course is more essential to a student's overall general education than another course from a department with robust enrollments. Prerequisites may likewise reflect a department's desire to bolster enrollment in a less popular course than the conviction, after careful thought, that the skills and knowledge of this less popular course are essential to successful completion of the course for which it is labeled a prerequisite. The number of undergraduate majors that cannot be completed using night and weekend classes, because the faculty members who teach certain required courses refuse those teaching times or places is another example where faculty priorities or budgetary considerations may take precedence over student constraints or desires.

While this observation cannot be taken to extremes, in the day to day decision-making in investor-owned institutions, what the student/the consumer/the customer needs is a more powerful consideration than in many older institutions, with established tenure policies, faculty hierarchies, and more balanced traditions of teaching, research and service.

4. Use Adjunct Faculty Purposefully

While some investor-owned postsecondary units rely of full-time faculty almost exclusively, especially in advanced professional programs, as do many not-for-profit institutions, there is generally a higher percentage of adjunct faculty members in large, investor-owned and other multi-campus institutions. Large state universities have increasingly relied on adjuncts to teach lower division courses, along with graduate assistants. Criticism of this practice is rampant in today's higher education literature.

One of the differences among the sectors is in the purposeful use of adjuncts as part of the educational model and the expectations of adjuncts to follow standardized curricula, syllabi and assignments. Where there is more standardization, the reliability of the adjunct faculty may be greater. This comes from the greater emphasis on consistency. It also comes from the applied nature of the fields taught in investor-owned institutions, typically business or another professional field. The model of the "practitioner-teacher," who is actively engaged in his or her profession and teaches future members of that profession as an additional responsibility, is dominant in many investor-owned institutions as a part of their professional education mission and model.

It is imperative that there be a core of full-time faculty in the institution to ensure consistency in educational approach. But for today's student with interest in an applied and rapidly changing field, the use of practicing professionals as central in the teaching of the skills and values of that profession may be of equal importance.

5. Measure Everything: Exert Financial Discipline Based on those Measures

Whether it's ISO 9000 (Quality), ISO 14000 (Environment), Baldrige or Continuous Quality Improvement, the corporate sector mantra is to quantify everything that can be quantified. Qualitative, peer review processes are more common in traditional higher education, but they produce less convincing evidence to a modern consumer. Many of the "standards" used in higher education, such as financial stability as determined by regional accreditors, are not sufficiently defined in the current environment of dramatic fiscal upheaval. The stress of investor-owned entities on careful quantification could help defuse some of the more contentious cases and certainly helps build a greater confidence in a skeptical general public that the institutions are self-assessing rigorously.

Whether it is the cost per internet inquiry, the number of "sign-ons" per week by online students that predicts course success, the number of square feet per admissions counselor needed in a new facility, the conversion rate from inquiry to admission of different marketing media, investor-owned institutions seem to measure, keep, and make decisions based on every conceivable aspect of performance measurement data. In this era of expanded accountability each of us may feel that we are also measuring everything that moves. The difference among the sectors in the centrality of measuring performance and cost data is dramatic. The culture of "if you can't measure it, you aren't managing it" pervades investor-owned higher education. What it means for a leader in higher education is often daily monitoring of factors such as inquiry rates, conversion rates, and costs associated with these factors. The culture is one where such information is deemed essential and understood by all and almost all important decisions are data driven or supported by extensive data driven information.

The culture of "measure everything" has a correlate, "treat each expense decision as if it were coming from your own pocket." Despite multi-hundreds of millions of dollars in annual revenue, discussions of even what would appear to be the smallest of expenditures, especially unbudgeted expenditures, receive extraordinary attention at very high organizational levels. Expenditures that might be in the decision authority of a department chair in a large state university might often end up being made at the highest institutional level in a large, multi-campus for-profit institution. One of the major reasons investor-owned institutions seem to fare better in these tight times is the discipline and rigor applied to even relatively small expenditure and investment decisions. Large scale institutions such as these look at even modest expenditures at one campus with an eye toward the impact of such a decision replicated many times at all campuses. Whether it is the visibility to investors of how such decisions are made or the fact that with incentives tied to the institution's financial wellbeing, the manager is in reality dealing in some ways with "his or her own money," the discipline applied to these decisions is dramatic.

6.   Focus on Growth

Since many of the investor-owned companies are privately held, there is limited documentation about the reinvestment habits of these entities. However, the publicly held Corinthian Colleges and ITT Educational Services report that 9 and 10 percent respectively of their funding comes from internal sources.[4]

A driving incentive for investor-owned higher education systems is growth, whether through organic growth of new campuses or growth by acquisitions. In a time where there are significant, recognized needs for expanded access to higher education this characteristic of investor-owned institutions provides opportunities for many popular higher education programs to be developed throughout the country, where people appear to need and want them. This has been described earlier as the "fourth wave of access in American higher education" after the Land Grant movement, the post war expansion of state colleges to university status, and the rapid growth and recognition of community colleges (O'Brien, 2006).[5]

At this time of severely limited and declining state and municipal revenues, the focus on predictable and systematic growth of investor-owned campuses is a meaningful way to address the limited access and financial support for growth in public and independent institutions. Strategic partnerships with investor-owned entities may offer state and independent institutions means to extend their impact during these times of dwindling or constrained resources. (See item 10 below).

7. Access Capital

When faced with an opportunity to grow that can realize positive results, an investor-owned institution may look to its investment community to provide the needed capital up-front to permit seizing that opportunity in a timely manner, rather than waiting for regular revenue streams to provide the resources to launch a potentially beneficial program, campus, or initiative. While access to new capital may often be tempered by the need to maintain a positive profile regarding institutional performance to its investment community, seeking such resources to foster growth or enhanced performance is a disciplined decision, usually made with long-term growth and wellbeing in mind.

One might think that this aspect of investor-owned university operations has less relevance to the independent or state institution. We would argue, however, that thinking about new initiatives from an investment-reward perspective is of critical importance to leaders in all sectors of higher education. Whether it is to a board of trustees, a foundation board or even a state university system office, discussion of new initiatives from a capital investment perspective may help leaders guide their institutions through these difficult times.

As will be discussed further below, one potential source of investment capital may be the investor-owned sector through collaborative projects that benefit all participants. These decisions too will be made on an assessment of the potential return on the capital investments and risks among all participants.

8. Mission Focus and Clarity

A very significant part of decision-making in all institutions is how does an initiative fit or alter the institution's mission. With all the focus on growth in investor-owned colleges and universities there is an understandable tendency toward institutional drift. Just as is the case with independent and state institutions who seek to expand or grow their mission to meet new student needs or to grow their impact on the communities they serve, investor-owned institutions are constantly confronted with opportunities to expand what they do or what they offer. Given the culture and focus on cost, modeling potential initiatives means that the pressures toward such mission expansion are tempered by the discipline of evaluating alternative uses of investment capital or energy away from what is working successfully.

The investor-owned institutions that have grown most visibly in the last decade are those that are clear about what market they are in, what niche in that market has been successful and how extensions or expansions from that "sweet spot" enhance or diminish their success in the "mission space" in which they are operating. This does not mean that these institutions don't try new initiatives that fail, they do; but it means that the discipline and agility values discussed above press these institutions to measure carefully whether a new initiative is enhancing or diminishing its position.

9.   Target Marketing

Knowing and targeting their market of potential students is a central tenet of investor-owned institutions. They spend more money identifying who responds to the institution's offerings, style of offering, schedules, and style than do colleges and universities in the other sectors. While considerable research is dedicated to identifying potential new student markets, considerable energy is also spent in understanding the priorities and needs of current student populations and how to reach these current student markets more effectively. The "measure everything" approach is perhaps most prominent in the marketing efforts of investor-owned universities. The discipline that these institutions use in knowing who their customers are and what motivates them can save scarce marketing resources and improve the effectiveness of most institutions' outreach efforts. For non-profit and public universities, potential contractual relationships with firms specialized in student marketing and acquisition may offer a smart use of limited resources or redirected resources during tough times.

10.   Collaborate while Competing

The future of higher education is likely to see new formats emerging. Principal among these may well be the joint venture or Public Private Partnership. As Michael Goldstein recently advocated, joint ventures can provide access to the capital markets for non-profit entities.[6] The asymmetrical nature of US regulation is that a not-for-profit may own a for-profit, but not the other way around. A not-for-profit can also contract with a for-profit for services. Over the last few years, universities have learned the advantages of outsourcing such functions as bookstores, food services, cleaning services and residence hall development. These functions were generally identified as the less "mission critical" ones, but the joint venture approach is proving successful at bringing private capital into more core areas such as marketing and recruitment.

The series of companies within the envelope of Education Dynamics, the boutique recruitment services of PowersEdu, the housing development services of American Campus Communities and over a dozen others in this field, are examples of the recent trend toward joint ventures. Other firms such as StudyBlue, Inc. offer academic support services and technologies that enhance student performance and retention dramatically. As Goldstein argues, there is a strong future for joint ventures in such areas as marketing and recruitment where investor-owned groups have proven the value of intense marketing campaigns funded at a level that most non-profits would find politically unacceptable in tight budget times.

Even in the actual delivery of instruction, joint ventures are appearing in such areas as distance education. Recently, Altius Education announced an $8 million offering to help smaller institutions develop their distance education potential. As the entrepreneurial President of St. Leo University in Florida recently pointed out about distance education, ". . .Still, not all colleges and universities will experience these benefits and advancements. The market has become so competitive – even cluttered – with educational providers of varying quality that new entrants will face steep challenges."[7]

In this "cluttered" landscape, a joint venture is likely to have greater chances of success and fewer negatives in the event of failure than a purely not-for-profit entity would normally enjoy. For small colleges facing the prospects of financial exigency, a joint venture in the form of a public private partnership may, in fact, be the only way to save the college. Experiments around this model are beginning to emerge and appear to have mixed blessings of regulators from the Department of Education to the regional accreditors.

In tough times, the smart leader looks around, sees what is working for others, learns about what works and adapts or replicates it. The growth of investor-owned higher education is not a fluke, nor is it a "flash in the pan." There are important elements in the model that are supporting the growth of this sector and leaders in all sectors of higher education (public, not-for-profit and investor-owned) need to look at the success of this sector to see what works and how these values and characteristics can be applied to help their students and advance their institutions.

NOTES

1. This chapter is an expansion of comments by Gregory O'Brien during the panel "Looking Ahead: Leading Successfully into the Future" during the 2009 Higher Education Leadership Conference, November 5–6, 2009, New York City, supplemented by contributions of Presidents Swenson and Bannister.
2. Wilson, Robin (2010), "For-profit colleges change higher education's landscape," Chronicle of Higher Education, February 7.
3. Gerber, Michael E. (1995), *The E-Myth Revisited*, NY: Harper Collins.
4. Ibid.
5. O'Brien, G. (2006), "What non-profit universities can learn from for-profit institutions, and vice versa," Keynote Address, Western Association of Colleges and Schools (WASC, Senior) Annual Meeting, Oakland, CA, April 2006 [also presented at the Higher Learning Commission Annual Meeting, Chicago, April 2005].
6. Goldstein, Michael (2010), "Cracking the Egg: Preserving the college while protecting the Core," *Trusteeship*, January/February, pp. 24–29.
7. Kirk, Arthur F. Jr. (2008), Saint Leo University Occasional Papers, vol. 2, issue 1, Fall, p. 1.

14. Cold comforts: questioning the habits of higher education

Stephen Joel Trachtenberg

Any two people who look back with a long perspective on American academia and then attempt to look forward as far as possible will tell you they see the same things though their perspectives or perhaps their interpretations will vary subtly. Ask a hundred people, the answers will be the same. Few people familiar with the workings of the Academy have anything new to say about the flaws in the machinery despite a great deal of novelty in course offerings, living arrangements, and student culture. This is not to say that the problems are obscure or that academics lack imagination: given the artfulness of their publications and grant proposals, their vision and creativity are beyond argument. But when academics – instructors and administrators alike – are confronted with the structural problems of university operations and governance and then asked what to do about them, they can see few if any new solutions, and what new things they may see are not lovable.

Our universities trace their roots to medieval Bologna and Paris, but the contemporary academic resistance to change is not, as Frederic Maitland put it, "aimless medievalism." The medieval remains are matters of superficial culture and ritual – the architecture of a few old and rich institutions, the robes and silly hats we wear at graduations, the Latin diplomas some of us still hand out, and a few administrative titles. If no longer a product of the middle ages, our root stocks are not all that new despite courses and disciplines that Abélard, Copernicus, Leibniz, Arnold, and Hutchins never could have imagined – and probably, for their wellbeing, so much the better.

American universities began taking their current shape and scope in the seventeenth and nineteenth centuries, presumably more enlightened eras. A few years after its founding in 1636, Harvard College was sickly and unlikely to survive. The unknown Henry Dunster, recently arrived from England to raise it from the living dead, looked homeward across the pond, specifically to Cambridge, where he had been a student at Magdalene College. (Of course it did not hurt that Magdalene and Harvard were both in cities called Cambridge.) The colleges of Cambridge at the time required undergraduates to spend four years to earn their degrees, and that seemed right to Dunster. A few years later, Cambridge decided three years would suffice, but Harvard College, the first and later foremost in America, did not change – and that is why to this day we have a four-year undergraduate system, with long vacations and a leisurely ascent towards knowledge combined with a slow assault on ignorance.

Unlike our ritual caps and gowns, the academic calendar is not benign or just silly. It is harmful to the enterprise of educating students. Earning a degree should not take four years. It is too much time spent at too high a cost for the value received. If the value were greater, I might agree it is worth the price and time, but that is not the case when not only the ablest students go on to graduate study, certainly in part for the prestige, but no less because their undergraduate preparation is not sufficient for what they would like to do afterwards. I believe that we can put the time to better use.

How this should be done need not be a single universal repair. Depending on the students' abilities, interests, and pocketbooks, I can think of several approaches. For example, a year or two of a low-cost community college followed by two more years in a major at a four-year institution. Or, a combined undergraduate and masters program in five years. Or three years straight through for the focused and determined students. Or combined undergraduate and legal or medical studies reducing the total time to final degrees by two years.[1] Or some other approach I have not yet thought about – but any new approach should also contemplate distance and online study. In any event, if the undergraduate calendar were to be reformed so that eight months a year instead of just six were spent in learning, the process would be better, less costly for students and the universities, and the outcomes, I am sure, would be better than they are now. There would be greater continuity of study: college students, no less than grade-school students, tend to forget a great deal during long summer vacations.

A further benefit of getting more time out of the calendar (hardly a paradox as I have described it) would be more complete use of physical facilities. If some students were studying year round, the cost of maintaining the plant would decline as would the unit cost of educating a student, and the students would have better opportunities to take courses they want to take or are required to take.

Of all the disappointments I had as a university president for thirty years – and there were enough to pave the Potomac – this one was the worst. The faculty at The George Washington University (GW) refused merely to consider the idea of altering the calendar, offering seventeen

separate arguments against *consideration* which amounted to a monu-
mentally loud No! Disappointed as I was, I was nonetheless not surprised.
The proposal to alter the calendar was not cosmetic: it would have altered
the rhythm of their academic life, and faculties are inclined to get comfortable with one rhythm and decline to hear another, let alone get up and
dance to it.[2]

The adherence to a calendar now 350 years old is not aimless medievalism or benign, as I have said. But the obduracy of the reluctance even
to consider a change grows out of the nineteenth century and the rise of
the research university. William Clark, in his strangely but aptly named
Academic Charisma, has written a fine chronicle of this phenomenon, and
I will briefly rifle his store with some thoughts of my own interspersed.[3]

From the founding of Harvard in the middle of the seventeenth century
until the middle of the nineteenth, American colleges and universities were
small, fairly quiet places, devoted to educating the few opulent young gen-
tlemen of their eras to be chiefly lawyers, preachers, doctors, and teachers.
Other trades and professions required little more than the equivalent of a
high school diploma or simply reading and an apprenticeship. That had
already begun to change radically in Europe and chiefly in Germany under
the leadership of Theodor Mommsen, a great and prolific scholar. He
believed that university professors should be researchers, should publish
mightily – he produced more than 1500 books and articles – or perish,
should inspire students to do the same or to take on the world in other
ways and beat it. Considering how urbanized Germany had become, how
middle class and settled as well, this was not a bad concept of higher education. Given how rural and still expanding and restless the United States
was in the middle of the nineteenth century, the research university made
little sense, but it caught on, I think because it made the faculty heroic
rather than bland: Mommsen himself was famous, a tourist attraction,
had both political and intellectual power, and won the Nobel in literature.[4]
Three new universities, founded in the generation after the Civil War
would not have been what they were without the influence, direct or not is
hard to say, of Mommsen. And certainly this model and outlook worked
for Johns Hopkins, the University of Chicago, and Stanford.

But it puzzles me that the land-grant schools, created by the Morill
Act in 1862 with emphases on agriculture, military preparation, and
the "mechanic arts," should have followed the old suit of the four-year
calendar with long intervals between semesters and the emergent model
of research and publication for their faculties.[5] It has suited Chicago,
Stanford, and Hopkins well, but I am unconvinced that most universities, where research, however defined, is the chief measure of worth and
of winning tenure, have profited from this approach. They have created

professors who conduct research because they have to, not because they have discovered something new and inspiring, or because it is more stimulating than teaching undergraduates. And they have largely turned undergraduate students over to graduate students, who are less learned and less seasoned and less well-trained in the art and science of teaching, or to adjuncts who teach in the hopes of homesteading in the groves of academe.

Blaming Henry Dunster or Theodor Mommsen is wrong, unkind, and beside the point. Both were great men, but I doubt either thought his decisions about the shape and governance of higher education were Holy Writ, subject to exegesis but not revision. But what they and others handed down, as if from Sinai in the academic mind, has acquired a kind of sanctity in the Academy. These old modalities are defended as tried and true, proven, traditional. Any suggestion that the calendar and the research university – or, for that matter, course loads and credits, tenure standards (or the continued existence of tenure), and departmental organization, among many other topics of governance – should be changed or at least examined with an eye toward change is met with resistance in most cases, intransigence in worse ones, and accusations of administrative venality in the worst. Comfort, once it is familiar, is wonderful and enduring.

I do not mean to suggest that there are not current or continuing trends in the administration of higher education that I find worse than mischievous and heartless, if not intentionally cruel or stupid. The broadening of higher education in the wake of World War II as a middle-class entitlement, further fueled by Lyndon Johnson's Great Society budgets, called for many new Ph.D.s to confront the rising tide of undergraduates. But enrollments began to shrink or stabilize around 1970. Even when they grew later, limited budgets did not permit adequate hiring to match previous levels. Nevertheless, graduate schools have continued for forty years to admit more doctoral candidates in the liberal arts and social sciences than are ever likely to find academic employment, yet still preparing them for work and a kind of life that will never be available to them.[6]

I am hardly the only person who has complained about this – even, at a meeting of the Council of Graduate Schools, in the lion's den – but a polite reception without action is worthless. It is probably not the case that graduate deans and admissions officers are simply building empires or job security, though a less mannerly observer might conclude as much.[7] Throughout academia, there has been endless degree inflation, not, as I understand, for purposes of furthering education but for adding an empty prestige. A friend, for example, went to have his hearing tested and was not examined by an audiologist with a B.A. and some additional training or a certificate, but by a doctor of audiology. If there is a demand, graduate schools will fill it; if the demand can be encouraged, they will cheer it on.

And while some administrators and academic bureaucrats like me tend to hold the professoriat accountable for many of the universities' problems, we are often in cahoots with them or at least have made a kind of peace, though I am nagged by Tacitus's phrase *Ubi solitudinem faciunt pacem appellant*. We have not created a desert, but still our peace looks to me like a slowly rising sea about to swamp us. I am thinking particularly of teaching loads for tenured professors. They naturally vary within and among institutions, but a senior professor who teaches only one course a semester, and sometimes only one a year, is an expensive proposition. The small pay of the adjuncts necessary to teach classes the *tenuratus* is not meeting mounts up when hundreds of them are necessary. This hardly, moreover, gives undergraduates the opportunity to study with the great men and women whom the university promotes as part of its value, nor consistent with the esteem it commands in the eyes of the world.

Whether the publications that senior faculty consequently produce because they teach scantily and have long vacations justify this system is not convincing, let alone dispositive, to me. I have always been pleased to congratulate faculty on their publications, but when I have read what they have written in a field about which I know something, I am usually disappointed and unimpressed. Years ago, I heard an aging and slightly sour professor of literature say that most books should have been articles and most articles should never have been written, a statement with an interesting ambiguity. Granted, many scholarly works offer something of value, but it is hard to measure against the value students should expect – and given the many publications which seem to offer next to nothing, it is even harder to defend this régime. I suspect that there is more personal glory and professional advancement at stake than the acquisition and dissemination of knowledge.[8] But administrators, in their reluctance to overthrow this dispensation, have colluded with the faculty.

I am not sure why this is, but I have thought for years of two things that are certainly at work in this case. The first is any administrator's distaste for a fight with faculty. Presidents and deans understand their roles as making things possible for faculty and students and assuring the institution's survival, not throwing down gauntlets. The second is that faculties have a great deal more power than they like to admit in public. On all but a few campuses – mainly military and religious institutions – senior faculty have veto power over changes in governance. And in recent years we have seen the turmoil a mutinous faculty can cause by voting no confidence in a president. This is an assumed or seized power, not scriptural, but real even so.

Administrations with the support – aggressive support may be what is really at issue – of their boards could change the pattern, but I am not aware of any campuses where this has happened. Even financial exigency has not, to my knowledge, been invoked except at schools that failed anyway. It is nothing any college or university ever wants to do because it makes the place look precarious if not in outright peril and could scare away donors and students. Only the board has that power.

I am not suggesting, however, that boards of trustees are a white-hatted posse, filled with reason and riding to the rescue. While my board supported me abundantly, it first balked when I proposed buying at a bargain price the campus of a failed college nearby for additional housing and to meet our Title IX obligations to women's sports, where we were lagging.

Yet even if a university board were to declare a state of exigency, no single entity – the board, the administration, the alumni, or the faculty – alone can save the modern university from the facts and pressures of economic life. The recession may be over or nearly over, but its rumbles will be felt under our foundations for years. After losing half their wealth, how agreeable will students' families be to write a check for $30,000, even if it does reflect a 40 percent discount, when the institution looks unlikely to thrive? No more willing, I imagine, than private donors or government agencies will feel. Moreover, higher education is capital and labor intensive, like neurosurgery and oil-well drilling, but unlike higher education they turn a profit and over time have always done so. Still, to invoke the WMD (weapons of mass destruction) option of financial exigency in the face of these facts, no matter how realistic, will look like backing the wrong horse.

And so it may be. But if no one ever backed the wrong horse there would be no horse races because the pay off on the winner would be negative – which is about where higher education is today. Defending failing ideas because we have accepted them for a hundred years or two hundred or nearly four hundred because these concepts or beliefs are familiar and traditional may point to the grand idea of higher education and its history. But the unwillingness to examine the university calendar, teaching obligations, departmental organization, admissions policies – among many other problems of governance – with an eye to change or a consideration of change and amelioration is insupportable financially and unsupported by reason. It prizes the familiar because it is comfortable, not because it works well.

If what I have written so far were new to anyone knowledgeable about higher education, that would be comforting to me. Ah, I could say, I have spoken and lifted the scales from the eyes of the Academy. But aside from a few personal anecdotes which simply illustrate known problems, there is nothing startling or novel here. Perhaps lining up a great deal of evidence reminds us of the obvious, which anyone can miss. Perhaps that helps.

It is a melancholic thought that the only way to assure the future of higher education, or perhaps to begin the process of assuring it, is to say "enough, we can't afford it, the old régime is beyond our means." It does not make sense to pay the most to professors who teach the least. It makes no sense to let an English department have staff to teach and direct dissertations on every topic from *Beowulf* to Larry Collins when half their classes are nearly empty, or for a philosophy department to admit (with administrative collusion) more graduate students than can ever find employment in the only field they are suited for. Ending departments or programs or anything else someone or other on campus is used to is unpleasant, but the alternative is much worse.[9] Better some should survive than all perish. Few academics, including economists, want to hear about creative destruction so close to home.

I wish I could see another way because merely thinking in these terms is terribly sad. If there is a better way that produces some reasonable belief in a happy future, it has my ardor and pledge of support. But time is short, and we need to act as soon as we can. I want to conclude that we will find a way, and I remain hopeful because American universities and colleges have been wellsprings of ideas and rockets of innovation. Nor is this our first grim moment that we have had to overcome. I want to think we will do it again.

NOTES

1. Some of these approaches are being tried here and there, but the most common model is overwhelmingly four years of undergraduate study followed generally by two years for a Masters and an indeterminate number of years to finish a Ph.D. *Vide* note 6 *infra*.
2. I do not mean to single out the GW faculty. Considering the number of institutions putting the summer to academic use (beyond summer school) can be counted on one hand or maybe two, it is clear that expanding the calendar is unwelcome everywhere.
3. Clark, William (2005), *Academic Charisma and the Rise of the Research University*, Chicago: Chicago Universitiy Press.
4. Here is Mark Twain, completely uncynical, describing a dinner in Germany in 1892: "Then we saw the end of the house rising to its feet; saw it rise abreast the advancing guard all along like a wave. This supreme honor had been offered to no one before. There was an excited whisper at our table – 'MOMMSEN!' – and the whole house rose. Rose and shouted and stamped and clapped and banged the beer mugs. Just simply a storm! Then the little man with his long hair and Emersonian face edged his way past us and took his seat. I could have touched him with my hand – Mommsen! – think of it!. . . *I would have walked a great many miles to get a sight of him*, and here he was, without trouble or tramp or cost of any kind. Here he was clothed in a titanic deceptive modesty which made him look like other men" (emphasis added). Cited on Wikipedia as Saunder and Collins, "Introduction" to their edition of Mommsen's *History of Rome* (Meridian Books 1958), at 1–17, 1.
5. Despite arguments to the contrary, I still like to believe that the academic calendar was influenced by the agricultural calendar; however, a vacation in the summer, which is

fairly leisurely on farms, with school work during the very busy planting and the harvest seasons, doesn't fit well at all with that notion.

6. I first delivered my own thoughts on this subject in a speech to the Council of Graduate Schools in 2007. It has since been expanded and printed in *Graduate Education in 2020* (Washington: CGS, 2009) under their title "Of Course It's Not Your Father's Oldsmobile – They Don't Make Them Any More." Louis Menand has published an article in the Harvard Magazine (November–December, 2009) dealing with this issue and others, available online at http://harvardmagazine.com/2009/11/professionalization-in-academy?page=0,4#commen. The Center for Innovation and Research in Graduate Education at the University of Washington has said that doctoral education in the social sciences needs to undergo a "paradigm shift" to reflect the realities of the job market. See http://chronicle.com/article/New-PhDs-in-Social-Sciences/267.

7. It is true that graduate programs in fields considered vocational rather than intellectual or academic are profitable for their universities.

8. In *Shakespeare, Einstein, and the Bottom Line: The Marketing of Higher Education* (Cambridge: Harvard UP, 2005), pp. 5, 67 *et alibi*, David Kirp observes that ambitious professors are not especially loyal to their departments or universities, but are liege to others in their field or sub-field whose praise and admiration will help them professionally. That they take little interest in university governance seems obvious.

9. GW has undertaken to reduce the number of doctoral programs from 48, many of which were weak, to about 20, giving those remaining a chance to flourish.

Index